W9-AHE-555

THE ARITHMETIC PRIMER

A Blueprint for Success in Basic Mathematics

Paul Shoecraft

Addison-Wesley Publishing Company

Menlo Park, California • Reading, Massachusetts
London • Amsterdam • Don Mills, Ontario • Sydney

To the many who have helped me with
this text and to my wife, Lynne, and my
daughters, Jessica and Bradlee.

"Arithmetic" from *The Complete Poems of Carl Sandburg,*
copyright 1950 by Carl Sandburg. Reprinted by
permission of Harcourt Brace Jovanovich, Inc.

This book is in the Addison-Wesley INNOVATIVE SERIES.

ISBN - 0 - 201 - 07321 - 8
ABCDEFGHIJ - WC - 821079

ARITHMETIC

Arithmetic is where numbers fly like pigeons in
  and out of your head.

Arithmetic tells you how many you lose or win
  if you know how many you had before
  you lost or won.

Arithmetic is seven eleven all good children
  go to heaven — or five six bundle of sticks.

Arithmetic is numbers you squeeze from your
  head to your hand to your pencil to your
  paper till you get the answer.

Arithmetic is where the answer is right and
  everything is nice and you can look
  out the window and see the blue sky —
  or the answer is wrong and you have to
  start all over and try again and see how
  it comes out this time.

Carl Sandburg

CONTENTS

INTRODUCTION

The Arithmetic Primer is about adding, subtracting, multiplying, and dividing at the speed of pencil and paper at the 99% level of mastery. Thus it is about what a pocket calculator can do at the speed of light at the 100% level of mastery. However, it is not just about adding, subtracting, multiplying, and dividing with less speed and accuracy than a pocket calculator. Rather, it is about doing so as a way of *thinking about the real world —* about the *right* buttons to push on a pocket calculator.

The Arithmetic Primer is for people who need to improve their computational skill. More than that, it is for people who need to do so *right now*. It consists of the items in Figures 1–6 and adheres to the format in Figure 7 (pages xv-xvii). Its most important characteristics as far as you are concerned are the following:

> It is effective. It has worked for everyone so far, and it will work for you. It will raise your computational skill to the 90% level of mastery.

> It is easy to use. It tells you what to do with "go to" statements. It shows you how to learn.

> It is efficient. It has you skipping the things you already know and working on just the things you do not know. It will *not* waste your time.

To begin, review the vocabulary items on the next page. Then turn to page xviii and proceed as directed. You will finish, sooner than you think, with an amazing amount of knowledge, and you will do so regardless of what you know at present. The only burden on you is that you be totally honest with yourself as you take the tests and check your work.

2 8	Addend	7 5	Subtrahend	3 8	Multiplicand
+ 1 7	Addend	− 4 9	Minuend	× 4	Multiplier
4 5	Sum	2 6	Difference	1 5 2	Product

$$\text{Divisor} \quad 4\overline{)30} \quad \begin{array}{l} 7R2 \quad \text{Quotient} \\ \text{Dividend} \end{array}$$

$\dfrac{4}{5}$ Numerator
Denominator

$\dfrac{2}{3}$ Proper fraction (numerator less than denominator)

$\dfrac{7}{3}$ Improper fraction (numerator greater than denominator)

$2\dfrac{3}{4}$ Mixed number (whole number and fraction in combination)

- Write your name in the space below.
- Write your name in the space on page xx.
- Take the test on page 1.

Continual Progress Report For _____

Skills	Subskills by Number and Page									
Addition of whole numbers	1	2	3	4	5	6	7	8		
	3	6	8	9	11	14	15	17		
Subtraction of whole numbers	1	2	3	4	5	6	7	8		
	21	23	25	27	29	31	33	36		
Multiplication of whole numbers	1	2	3	4	5	6	7	8	9	10
	39	43	45	48	50	52	54	56	59	62
Division of whole numbers	1	2	3	4	5	6	7	8	9	10
	66	68	71	73	75	77	80	82	84	86
Fractions: basic concepts	1	2	3	4	5	6	7	8	9	10
	97	100	103	106	108	110	114	116	119	121
	11	12	13	14	15	16	17	18	19	
	122	124	126	127	129	131	132	133	135	
Addition of fractions	1	2	3	4						
	139	142	146	149						
Subtraction of fractions	1	2	3	4						
	153	156	160	163						

Figure 1 Continual progress report. Keeps track of what you know and do not know. Aids with self-management.

Growth Record For _____

Scores on general survey tests for whole numbers:

    Pretest _____   Date _____

    Post test _____   Date _____

    Growth _____

Scores on general survey tests for fractions:

    Pretest _____   Date _____

    Post test _____   Date _____

    Growth _____

Scores on general survey tests for decimals and percents:

    Pretest _____   Date _____

    Post test _____   Date _____

    Growth _____

Scores on general survey tests for estimation, integers, less than, greater than, exponents, and square roots:

    Pretest _____   Date _____

    Post test _____   Date _____

    Growth _____

Figure 2 Growth record. Provides proof of progress. Develops confidence.

General Survey Pretest for Whole Numbers

1. $6 + 9 = ?$

2. $\begin{array}{r} 43 \\ +25 \end{array}$

3. $\begin{array}{r} 67 \\ +28 \end{array}$

4. $\begin{array}{r} 354 \\ +168 \end{array}$

5. $\begin{array}{r} 24036 \\ 31802 \\ +12791 \end{array}$

6. $15 - 8 = ?$

7. $\begin{array}{r} 38 \\ -14 \end{array}$

8. $\begin{array}{r} 92 \\ -47 \end{array}$

9. $\begin{array}{r} 741 \\ -358 \end{array}$

10. $\begin{array}{r} 30100 \\ -15921 \end{array}$

11. $6 \times 9 = ?$

12. $\begin{array}{r} 27 \\ \times 3 \end{array}$

13. $\begin{array}{r} 59 \\ \times 4 \end{array}$

14. $\begin{array}{r} 2016 \\ \times \ 58 \end{array}$

15. $\begin{array}{r} 2418 \\ \times 5300 \end{array}$

16. $17 \div 3 = ?$

17. $8\overline{)98}$

18. $6\overline{)542}$

19. $37\overline{)7528}$

20. Divide 36 into 548 and write the remainder as a fraction. Simplify if you know how.

- *STOP*
- Check your answers on page 331.
- Enter the number correct and today's date in the spaces provided on page xx.
- If you got 18 or more right, take the test on page 92.
- If you got less than 18 right, take the test on page 3.

Figure 3 General survey pretests and post tests. Provide for proper placement in text. Advancement by "go to" directives.

SECTION 3

SKILL

Addition of Whole Numbers

Inventory Pretest for
Addition of Whole Numbers

1. $5 + 8 = ?$
2. $5 + 7 + 2 = ?$

3. $\begin{array}{r} 37 \\ +12 \end{array}$

4. $\begin{array}{r} 46 \\ +37 \end{array}$

5. $\begin{array}{r} 276 \\ +352 \end{array}$

6. $\begin{array}{r} 473 \\ +289 \end{array}$

7. $\begin{array}{r} 487 \\ 29 \\ +315 \end{array}$

8. $\begin{array}{r} 31098 \\ 28736 \\ +10596 \end{array}$

- *STOP*
- Check your answers on page 331.
- Shade the boxes opposite "addition of whole numbers" on page xviii which correspond to the problems you got right.
- If you got all of them right, take the test on page 21.
- If you missed some of them, start working on the subskills in this section which correspond to the ones you missed.
- For each subskill, look at the example, study the solution, think about the lesson, and work the *odd* drill-and-practice problems.

Figure 4 Inventory pretests and post tests. Pinpoint deficiencies. Items keyed to subskills. Advancement by "go to" directives.

SUBSKILL 5: Two Addends with Exchanging of Tens

Problem: 2 7 5
    + 1 5 3

Solution:
- Add vertically from right to left.
- Exchange ten of a kind for one of next larger kind.

①
2 7 5
+ 1 5 3
4 2 8

Lesson: Combine like quantities. Exchange ten tens for a hundred.

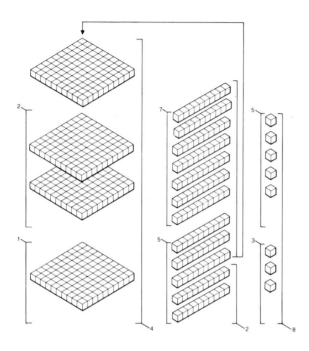

Drill and Practice:

Set 1
| 1. 461 | 2. 283 | 3. 395 | 4. 478 | 5. 2475 |
| +283 | +461 | +264 | +51 | +372 |

- *STOP.*
- Check your answers on page 331.
- Correct the problems you missed.
- Go on to Set 2.

Set 2
| 1. 264 | 2. 382 | 3. 111 | 4. 62 | 5. 1094 |
| +354 | +475 | +591 | +453 | +45285 |

- *STOP.*
- Check your answers on page 331.
- Correct the problems you missed.
- Go on to Set 3 or 4.

Set 3
| 1. 377 | 2. 188 | 3. 253 | 4. 887 | 5. 306873 |
| +261 | +331 | +253 | + 32 | + 2045 |

- *STOP.*
- Check your answers on page 331.
- Correct the problems you missed.
- Go on to Set 4.

Set 4

1. Add the digits on the license plates.

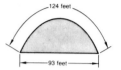

PAU 180

LYN 479

2. How many feet of fencing would you need for the garden plot?

124 feet — 93 feet

3. Chismo earned $183 for laying a brick wall and $45 for landscaping a backyard. How much did he earn all together?

4. Drone held a Sou weighing 83 grammins in his left hand and an Ardwelt weighing 46 grammins in his right hand. How many Sous was he holding?

5. You are having dinner at a fish and chips place. You order one serving of chips and two pieces of fish. One serving of chips contains 274 calories. Two pieces of fish contain 344 calories. How many calories will you consume?

- *STOP*
- Check your answers on page 331.
- Correct the problems you missed.
- Shade box 5 opposite "addition of whole numbers" on page xviii.
- If this was the last subskill you had to work on in this section, take the test on page 20.
- If you have other subskills to work on in this section, go on to the next one.

Figure 5 Remediation exercises, four sets for each subskill. Exercises keyed to items on inventory pre-tests and post tests. Advancement by "go to" directives.

ANSWERS

General Survey Pretest for Whole Numbers:

1. 15   *2.* 68   *3.* 95   *4.* 522   *5.* 68,629
6. 7   *7.* 24   *8.* 45   *9.* 383   *10.* 14,179
11. 54   *12.* 81   *13.* 236   *14.* 116,928
15. 12,815,400   *16.* 5R2   *17.* 12R2
18. 90R2   *19.* 203R17   *20.* 15$\frac{8}{36}$ or 15$\frac{2}{9}$

SKILL
Addition of Whole Numbers

Inventory Pretest:

1. 13   *2.* 14   *3.* 49   *4.* 83   *5.* 628
6. 762   *7.* 831   *8.* 70,430

Drill and Practice Sets by Subskill:

SUBSKILL 1:

Set 1
1. 11   *3.* 12   *5.* 16   *7.* 8   *9.* 9
Set 2
1. 18   *3.* 10   *5.* 15   *7.* 9   *9.* 14
Set 3
1. 17   *3.* 15   *5.* 10   *7.* 2   *9.* 8
Set 4
1. 8   *3.* (a) 13   (b) 14   *5.* $3

SUBSKILL 2:

Set 1
1. 16   *3.* 12   *5.* 15
Set 2
1. 14   *3.* 9   *5.* 14
Set 3
1. 24   *3.* 27   *5.* 20
Set 4
1. 14   *3.* Every sum is 15.   *5.* 22 cents

SUBSKILL 3:

Set 1
1. 597   *3.* 75   *5.* 4599

Set 2
1. 879   *3.* 99   *5.* 93,399
Set 3
1. 638   *3.* 77   *5.* 455,308
Set 4
1. 58 cents   *3.* Eight miles per hour
5. 12 feet, seven inches

SUBSKILL 4:

Set 1
1. 61   *3.* 67   *5.* 391
Set 2
1. 50   *3.* 80   *5.* 8671
Set 3
1. 40   *3.* 92   *5.* 66,962
Set 4
1. 40 cents   *3.* Twenty-fifth floor   *5.* 552

SUBSKILL 5:

Set 1
1. 744   *3.* 659   *5.* 2847
Set 2
1. 618   *3.* 702   *5.* 46,379
Set 3
1. 638   *3.* 506   *5.* 308,918
Set 4
1. 659   *3.* $228   *5.* 618

SUBSKILL 6:

Set 1
1. 834   *3.* 610   *5.* 1830
Set 2
1. 410   *3.* 902   *5.* 15,898
Set 3
1. 900   *3.* 443   *5.* 574,921
Set 4
1. $1   *3.* 211 pounds   *5.* 918

Figure 6 Answers. Provide for self-checking. Location by "go to" directives.

An Instructor's Manual, available to teachers, shows how to use The Arithmetic Primer *as a consumable or non-consumable basal, supplementary, or self-instructional text. Includes black-line masters of continual progress report, growth record, three forms of a 50-item proficiency test, a set of base ten blocks, a set of fraction discs, a set of fraction dominoes, and a set of math rummy cards.*

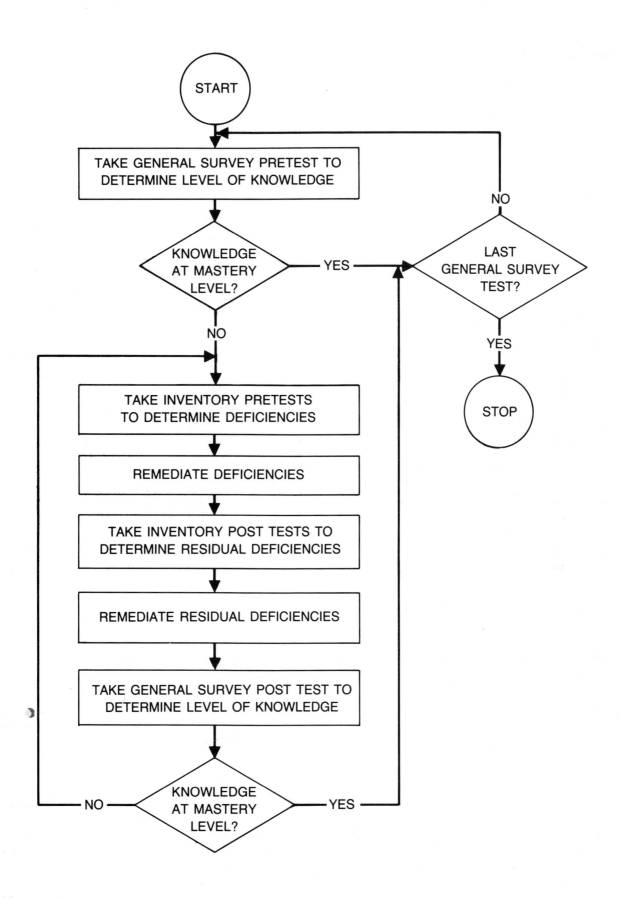

Figure 7 Program of instruction. Loops guarantee *mastery.*

Section 1 Continual Progress Report and Growth Record

- Write your name in the space below.
- Write your name in the space on page xx.
- Take the test on page 1.

Continual Progress Report For _____

Skills	Subskills by Number and Page									
Addition of whole numbers	1	2	3	4	5	6	7	8		
	3	6	8	9	11	14	15	17		
Subtraction of whole numbers	1	2	3	4	5	6	7	8		
	21	23	25	27	29	31	33	36		
Multiplication of whole numbers	1	2	3	4	5	6	7	8	9	10
	39	43	45	48	50	52	54	56	59	62
Division of whole numbers	1	2	3	4	5	6	7	8	9	10
	66	68	71	73	75	77	80	82	84	86
Fractions: basic concepts	1	2	3	4	5	6	7	8	9	10
	97	100	103	106	108	110	114	116	119	121
	11	12	13	14	15	16	17	18	19	
	122	124	126	127	129	131	132	133	135	
Addition of fractions	1	2	3	4						
	139	142	146	149						
Subtraction of fractions	1	2	3	4						
	153	156	160	163						

Multiplication of fractions	1	2	3	4	5					
	167	171	174	177	181					
Division of fractions	1	2	3	4	5	6				
	187	190	192	194	196	198				
Working with decimals	1	2	3	4	5	6	7	8	9	10
	206	209	212	213	216	218	221	222	227	231
	11	12	13	14						
	236	238	241	243						
Working with percents	1	2	3	4	5	6	7	8		
	248	251	252	254	256	257	259	261		
Estimation	1	2	3	4						
	270	273	275	277						
Integers	1	2	3	4	5	6				
	282	285	288	291	293	295				
Less than and greater than	1	2	3	4	5					
	298	300	301	303	304					
Exponents and roots	1	2	3	4	5	6	7	8	9	
	308	310	312	314	316	317	320	323	325	

Growth Record For _____

    Scores on general survey tests for whole numbers:

        Pretest _____   Date _____

        Post test _____   Date _____

        Growth _____

    Scores on general survey tests for fractions:

        Pretest _____   Date _____

        Post test _____   Date _____

        Growth _____

    Scores on general survey tests for decimals and percents:

        Pretest _____   Date _____

        Post test _____   Date _____

        Growth _____

    Scores on general survey tests for estimation, integers, less than, greater than, exponents, and square roots:

        Pretest _____   Date _____

        Post test _____   Date _____

        Growth _____

General Survey Pretest
for Whole Numbers

1. $6 + 9 = ?$

2. $\begin{array}{r} 43 \\ +25 \\ \hline \end{array}$

3. $\begin{array}{r} 67 \\ +28 \\ \hline \end{array}$

4. $\begin{array}{r} 354 \\ +168 \\ \hline \end{array}$

5. $\begin{array}{r} 24036 \\ 31802 \\ +12791 \\ \hline \end{array}$

6. $15 - 8 = ?$

7. $\begin{array}{r} 38 \\ -14 \\ \hline \end{array}$

8. $\begin{array}{r} 92 \\ -47 \\ \hline \end{array}$

9. $\begin{array}{r} 741 \\ -358 \\ \hline \end{array}$

10. $\begin{array}{r} 30100 \\ -15921 \\ \hline \end{array}$

11. $6 \times 9 = ?$

12. $\begin{array}{r} 27 \\ \times 3 \\ \hline \end{array}$

13. $\begin{array}{r} 59 \\ \times 4 \\ \hline \end{array}$

14. $\begin{array}{r} 2016 \\ \times 58 \\ \hline \end{array}$

15. $\begin{array}{r} 2418 \\ \times 5300 \\ \hline \end{array}$

16. $17 \div 3 = ?$

17. $8 \overline{)98}$

18. $6 \overline{)542}$

19. $37 \overline{)7528}$

20. Divide 36 into 548 and write the remainder as a fraction. Simplify if you know how.

- *STOP*
- Check your answers on page 331.
- Enter the number correct and today's date in the spaces provided on page xx.
- If you got 18 or more right, take the test on page 92.
- If you got less than 18 right, take the test on page 3.

SKILL
Addition of Whole Numbers

Inventory Pretest for Addition of Whole Numbers

1. 5 + 8 = ?

2. 5 + 7 + 2 = ?

3. 37	4. 46	5. 276	6. 473	7. 487	8. 31098
+12	+37	+352	+289	29	28736
				+315	+10596

- *STOP*

- Check your answers on page 331.

- Shade the boxes opposite "addition of whole numbers" on page xviii which correspond to the problems you got right.

- If you got all of them right, take the test on page 21.

- If you missed some of them, start working on the subskills in this section which correspond to the ones you missed.

- For each subskill, look at the example, study the solution, think about the lesson, and work the *odd* drill-and-practice problems.

SUBSKILL 1: Addition Facts

Problem: 4 + 8 = ?

Solution: • Memorize addition facts in Table 3.1.

• When in doubt, count.

4 + 8 = 12

Table 3.1 Addition Facts

+	0	1	2	3	4	5	6	7	8	9
0	0	1	2	3	4	5	6	7	8	9
1	1	2	3	4	5	6	7	8	9	10
2	2	3	4	5	6	7	8	9	10	11
3	3	4	5	6	7	8	9	10	11	12
4	4	5	6	7	8	9	10	11	12	13
5	5	6	7	8	9	10	11	12	13	14
6	6	7	8	9	10	11	12	13	14	15
7	7	8	9	10	11	12	13	14	15	16
8	8	9	10	11	12	13	14	15	16	17
9	9	10	11	12	13	14	15	16	17	18

3

Lesson: Combine ones. Exchange ten ones for a ten.

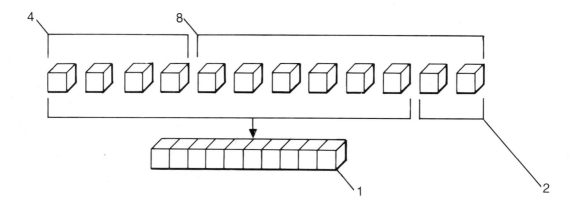

Drill and Practice:

Set 1

    1. 5 + 6 = ?
    2. 8 + 9 = ?
    3. 3 + 9 = ?

4. 7   5. 9   6. 0   7. 4   8. 2   9. 5 10. 1
  +6   +7   +5   +4   +1   +4   +0

- *STOP.*
- Check your answers on page 331.
- Correct the problems you missed.
- Go on to Set 2.

Set 2.

    1. 9 + 9 = ?
    2. 7 + 7 = ?
    3. 6 + 4 = ?

4. 2   5. 8   6. 2   7. 3   8. 2   9. 8 10. 2
  +9   +7   +4   +6   +2   +6   +5

- *STOP.*
- Check your answers on page 331.
- Correct the problems you missed.
- Go on to Set 3 or 4.

Set 3

    1. 9 + 8 = ?
    2. 8 + 8 = ?
    3. 6 + 9 = ?

4. 6   5. 3   6. 4   7. 1   8. 6   9. 5 10. 0
  +6   +7   +3   +1   +7   +3   +0

- *STOP.*
- Check your answers on page 331.
- Correct the problems you missed.
- Go on to Set 4.

Set 4

1. Total the dice.

2. Count the dots.

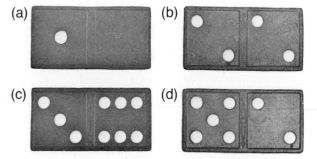

(a)   (b)

(c)   (d)

3. Count the dots.

(a)

(b)

4. Write two addition sentences for the tacks.

5. How much for one can of washer spray and one dish drainer?

16 OZ. WASHER SPRAY

$1

Stubborn stains disappear as you wash. Just spray on and throw in the washer.

5 PC. DISH DRAIN

$2

Plastic drain tray, silverware, cup, soap dish, spatula, & mat.

- *STOP*

- Check your answers on page 331.

- Correct the problems you missed.

- Shade box 1 opposite "addition of whole numbers" on page xviii.

- If this was the only subskill you had to work on in this section, take the test on page 20.

- If you have other subskills to work on in this section, go on to the next one.

SUBSKILL 2: Three Single-Digit Addends

Problem: 4 + 3 + 6 = ?

Solution:
- Memorize addition facts in Table 3.2.
- Add two at a time.
- When in doubt, count.

4 + 3 + 6 = ⑦ + 6 = 13

Table 3.2 Addition Facts

+	0	1	2	3	4	5	6	7	8	9
0	0	1	2	3	4	5	6	7	8	9
1	1	2	3	4	5	6	7	8	9	10
2	2	3	4	5	6	7	8	9	10	11
3	3	4	5	6	7	8	9	10	11	12
4	4	5	6	⑦	8	9	10	11	12	13
5	5	6	7	8	9	10	11	12	13	14
6	6	7	8	9	10	11	12	13	14	15
7	7	8	9	10	11	12	13	14	15	16
8	8	9	10	11	12	13	14	15	16	17
9	9	10	11	12	13	14	15	16	17	18

Lesson: Combine ones. Exchange ten ones for a ten.

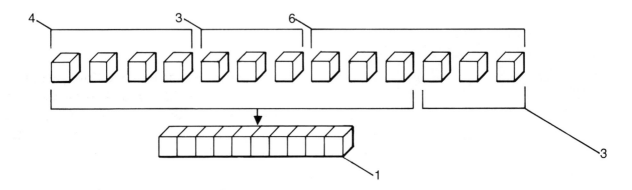

Drill and Practice:

Set 1

1. 6 + 2 + 8 = ?   2. 3 + 5 + 7 = ?

3. 4   4. 2   5. 7
    5   5   1
  + 3   + 1   + 7

- *STOP.*
- Check your answers on page 331.
- Correct the problems you missed.
- Go on to Set 2.

Set 2

1. 5 + 8 + 1 = ?   2. 9 + 2 + 4 = ?

3. 2   4. 1   5. 6
    3   2   3
  + 4   + 7   + 5

- *STOP.*
- Check your answers on page 331.
- Correct the problems you missed.
- Go on to Set 3 or 4.

Set 3

1. 7 + 8 + 9 = ?   2. 1 + 7 + 8 = ?

3. 9   4. 2   5. 7
    9   1   6
  + 9   + 4   + 7

- *STOP.*
- Check your answers on page 331.
- Correct the problems you missed.
- Go on to Set 4.

Set 4

1. Count the dots.

2. Total the score on the dartboard.

3. The following array of numbers is called a magic square. To see why, add the numbers in each row, each column, and along both diagonals.

6	7	2
1	5	9
8	3	4

4. It takes a snake 30 minutes to slither one mile. It takes a turtle two hours to walk one mile. And it takes a snail five hours to crawl one mile. How long would it take all three creatures to travel one mile?

5. One pear costs five cents. Four pieces of celery cost eight cents. And two apples cost nine cents. How much would one pear, four pieces of celery, and two apples cost?

- *STOP*

- Check your answers on page 331.

- Correct the problems you missed.

- Shade box 2 opposite "addition of whole numbers" on page xviii.

- If this was the last subskill you had to work on in this section, take the test on page 20.

- If you have other subskills to work on in this section, go on to the next one.

SUBSKILL 3: Addition Without Exchanging

Problem:
```
  2 3 5
+ 1 2 4
```

Solution: ● Add vertically from right to left.

```
  2 3 5
+ 1 2 4
───────
┌─────┐
│3 5 9│
└─────┘
```

Lesson: Combine like quantities.

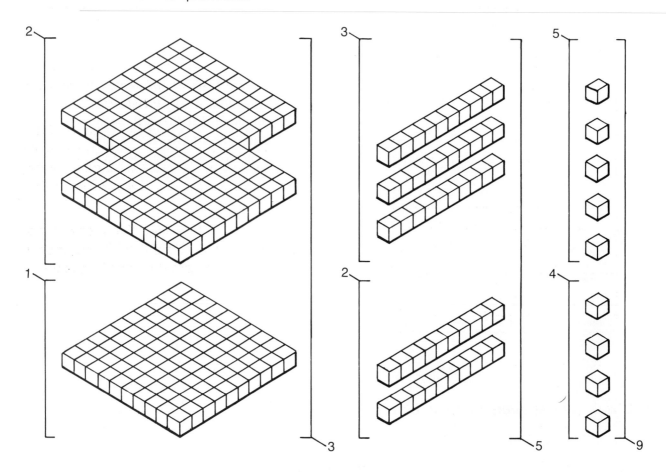

Drill and Practice:

Set 1

1. 172	2. 271	3. 43	4. 32	5. 3078
+425	+ 14	+32	+ 3	+1521

Set 2

1. 608	2. 45	3. 55	4. 6	5. 43182
+271	+124	+44	+41	+50217

● *STOP.*
● Check your answers on page 331.
● Correct the problems you missed.
● Go on to Set 2.

● *STOP.*
● Check your answers on page 331.
● Correct the problems you missed.
● Go on to Set 3 or 4.

Set 3

1. 425   2. 530   3. 25   4. 14   5. 420105
    +213   + 27   +52   + 5   + 35203

● *STOP.*
● Check your answers on page 331.
● Correct the problems you missed.
● Go on to Set 4.

Set 4

1. Total the cashier's slip.

PLEASE PAY CASHIER	
sm coke	25
sm fries	30
total	
Tax	3

CHECK NUMBER GUESTS ATTENDANT TOTAL
40903

5F650 Rediform A B C D E F G H I

2. What was the original cost of the open hearth bedroom?

3. A man jogs eight miles per hour. A woman jogs eight miles per hour. How fast would they jog together?

4. The distance from Basuraville to Conckshell is 12 miles. The distance from Conckshell to Oprystar is 35 miles. What is the distance from Basuraville to Oprystar?

5. One board is four feet, five inches long. Another board is eight feet, two inches long. How long are the boards together?

● *STOP*

● Check your answers on page 331.

● Correct the problems you missed.

● Shade box 3 opposite "addition of whole numbers" on page xviii.

● If this was the last subskill you had to work on in this section, take the test on page 20.

● If you have other subskills to work on in this section, go on to the next one.

SUBSKILL 4: Two Addends with Exchanging of Ones

Problem: 3 5
            + 4 7

Solution: ● Add vertically from right to left.

- Exchange ten of a kind for one of next larger kind.

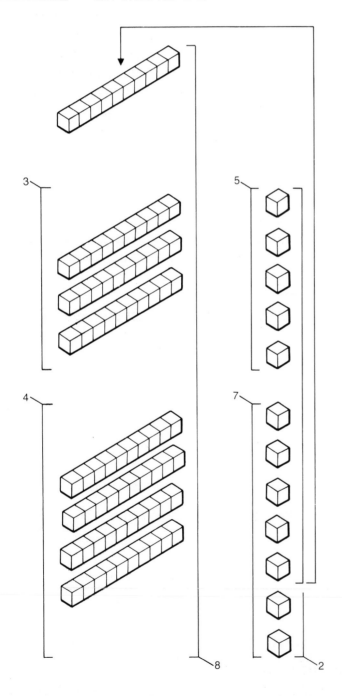

Lesson: Combine like quantities. Exchange ten ones for a ten.

Drill and Practice:

Set 1

1.　27　2.　43　3.　29　4.　7　5.　234
　+34　　+ 7　　+38　　+25　　+157

- *STOP.*
- Check your answers on page 331.
- Correct the problems you missed.
- Go on to Set 2.

Set 2

1.　15　2.　3　3.　46　4.　17　5.　5042
　+35　　+29　　+34　　+ 8　　+3629

- *STOP.*
- Check your answers on page 331.
- Correct the problems you missed.
- Go on to Set 3 or 4.

Set 3

1.　26　2.　28　3.　66　4.　1　5.　61034
　+14　　+ 4　　+26　　+19　　+ 5928

- *STOP.*
- Check your answers on page 331.
- Correct the problems you missed.
- Go on to Set 4.

Set 4

1. Add the values of the coins.

2. Total the cashier's slip.

PLEASE PAY CASHIER

Hot cakes	39
Sm coffee c/s	25
total	
Tax	3

CHECK NUMBER	GUESTS	ATTENDANT	TOTAL
40903			

5F650 Rediform   A B C D E F G H I

3. Four men and two women got on an elevator at ground level. The elevator went up seventeen floors. Three men and one woman got off the elevator. Five men and one woman got on the elevator. The elevator went up eight floors. Three men and two women got off the elevator. Two men and four women got on the elevator. The elevator is on what floor?

4. Kipp was 38 inches tall. He grew four inches. How tall is he now?

5. You are having breakfast at a restaurant. You order scrambled eggs and one order of pork sausage. One order of scrambled eggs contains 317 calories. One order of pork sausage contains 235 calories. How many calories will you consume?

- *STOP*

- Check your answers on page 331.

- Correct the problems you missed.

- Shade box 4 opposite "addition of whole numbers" on page xviii.

- If this was the last subskill in this section you had to work on, take the test on page 20.

- If you have other subskills in this section to work on, go on to the next one.

SUBSKILL 5: Two Addends with Exchanging of Tens

Problem:
    2 7 5
  + 1 5 3

Solution:
- Add vertically from right to left.

- Exchange ten of a kind for one of next larger kind.

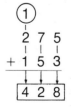

Lesson: Combine like quantities. Exchange ten tens for a hundred.

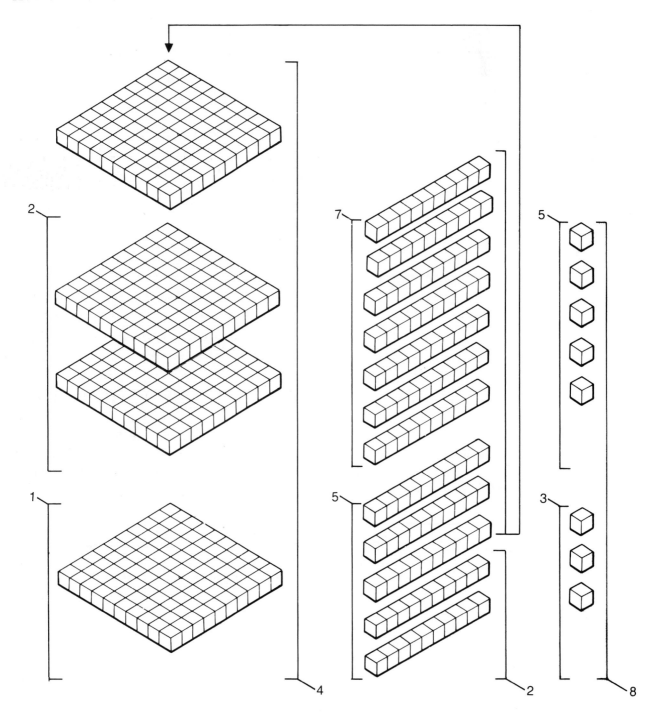

Drill and Practice:

Set 1

1. 461	2. 283	3. 395	4. 478	5. 2475
+283	+461	+264	+ 51	+ 372

- *STOP.*
- Check your answers on page **331**.
- Correct the problems you missed.
- Go on to Set 2.

Set 2

1. 264	2. 382	3. 111	4. 62	5. 1094
+354	+475	+591	+453	+45285

- *STOP.*
- Check your answers on page **331**.
- Correct the problems you missed.
- Go on to Set 3 or 4.

Set 3

1. 377 2. 188 3. 253 4. 887 5. 306873
   +261   +331   +253   + 32   + 2045

- *STOP.*
- Check your answers on page 331.
- Correct the problems you missed.
- Go on to Set 4.

Set 4

1. Add the digits on the license plates.

PAU 180

LYN 479

2. How many feet of fencing would you need for the garden plot?

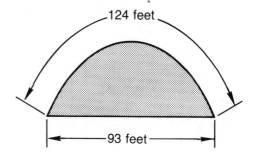
124 feet

93 feet

3. Chismo earned $183 for laying a brick wall and $45 for landscaping a backyard. How much did he earn all together?

4. Drone held a Sou weighing 83 grammins in his left hand and an Ardwell weighing 46 grammins in his right hand. How many Sous was he holding?

5. You are having dinner at a fish and chips place. You order one serving of chips and two pieces of fish. One serving of chips contains 274 calories. Two pieces of fish contain 344 calories. How many calories will you consume?

- *STOP*
- Check your answers on page 331.
- Correct the problems you missed.
- Shade box 5 opposite "addition of whole numbers" on page xviii.
- If this was the last subskill you had to work on in this section, take the test on page 20.
- If you have other subskills to work on in this section, go on to the next one.

SUBSKILL 6: Two Addends with Exchanging of Ones and Tens

Problem:

$$\begin{array}{r} 5\ 7\ 6 \\ +\ 3\ 4\ 7 \\ \hline \end{array}$$

Solution:

- Add vertically from right to left.

- Exchange ten of a kind for one of next larger kind.

$$\begin{array}{r} \textcircled{1}\,\textcircled{1} \\ 5\ 7\ 6 \\ +\ 3\ 4\ 7 \\ \hline \boxed{9\ 2\ 3} \end{array}$$

Lesson: Combine like quantities. Exchange ten ones for a ten and ten tens for a hundred.

	Hundreds	Tens	Ones
	1 ←	1 ←	
	5	7	6
	3	4	7
+			
	9	①2	①3

Drill and Practice:

Set 1

1. 478   2. 123   3. 355   4. 476   5. 1296
   +356   +479   +255   + 58   + 534

- *STOP.*
- Check your answers on page 331.
- Correct the problems you missed.
- Go on to Set 2.

Set 2

1. 136   2. 454   3. 377   4. 36   5. 5599
   +274   +268   +525   +899   +10299

- *STOP.*
- Check your answers on page 331.
- Correct the problems you missed.
- Go on to Set 3 or 4.

Set 3

1. 444   2. 369   3. 176   4. 765   5. 421045
   +456   +258   +267   + 46   +153876

- *STOP.*
- Check your answers on page 331.
- Correct the problems you missed.
- Go on to Set 4.

Set 4

1. Add the values of the coins.

2. How much for one of each?

3. Torpo weighed 173 pounds. He gained 38 pounds. How much does he weigh now?

4. One board is one yard, two feet, eight inches long. Another board is four yards, one foot, seven inches long. How long are the boards together?

5. You are breaking a fast at a pizza parlor. You order two ten-inch pepperoni pizzas at 459 calories each. How many calories will you consume?

- *STOP*
- Check your answers on page 331.
- Correct the problems you missed.
- Shade box 6 opposite "addition of whole numbers" on page xviii.
- If this was the last subskill you had to work on in this section, take the test on page 20.
- If you have other subskills to work on in this section, go on to the next one.

SUBSKILL 7: Three Addends with Exchanging of Ones and Tens

Problem:
```
    5 7 8
      6 9
  + 2 3 4
```

Solution:
- Add vertically from right to left.
- Exchange ten of a kind for one of next larger kind.

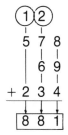

Lesson: Combine like quantities. Exchange ten ones for a ten and ten tens for a hundred.

Hundreds	Tens	Ones
1 ←	2 ←	
5	7	8
	6	9
2	3	4
+		
8	① 8	② 1

Drill and Practice:

Set 1

1. 456	2. 18	3. 389	4. 121	5. 2378
31	543	298	321	1359
+275	+257	+ 74	+458	+ 198

- *STOP.*
- Check your answers on page 332.
- Correct the problems you missed.
- Go on to Set 2.

Set 2

1. 36	2. 132	3. 453	4. 432	5. 11243
457	43	165	145	187
+182	+355	+ 12	+254	+ 2299

- *STOP.*
- Check your answers on page 332.
- Correct the problems you missed.
- Go on to Set 3 or 4.

Set 3

1. 245	2. 531	3. 93	4. 543	5. 100199
597	35	277	179	30288
+ 68	+234	+419	+163	+ 377

- *STOP.*
- Check your answers on page 332.
- Correct the problems you missed.
- Go on to Set 4.

Set 4

1. Complete the deposit slip.

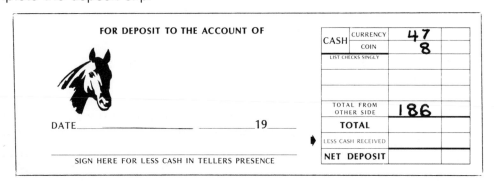

2. Jessica got three A's, three B's, one C, and one E on her report card. She was given 25 cents for each A, ten cents for each B, five cents for each C, and a discussion for each D or E. How much was she given?

3. A man and woman contributed $45 to the Christian Childrens' Fund, $12 to the Salvation Army, and $54 to the church. How much did they contribute?

4. Lynne twirled around twice and dropped her baton seven times. Jessica twirled around three times and dropped her baton six times. And Bradlee twirled around four times and dropped her baton five times. Which of them was the best twirler?

5. You are having lunch at a taco place. You order one enchirito, one taco, and one tostado. One enchirito contains 391 calories. One taco contains 146 calories. And one tostado contains 206 calories. How many calories will you consume?

6. How many inches of trim would you need for the table top?

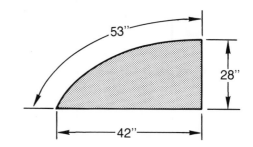

- *STOP*

- Check your answers on page 332.

- Correct the problems you missed.

- Shade box 7 opposite "addition of whole numbers" on page xviii.

- If this was the last subskill you had to work on in this section, take the test on page 20.

- If you have other subskills to work on in this section, go on to the next one.

SUBSKILL 8: Addition with Exchanging of Ones, Tens, Hundreds, and Thousands

Problem:

```
  2 7 9 0 7
  1 8 5 4 9
+ 3 8 6 5 0
```

Solution:

- Add vertically from right to left.

- Exchange ten of a kind for one of next larger kind.

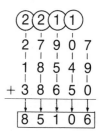

Lesson: Combine like quantities. Exchange ten ones for a ten, ten tens for a hundred, ten hundreds for a thousand, and ten thousands for a ten thousand.

Ten Thousands	Thousands	Hundreds	Tens	Ones
2 ←	2 ←	1 ←	1 ←	
2	7	9	0	7
1	8	5	4	9
3	8	6	5	0
8	(2) 5	(2) 1	(1) 0	(1) 6

+

Drill and Practice:

Set 1

```
1.  34657   2.  58739   3.  23013   4. 930254
    21967        4192        2584      85843
   +11728      +13129      +45103       7630
                                    + 10391
```

- *STOP.*
- Check your answers on page 332.
- Correct the problems you missed.
- Go on to Set 2.

Set 2

```
1.  23232   2.  3007   3.   376   4. 6592147
    15463       49876      49231      30706
   +46590      +32579     + 5508    1490375
                                       2103
                                   + 765251
```

- *STOP.*
- Check your answers on page 332.
- Correct the problems you missed.
- Go on to Set 3 or 4.

Set 3

```
1.  19270   2.    398   3. 43987   4. 86981213
    23465       3109        2986      97639302
   +27297     +45672      +   45      8976846
                                        30211
                                      4008139
                                   +40003156
```

- *STOP.*
- Check your answers on page 332.
- Correct the problems you missed.
- Go on to Set 4.

Set 4

1. Balance the check register.

CHECK NO.	DATE	CHECK ISSUED TO	AMOUNT OF CHECK	√	DATE OF DEP.	AMOUNT OF DEPOSIT	BALANCE
					BALANCE BROUGHT FORWARD →		4855
612	7/24	A & P	62				62
							4793
613	7/27	Shell Oil	85				85
							4708
		Deposit			8/1	5493	

2. Complete the deposit slip.

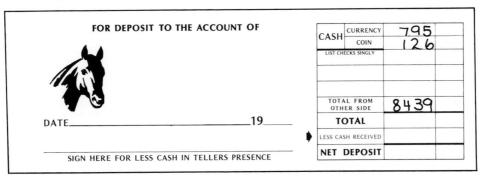

3. In one month Macho earned $895 at his regular occupation and $407 at his after-hours occupation. How much did he earn all together?

895
+407
1302

4. The distance from Phoenix, Arizona to Amarillo, Texas is 752 miles. The distance from Amarillo, Texas to St. Louis, Missouri is 785 miles. The distance from St. Louis, Missouri to Indianapolis, Indiana is 235 miles. The distance from Indianapolis, Indiana to New York, New York is 765 miles. And the distance from New York, New York to Augusta, Maine is 370 miles. What is the distance from Phoenix, Arizona, to Augusta, Maine?

5. For lunch you order one large hamburger, one large chocolate malt, and one serving of onion rings. One large hamburger contains 850 calories. One large chocolate malt contains 830 calories. And one serving of onion rings contains 300 calories. How many calories will you consume?

6. Solve the problems in Set 1 with the following addition facts algorithm.

$$
\begin{array}{r}
8\ 9\ 3\ 4 \\
5\ 7\ 1\ 6 \\
+\ 3\ 8\ 8\ 9 \\
\end{array}
\qquad
\begin{array}{r}
{}_1 8_0\ {}^2 9_0\ {}^1 3\ {}^1 4 \\
5_5\ 7\ 1_5\ 6_0 \\
+\ 3_8\ 8_5\ 8_3\ 9_9 \\
\hline
1\ 8\ 5\ 3\ 9 \\
\end{array}
$$

- *STOP*

- Check your answers on page 332.

- Correct the problems you missed.

- Shade box 8 opposite "addition of whole numbers" on page xviii.

- Take the test on page 20.

Inventory Post Test for
Addition of Whole Numbers

1. 7 + 6 = ?
2. 4 + 8 + 2 = ?

3. 25	4. 58	5. 364	6. 325	7. 104	8. 14573
+34	+23	+295	+497	65	40723
				+358	+28819

- *STOP*

- Check your answers with the instructor.

- As before, work through the subskills in this section which correspond to the problems you missed, except work the *even* drill-and-practice problems.

- Take the test on page 21.

SKILL
Subtraction of Whole Numbers

Inventory Pretest for
Subtraction of Whole Numbers

1. $7 - 3 = ?$
2. $14 - 8 = ?$

3. 746	4. 73	5. 537	6. 752	7. 52371	8. 70500
−425	−28	−154	−386	−14796	−32954

- *STOP*

- Check your answers on page 332.

- Shade the boxes opposite "subtraction of whole numbers" on page xviii which correspond to the problems you got right.

- If you got all of them right, take the test on page 39.

- If you missed some of them, start working on the subskills in this section which correspond to the ones you missed.

- For each subskill, look at the example, study the solution, think about the lesson, and work the *odd* drill-and-practice problems.

SUBSKILL 1: Subtraction Facts

Problem: $8 - 5 = ?$

Solution: • Memorize subtraction facts in Table 4.1. Row number is subtrahend. Column number is minuend.

• When in doubt, count.

$8 - 5 = \boxed{3}$

Table 4.1 Subtraction Facts

−	0	1	2	3	4	5	6	7	8	9
0	0									
1	1	0								
2	2	1	0							
3	3	2	1	0						
4	4	3	2	1	0					
5	5	4	3	2	1	0				
6	6	5	4	3	2	1	0			
7	7	6	5	4	3	2	1	0		
8	8	7	6	5	4	3̄	2	1	0	
9	9	8	7	6	5	4	3	2	1	0

Lesson: Separate minuend from subtrahend.

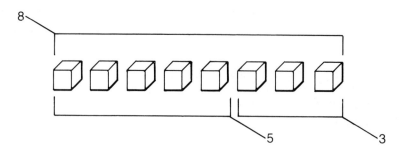

Drill and Practice:

Set 1

1. 9 − 6 = ?
2. 8 − 4 = ?

1.	5	4.	6	5.	9
	−2		−5		−1

- STOP.
- Check your answers on page 332.
- Correct the problems you missed.
- Go on to Set 2.

Set 2

1. 8 − 1 = ?
2. 5 − 5 = ?

3.	3	4.	8	5.	9
	−2		−6		−5

- STOP.
- Check your answers on page 332.
- Correct the problems you missed.
- Go on to Set 3 or 4.

Set 3

1. 9 − 3 = ?
2. 7 − 5 = ?

3.	9	4.	8	5.	3
	−0		−3		−3

- STOP.
- Check your answers on page 332.
- Correct the problems you missed.
- Go on to Set 4.

Set 4

1. Write two subtraction sentences for the dice.

2. Write two subtraction sentences for each domino.

(a)  (b)

(c)  (d)

3. Broadnoggin had nine pennies. He ate five of them. How many did he have left?

4. A snake can slither two miles per hour. A bee can fly six miles per hour. How much faster than a snake is a bee?

5. Yardsworth can jump four feet. Milestrung can jump seven feet. Yardsworth jumps how many feet fewer than Milestrung?

6. Fas and Slo finished third and fifth, respectively, in a race. How many people finished between them?

- *STOP*
- Check your answers on page 332.
- Correct the problems you missed.
- Shade box 1 opposite "subtraction of whole numbers" on page xviii.
- If this was the only subskill you had to work on in this section, take the test on page 37.
- If you have other subskills to work on in this section, go on to the next one.

SUBSKILL 2: Exchanging Facts

Problem: 13 − 7 = ?

Solution:
- Memorize exchanging facts in Table 4.2. Row number is subtrahend. Column number is minuend.

- When in doubt, count.

  13 − 7 = 6

Table 4.2 Exchanging Facts

−	1	2	3	4	5	6	7	8	9
10	9	8	7	6	5	4	3	2	1
11		9	8	7	6	5	4	3	2
12			9	8	7	6	5	4	3
13				9	8	7	6	5	4
14					9	8	7	6	5
15						9	8	7	6
16							9	8	8
17								9	8
18									9

Lesson: Exchange the ten for ten ones. Separate minuend from subtrahend.

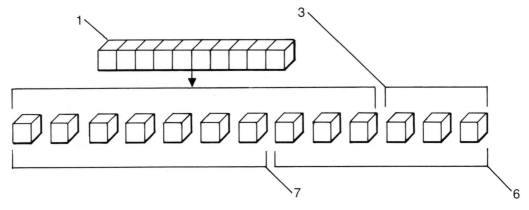

Drill and Practice:

Set 1

    1. 12 − 3 = ?

    2. 15 − 9 = ?

3. 13
   − 6

4. 14
   − 5

5. 17
   − 9

- STOP.
- Check your answers on page 332.
- Correct the problems you missed.
- Go on to Set 2.

Set 2

    1. 12 − 8 = ?

    2. 11 − 9 = ?

3. 10
   − 9

4. 14
   − 9

5. 12
   − 7

- STOP.
- Check your answers on page 332.
- Correct the problems you missed.
- Go on to Set 3 or 4.

Set 3

    1. 14 − 7 = ?

    2. 11 − 8 = ?

3. 11
   − 8

4. 16
   − 8

5. 15
   − 9

- STOP.
- Check your answers on page 332.
- Correct the problems you missed.
- Go on to Set 4.

Set 4

1. Write two subtraction sentences for each domino.

(a)

(b)

2. Write two subtraction sentences for the tacks.

3. Three men, one woman, and two children got off an elevator on the eighth floor. Two men, four women, and one child got on. The elevator went up to the thirteenth floor. Two men, three women, and three children got off the elevator. Four men and two women got on. The elevator traveled how many floors?

4. Jessica had 14 pennies. She spent eight of them. How many did she have left?

5. A sports event lasted from 9:00 A.M. to 12:00 A.M. How many hours did it last?

- *STOP*

- Check your answers on page 332.

- Correct the problems you missed.

- Shade box 2 opposite "subtraction of whole numbers" on page xviii.

- If this was the last subskill you had to work on in this section, take the test on page 37.

- If you have other subskills to work on in this section, go on to the next one.

SUBSKILL 3: Subtraction Without Exchanging

Problem:

$$\begin{array}{r} 3\ 7\ 6 \\ -\ 1\ 3\ 4 \\ \hline \end{array}$$

Solution:
- Subtract vertically from right to left.

$$\begin{array}{r} 3\ 7\ 6 \\ -\ 1\ 3\ 4 \\ \hline \boxed{2\ 4\ 2} \end{array}$$

Lesson: Separate minuend from subtrahend.

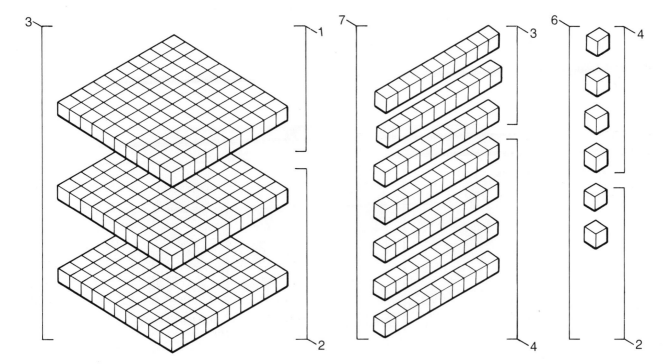

Drill and Practice:

Set 1

1. 485	2. 789	3. 85	4. 48	5. 4302
−132	− 56	−23	− 3	−2101

- *STOP*
- Check your answers on page 332.
- Correct the problems you missed.
- Go on to Set 2.

Set 2

1. 378	2. 385	3. 79	4. 58	5. 832573
−254	− 52	−34	− 6	−421320

- *STOP.*
- Check your answers on page 332.
- Correct the problems you missed.
- Go on to Set 3 or 4.

Set 3

1. 805	2. 435	3. 43	4. 24	5. 83452006
−401	− 21	−32	− 3	− 320005

- *STOP.*
- Check your answers on page 332.
- Correct the problems you missed.
- Go on to Set 4.

Set 4

1. Figure the change for the purchase.

2. Figure the savings on the potting soil.

IT'S FOR YOUR GARDEN!

5 LB. PLANT FOOD **96**c ea. REG. 1.29 — Choose from citrus/ avocado food, azalea/ camelia, all purpose, tomato food, rose food.

VITAMIN B-1 **77**c REG. 1.19 PINT VITAMIN B-1 Helps prevent the transplant shock.

LIQUID PLANT FOOD **1**68 REG. 2.29 Gallon size. Lets you fertilize the easy way.

POTTING MIX FOR PLANTS **59**c REG. 89c Helps plant hold moisture. 4 qt. for house or garden.

3. At the beginning of summer Pax was 45 inches tall. At the end of summer he was 48 inches tall. How much did he grow during the summer?

4. The paperback edition of *A Tale of Two Cities* by Charles Dickens is 367 pages long. Jessica read 243 pages of it. How many pages does she have left to read?

5. You are running a mile against time. Your watch shows 1:41.40 (one hour, 41 minutes, and 40 seconds) when you begin. It shows 1:47.52 when you finish. What was your time for the mile?

- *STOP*
- Check your answers on page 332.
- Correct the problems you missed.
- Shade box 3 opposite "subtraction of whole numbers" on page xviii.
- If this was the last subskill you had to work on in this section, take the test on page 37.
- If you have other subskills to work on in this section, go on to the next one.

SUBSKILL 4: Subtraction with Exchanging of Tens

Problem:
$$\begin{array}{r} 7\,2 \\ -\,4\,9 \\ \hline \end{array}$$

Solution:
- Subtract vertically from right to left.
- Exchange if lower digit is greater than upper digit.

$$\begin{array}{r} \overset{6}{\cancel{7}}\,\overset{12}{2} \\ -\,4\,9 \\ \hline \boxed{2\;3} \end{array}$$

Lesson: Exchange a ten for ten ones. Separate minuend from subtrahend.

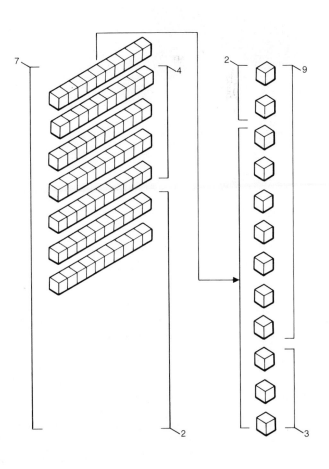

Drill and Practice:

Set 1

1. 54	2. 73	3. 47	4. 23	5. 475
−25	−38	−18	−8	−349

- *STOP.*
- Check your answers on page 332.
- Correct the problems you missed.
- Go on to Set 2.

Set 2

1. 36	2. 45	3. 73	4. 42	5. 3871
−17	−28	−46	− 4	−157

- *STOP.*
- Check your answers on page 332.
- Correct the problems you missed.
- Go on to Set 3 or 4.

Set 3

1. 55	2. 81	3. 50	4. 57	5. 10982
−28	−73	−27	− 8	−10435

- *STOP.*
- Check your answers on page 332.
- Correct the problems you missed.
- Go on to Set 4.

Set 4

1. Figure the change for the purchase.

2. A woman weighing 132 pounds lost nine pounds. How much does she weigh now?

3. A very fast person can run 18 miles per hour. A very fast horse can run 45 miles per hour. How much faster than a very fast person is a very fast horse?

4. Lynne is 66 inches tall. Paul is 70 inches tall. How much taller than Lynne is Paul?

5. A gravestone reads "Born July 7, 1924, Died September 24, 1972." How many years old was the person when he or she died?

- *STOP*
- Check your answers on page 332.
- Correct the problems you missed.
- Shade box 4 opposite "subtraction of whole numbers" on page xviii.
- If this was the last subskill you had to work on in this section, take the test on page 37.
- If you have other subskills to work on in this section, go on to the next one.

SUBSKILL 5: Subtraction with Exchanging of Hundreds

Problem:
```
  4 2 8
- 2 4 3
```

Solution:
- Subtract vertically from right to left.

- Exchange if lower digit is greater than upper digit.

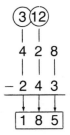

Lesson: Exchange a hundred for ten tens. Separate minuend from subtrahend.

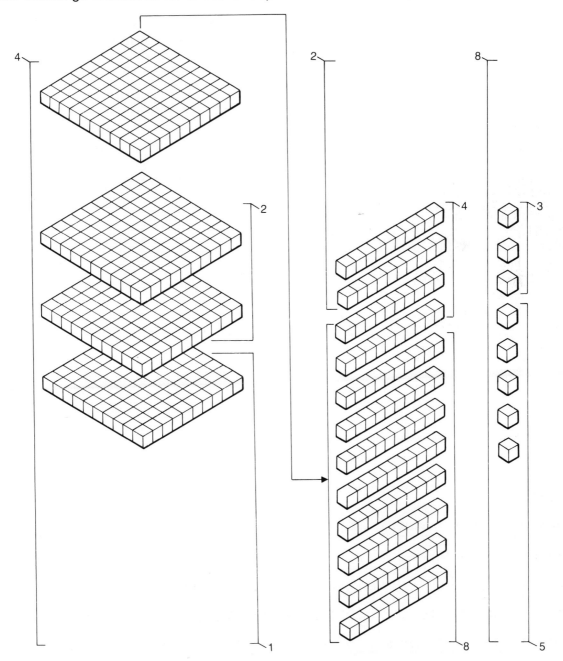

Drill and Practice:

Set 1

1. 456	2. 359	3. 518	4. 208	5. 4736
−283	− 84	−235	− 47	− 395

- *STOP.*
- Check your answers on page **332.**
- Correct the problems you missed.
- Go on to Set 2.

Set 2

1. 555	2. 273	3. 936	4. 321	5. 48437
−264	− 82	−263	− 50	− 2255

- *STOP.*
- Check your answers on page **332.**
- Correct the problems you missed.
- Go on to Set 3 or 4.

Set 3

1. 543	2. 866	3. 209	4. 586	5. 574567
−262	− 81	−183	− 95	−570283

- *STOP.*
- Check your answers on page **332.**
- Correct the problems you missed.
- Go on to Set 4.

Set 4

1. Balance the check register.

CHECK NO.	DATE	CHECK ISSUED TO	AMOUNT OF CHECK	DATE OF DEP	AMOUNT OF DEPOSIT	BALANCE
		BALANCE BROUGHT FORWARD ➔				428
501	6/20	SAFEWAY	62			62 / 366
502	7/1	PENNEYS	91			91 / 275
503	7/3	MASTER CHARGE	85			

2. Complete the receipt.

No. _____   _____ 19 ____

Received of _____

Eighty One and no/100 ~~~~~~~ **Dollars**

Amt of Account	1432	
Amt Paid	81	
Balance Due		

$ 81 _____

3. In taking an engine apart, you ended up with 228 nuts and bolts. In putting the engine back together, you used 196 of them. How many nuts and bolts did you have left over?

4. The distance from Phoenix, Arizona to New York, New York is 2537 miles. And the distance from Phoenix, Arizona to Augusta, Maine is 2907 miles. What is the distance from New York, New York to Augusta, Maine?

- *STOP*

- Check your answers on page 332.

- Correct the problems you missed.

- Shade box 5 opposite "subtraction of whole numbers" on page xviii.

- If this was the last subskill in this section you had to work on, take the test on page 37.

- If you have other subskills in this section to work on, go on to the next one.

SUBSKILL 6: Subtraction with Exchanging of Tens and Hundreds

Problem:
```
  8 3 7
- 6 7 9
```

Solution: • Subtract vertically from right to left.

• Exchange if lower digit is greater than upper digit.

```
        (12)
  (7)(2)(17)
   8  3  7
  -6  7  9
  -----------
  | 1  5  8 |
```

Hundreds	Tens	Ones
7 8	12 2 3	17 7
− 6	7	9
1	5	8

Lesson: Exchange a ten for ten ones and a hundred for ten tens. Subtract.

Drill and Practice:

Set 1

1. 523   2. 473   3. 325   4. 764   5. 4788
  −276   −189   −136   − 86   −2699

- *STOP.*
- Check your answers on page 332.
- Correct the problems you missed.
- Go on to Set 2.

Set 2

1. 831   2. 670   3. 911   4. 175   5. 35417
   −652   −384   −222   − 87   −12368

Set 3

1. 617   2. 526   3. 460   4. 318   5. 672231
   −328   −339   −273   − 29   −670143

- STOP.
- Check your answers on page 332.
- Correct the problems you missed.
- Go on to Set 3 or 4.

- STOP.
- Check your answers on page 332.
- Correct the problems you missed.
- Go on to Set 4.

Set 4

1. Balance the check register.

CHECK NO.	DATE	CHECK ISSUED TO	AMOUNT OF CHECK	DATE OF DEP	AMOUNT OF DEPOSIT	BALANCE
		BALANCE BROUGHT FORWARD ➤				*1517*
521	*9/20*	*WOOLWORTH'S*	*21*			*21* *1496*
522	*9/27*	*HOWARD JOHNSON'S*	*48*			*48* *1448*
523	*10/1*	*SEARS*	*79*			

2. Complete the receipt.

No. _____	_____ 19 ___

Received of _____

SEVEN HUNDRED SIXTY THREE AND ^*NO*/*100* Dollars

Amt of Account	*951*
Amt Paid	*763*
Balance Due	

$ *763*

3. The paperback edition of *Moby Dick* by Herman Melville is 536 pages long. Bradlee read 79 pages of it. How many pages does she have left to read?

4. The distance around a back yard is 230 feet. One hundred forty-seven feet of fencing have been purchased for the yard. How many feet of fencing remain to be purchased?

5. A gravestone reads "Born August 29, 1897, Died May 15, 1964." How many years old was the person when he or she died?

6. A 120-pound woman uses about 240 calories per hour when doing active housework such as using a vacuum cleaner. She uses about 84 calories per hour when resting such as reading. How many more calories does she use when doing active housework than when resting?

7. Solve the problems in Set 1 with the following equal additions algorithm.

$$
\begin{array}{r} 9\ 3\ 2 \\ -\ 5\ 4\ 7 \\ \hline \end{array}
\rightarrow
\begin{array}{r} 9\ 3\ 2 \\ {\scriptstyle 6\ 5} \\ -\ \not{5}\ \not{4}\ 7 \\ \hline 3\ 8\ 5 \end{array}
$$

• *STOP*

• Check your answers on page 333.

• Correct the problems you missed.

• Shade box 6 opposite "subtraction of whole numbers" on page xviii.

• If this was the last subskill you had to work on in this section, take the test on page 37.

• If you have other subskills to work on in this section, go on to the next one.

SUBSKILL 7: Subtraction with Exchanging of Tens, Hundreds, Thousands, and Ten Thousands

Problem:
$$
\begin{array}{r} 6\ 3\ 5\ 7\ 2 \\ -\ 2\ 5\ 6\ 9\ 8 \\ \hline \end{array}
$$

Solution:
• Subtract vertically from right to left.

• Exchange if lower digit is greater than upper digit.

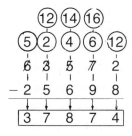

Lesson: Exchange a ten for ten ones, a hundred for ten tens, a thousand for ten hundreds, and a ten thousand for ten thousands. Subtract.

Ten Thousands	Thousands	Hundreds	Tens	Ones
5 ⤦ 6̸	12 ⤦ 2 3	14 ⤦ 4 5	16 ⤦ 6 7	12 ⤦ 2
2	5	6	9	8
3	7	8	7	4

Drill and Practice:

Set 1

1. 43210   2. 37421   3. 84762   4. 739483
  −14563   −18745   −35989   −256567

- *STOP.*
- Check your answers on page **333.**
- Correct the problems you missed.
- Go on to Set 2.

Set 2

1. 84837   2. 96340   3. 65314   4. 8937246
  −45949   −58581   −46728   −5456858

- *STOP.*
- Check your answers on page **333.**
- Correct the problems you missed.
- Go on to Set 3 or 4.

Set 3

1. 43214   2. 87538   3. 67340   4. 43216327
  −24936   −48859   −18495   −25763285

- *STOP.*
- Check your answers on page **333.**
- Correct the problems you missed.
- Go on to Set 4.

Set 4

1. Complete the deposit slip.

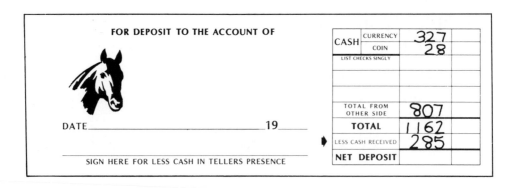

FOR DEPOSIT TO THE ACCOUNT OF		
CASH	CURRENCY	327
	COIN	28
LIST CHECKS SINGLY		
TOTAL FROM OTHER SIDE		807
TOTAL		1162
LESS CASH RECEIVED		285
NET DEPOSIT		

DATE_____ 19____

_____
SIGN HERE FOR LESS CASH IN TELLERS PRESENCE

2. Determine the savings for each automobile.

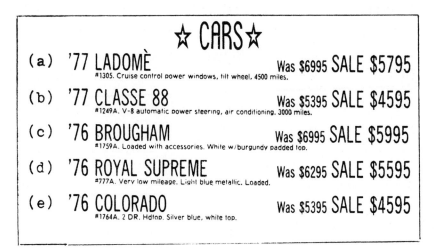

☆ CARS ☆

(a) '77 LADOMÈ
#1305. Cruise control power windows, tilt wheel, 4500 miles.
Was $6995 SALE $5795

(b) '77 CLASSE 88
#1249A. V-8 automatic power steering, air conditioning. 3000 miles.
Was $5395 SALE $4595

(c) '76 BROUGHAM
#1759A. Loaded with accessories. White w/burgundy padded top.
Was $6995 SALE $5995

(d) '76 ROYAL SUPREME
#777A. Very low mileage. Light blue metallic. Loaded.
Was $6295 SALE $5595

(e) '76 COLORADO
#1764A. 2 DR. Hdtop. Silver blue, white top.
Was $5395 SALE $4595

3. The paperback edition of *The Brothers Karamazov* by Dostoyevsky is 701 pages long. The paperback edition of *War and Peace* by Tolstoy is 1455 pages long. How much longer than *The Brothers Karamazov* is *War and Peace?*

4. You have traveled 1958 miles of a 2917 mile trip. How far away is your destination?

5. You are flying a kite with a 1510-foot ball of string. You let the kite out to where only 532 feet of string is left. How far away is the kite?

6. You are running a mile against time. Your watch shows 1:33.35 (one hour, 33 minutes, and 35 seconds) when you begin. It shows 1:41.20 when you finish. What was your time for the mile?

- *STOP*

- Check your answers on page 333.

- Correct the problems you missed.

- Shade box 7 opposite "subtraction of whole numbers" on page xviii.

- If this was the last subskill you had to work on in this section, take the test on page 37.

- If you have other subskills to work on in this section, go on to the next one.

SUBSKILL 8: Exchanging Across Zeros

Problem:

```
  5 0 7 0 0
- 2 3 8 5 6
```

Solution:
- Subtract vertically from right to left.
- Exchange if lower digit is greater than upper digit.

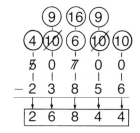

Lesson: Exchange a ten thousand for ten thousands, a thousand for ten hundreds, a hundred for ten tens, and a ten for ten ones. Subtract.

Ten Thousands	Thousands	Hundreds	Tens	Ones
4 / 5	9 / 10 / 0	16 / 6 / 7	9 / 10 / 0	10 / 0
− 2	3	8	5	6
2	6	8	4	4

Drill and Practice:

Set 1

1. 60800
   −23941

2. 7400
   −2536

3. 502
   −236

4. 600000
   −125483

- *STOP.*
- Check your answers on page 333.
- Correct the problems you missed.
- Go on to Set 2.

Set 2

1. 40200
   −12538

2. 3100
   − 243

3. 500
   − 19

4. 8000056
   −4139198

- *STOP.*
- Check your answers on page 333.
- Correct the problems you missed.
- Go on to Set 3 or 4.

Set 3

1. 50300
   −31465

2. 5604
   −3819

3. 300
   −173

4. 80403080
   −34526090

- *STOP.*
- Check your answers on page 333.
- Correct the problems you missed.
- Go on to Set 4.

Set 4

1. Two hundred ninety-three pieces of a 500-piece puzzle have been put together. How many pieces remain to be put together?

2. An automobile costing $6000 is marked down to $5999. How much of a savings is that?

3. How much more than one thousand is one million?

4. How many years from the year 1978 to the year 2000?

5. You are driving. The odometer on your car reads 48,027. You will have reached your destination when it reads 49,132. How much further do you have to go?

- *STOP*
- Check your answers on page 333.
- Correct the problems you missed.
- Shade box 8 opposite "subtraction of whole numbers" on page XViii.
- Take the test on page 37.

Inventory Post Test for Subtraction of Whole Numbers

$$1.\ 9 - 4 = ?$$
$$2.\ 13 - 7 = ?$$

3. 478	4. 52	5. 318	6. 732	7. 63107	8. 30700
-352	-37	-124	-569	-23288	-12852

- *STOP*
- Check your answers with the instructor.
- As before, work through the subskills in this section which correspond to the problems you missed, except work the *even* drill-and-practice problems.
- Take the test on page 39.

SKILL
Multiplication of Whole Numbers

Inventory Pretest for
Multiplication of Whole Numbers

1. $8 \times 7 = ?$

2. 34	3. 28	4. 152	5. 247	6. 13248	7. 3615	8. 7083	9. 42859	10. 7814
$\times\ 2$	$\times\ 3$	$\times\ 4$	$\times\ 3$	$\times\ \ \ \ 5$	$\times\ \ 24$	$\times\ 235$	$\times 35000$	$\times 2006$

- *STOP*

- Check your answers on page **333**.

- Shade the boxes opposite "multiplication of whole numbers" on page xviii which correspond to the problems you got right.

- If you got all of them right, take the test on page 65.

- If you missed some of them, start working on the subskills in this section which correspond to the ones you missed.

- For each subskill, look at the example, study the solution, think about the lesson, and work the *odd* drill-and-practice problems.

SUBSKILL 1: Multiplication Facts

Problem: $6 \times 8 = ?$

Solution:
- Memorize multiplication facts in Table 5.1.

- Learn finger method of multiplication for factors greater than five.

Count to six on fingers of one hand and put down finger touched twice. Count to eight on fingers of other hand and put down fingers touched twice. Read "down" fingers as tens and "up" fingers as ones and add tens to *product* of ones.

$$6 \times 8 = 10 + 10 + 10 + 10 + 4 \times 2 = \boxed{48}$$

Table 5.1 Multiplication Facts

×	0	1	2	3	4	5	6	7	8	9
0	0	0	0	0	0	0	0	0	0	0
1	0	1	2	3	4	5	6	7	8	9
2	0	2	4	6	8	10	12	14	16	18
3	0	3	6	9	12	15	18	21	24	27
4	0	4	8	12	16	20	24	28	32	36
5	0	5	10	15	20	25	30	35	40	45
6	0	6	12	18	24	30	36	42	48	54
7	0	7	14	21	28	35	42	49	56	63
8	0	8	16	24	32	40	48	56	64	72
9	0	9	18	27	36	45	54	63	72	81

Lesson: Six groups of eight ones.

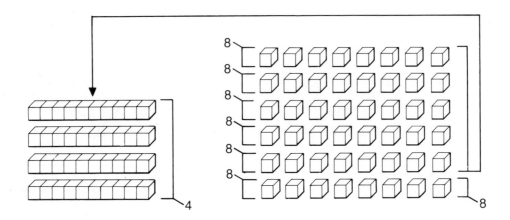

Drill and Practice:

Set 1

    1. 7 × 8 = ?   2. 3 × 5 = ?

3. 9	4. 3	5. 6	6. 7
×7	×0	×4	×2

7. 7	8. 3	9. 8	10. 7
×7	×2	×6	×4

Set 2

    1. 9 × 0 = ?   2. 1 × 7 = ?

3. 1	4. 7	5. 3	6. 8
×8	×6	×9	×5

7. 4	8. 8	9. 9	10. 6
×4	×4	×9	×5

- *STOP.*
- Check your answers on page 333.
- Correct the problems you missed.
- Go on to Set 2.

- *STOP.*
- Check your answers on page 333.
- Correct the problems you missed.
- Go on to Set 3 or 4.

Set 3

   1. $5 \times 2 = ?$ 2. $9 \times 5 = ?$

3. 7   4. 4   5. 8   6. 8
  $\times 3$ $\times 9$ $\times 6$ $\times 9$

7. 8   8. 4   9. 9   10. 6
  $\times 7$ $\times 5$ $\times 2$ $\times 9$

- *STOP.*
- Check your answers on page **333**.
- Correct the problems you missed.
- Go on to Set 4.

Set 4

1. Count the eggs.

2. Write two multiplication sentences for the cola bottles.

3. Count the paths from A to C.

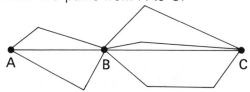

4. Write two multiplication sentences for all possible combinations of the following first and last names.

   First names: Lob, Zlu

   Last names: Tubbit, Gorf, Charlz

5. How many pennies could you get for the nickels?

6. Complete the sales slip.

| No. 166- 6 Date_____19__ |
| Name_____ |
| Address_____ |

SOLD BY	CASH	C. O. D.	CHARGE	ON ACCT.	MDSE. RETD.	PAID OUT

QUAN.		DESCRIPTION	AMOUNT
6	1	$\frac{1}{4}''$ HEX NUTS @ 4¢ EA	
7	2	9×2 WOOD SCREWS @ 5¢ EA	
8	3	$\frac{6}{32} \times \frac{3}{8}$ MAC SCREWS @ 2¢ EA	
9	4	$\frac{1}{4}''$ WING NUTS @ 7¢ EA	
6	5	$\frac{6}{32} \times \frac{3}{4}$ MAC SCREWS @ 3¢ EA	
	6		
	7	TOTAL	
	8		
	9		
	10		
	11		
	12		

| Customer's Order No. | Rec'd By |

7. Jessica has four skirts and six blouses. How many skirt-blouse combinations can she try on?

8. An orchard has one row of three apple trees, one row of four apple trees, and one row of five apple trees. How many rows of apple trees does it have?

9. There are two cups in one pint. How many cups are in

    (a) one quart (two pints)?

    (b) one gallon (four quarts)?

10. The following recipe is for one cup of homemade peanut butter. How much would you need to make four cups of it?

HOMEMADE PEANUT BUTTER

EQUIPMENT
Baking sheet
Measuring cup and spoons
Blender, plastic scraper

INGREDIENTS
2 cups shelled peanuts (dry-roasted, roasted in the shell or raw)
About 1 tablespoon vegatable oil
About 1 teaspoon salt

11. A classroom contains six rows of eight chairs each. How many chairs does it contain?

12. A fence is strung along ten fence posts. The fence posts are six meters apart. How long is the fence?

13. Find the area of the rectangle if the area of the shaded square is one.

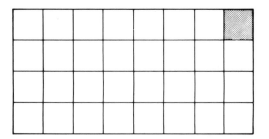

14. Find the area of the rectangle using $A = lw$ for the area A of a rectangle of length l and width w.

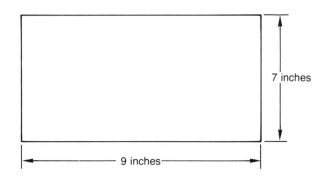

7 inches

9 inches

- *STOP*

- Check your answers on page 333.

- Correct the problems you missed.

- Shade box 1 opposite "multiplication of whole numbers" on page xviii.

- If this was the only subskill you had to work on in this section, take the test on page 64.

- If you have other subskills to work on in this section, go on to the next one.

SUBSKILL 2: Single-Digit Multiplier Without Exchanging

Problem:
$$\begin{array}{r} 4\ 3 \\ \times\ 2 \end{array}$$

Solution:
- Multiply top numbers by bottom number.
- Work from right to left.

$$\begin{array}{r} 4\ 3 \\ \times\ 2 \\ \hline \boxed{8\ 6} \end{array}$$

Lesson: Two groups of four tens and three ones.

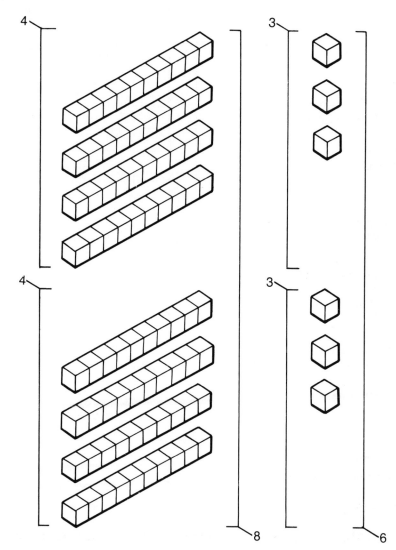

Drill and Practice:

Set 1

1. $\begin{array}{r} 32 \\ \times\ 2 \end{array}$ 2. $\begin{array}{r} 43 \\ \times\ 1 \end{array}$ 3. $\begin{array}{r} 20 \\ \times\ 3 \end{array}$ 4. $\begin{array}{r} 231 \\ \times\ 3 \end{array}$ 5. $\begin{array}{r} 21343 \\ \times\ 2 \end{array}$

- *STOP.*
- Check your answers on page **333**.
- Correct the problems you missed.
- Go on to Set 2.

Set 2

1. 21
   × 4

2. 43
   × 0

3. 40
   × 2

4. 222
   × 4

5. 312302
   ×   3

- *STOP.*
- Check your answers on page 333.
- Correct the problems you missed.
- Go on to Set 3 or 4.

Set 3

1. 23
   × 1

2. 14
   × 2

3. 24
   × 0

4. 123
   × 2

5. 4444444
   ×   2

- *STOP.*
- Check your answers on page 333.
- Correct the problems you missed.
- Go on to Set 4.

Set 4

1. How many pennies could you get for the dimes?

2. Complete the sales slip.

| No. 166- 6 Date_____19__ |
| Name_____ |
| Address_____ |

SOLD BY	CASH	C. O. D.	CHARGE	ON ACCT.	MDSE. RETD.	PAID OUT

QUAN.		DESCRIPTION	AMOUNT
12	1	$\frac{6}{32}$ ×2 Mac Screws @ 4¢ EA	
11	2	9×1$\frac{3}{4}$ Wood Screws @ 5¢ EA	
34	3	$\frac{6}{32}$ × $\frac{3}{8}$ Mac Screws @ 2¢ EA	
23	4	$\frac{6}{32}$ ×$\frac{3}{4}$ Mac Screws @ 3¢ EA	
	5		
	6	TOTAL	
	7		
	8		
	9		
	10		
	11		
	12		
Customer's Order No.		Rec'd By	

3. A flash of lightning is seen and three seconds later a clap of thunder is heard. How far away was the lightning if sound travels at 332 meters per second?

4. There are 12 inches in one foot. How many inches are in one yard (three feet)?

5. One scoop of ice cream contains 133 calories. How many calories would be contained in
   (a) one double scoop?
   (b) one triple scoop?

6. An ant weighs 1/100 of an ounce. It can pull loads weighing five times as much as it weighs. How much could a 100-pound ant pull?

- *STOP*

- Check your answers on page 333.

- Correct the problems you missed.

- Shade box 2 opposite "multiplication of whole numbers" on page xviii.

- If this was the last subskill you had to work on in this section, take the test on page 64.

- If you have other subskills to work on in this section, go on to the next one.

SUBSKILL 3: Single-Digit
Multiplier with
Exchanging of Ones

Problem: $\begin{array}{r} 2\ 3 \\ \times\ 4 \end{array}$ *Solution:*
- Multiply top numbers by bottom number.

- Work from right to left.

- Exchange ten of a kind for one of next larger kind.

① $\begin{array}{r} 2\ 3 \\ \times\ 4 \\ \hline 9\ 2 \end{array}$

Lesson: Four groups of two tens and three ones.

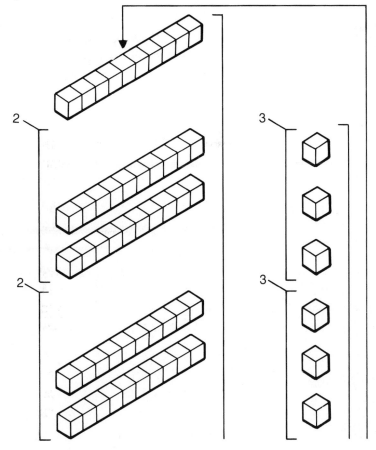

(Figure continued next page)

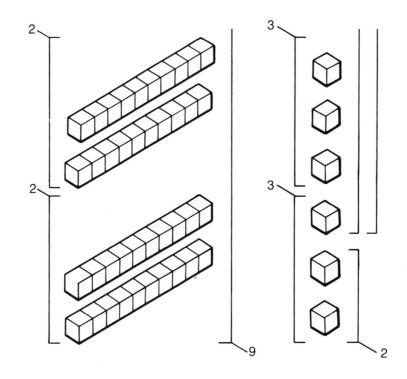

Drill and Practice:

Set 1

1.	35	2.	46	3.	28	4.	136	5.	1224
	× 2		× 2		× 3		× 2		× 3

- *STOP.*
- Check your answers on page **333**.
- Correct the problems you missed.
- Go on to Set 2.

Set 2

1.	26	2.	39	3.	19	4.	117	5.	30125
	× 3		× 2		× 5		× 3		× 3

- *STOP.*
- Check your answers on page **333**.
- Correct the problems you missed.
- Go on to Set 3 or 4.

Set 3

1.	14	2.	15	3.	24	4.	102	5.	401327
	× 7		× 6		× 4		× 5		× 2

- *STOP.*
- Check your answers on page **333**.
- Correct the problems you missed.
- Go on to Set 4.

Set 4

1. How many pennies could you get for the quarters?

2. Determine the cost of two square feet of the tile.

SOLID VINYL TILE
* FLEXIBLE — EASY TO CUT, FIT!
* MARBLE CHIP PATTERN WITH HI-GLOSS FINISH!

12 x 12" *Only* **37**¢ SQ. FT.

3. Complete the sales slip.

No. 166-6 Date _____ 19___
Name_____
Address_____

SOLD BY	CASH	C. O. D.	CHARGE	ON ACCT.	MDSE. RETD.	PAID OUT

QUAN.		DESCRIPTION	AMOUNT	
6	1	½" Hex Nuts @ 12¢ Ea		
14	2	14×1½ WoodScrews@7¢ Ea		
4	3	¼×4 Car Screws @15¢ Ea		
19	4	7/16" Washers @ 5¢ Ea		
	5			
	6	Total		
	7			
	8			
	9			
	10			
	11			
	12			
Customer's Order No.		Rec'd By		

4. An auditorium contains eight rows of 12 chairs each. How many chairs does it contain?

5. Ants have six legs. How many legs do 13 ants have?

6. Find the volume of the boxes if the volume of the shaded box is 1.

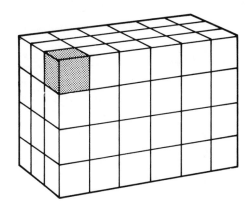

7. Find the volume of the box using $V = lwh$ for the volume V of a box of length l, width w, and height h.

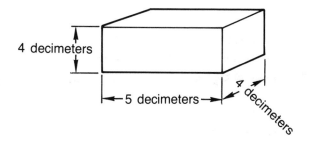

4 decimeters

5 decimeters

4 decimeters

* *STOP*

* Check your answers on page 333.

* Correct the problems you missed.

* Shade box 3 opposite "multiplication of whole numbers" on page xviii.

* If this was the last subskill in this section you had to work on, take the test on page 64.

* If you have other subskills in this section to work on, go on to the next one.

SUBSKILL 4: Single-Digit Multiplier with Exchanging of Tens

Problem: 1 6 4
         ×   2

Solution:
- Multiply top numbers by bottom number.

- Work from right to left.

- Exchange ten of a kind for one of next larger kind.

①
1 6 4
×   2

3 2 8

Lesson: Two groups of a hundred, six tens, and four ones.

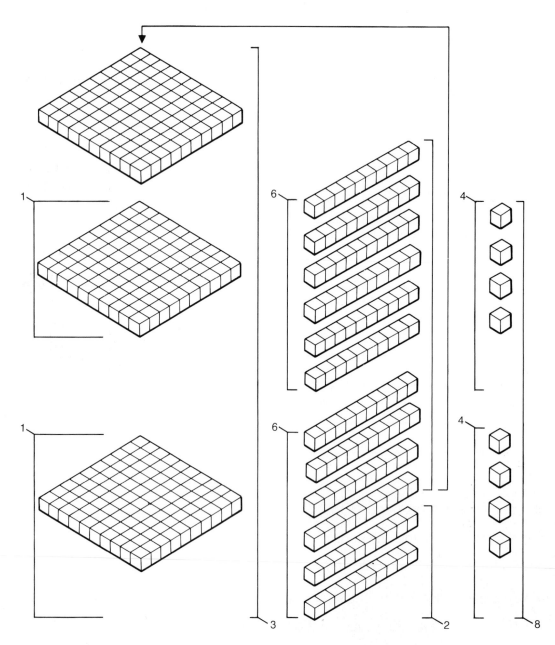

1   6   4

3   2   8

Drill and Practice:

Set 1

1. 153	2. 272	3. 180	4. 92	5. 1142
× 3	× 2	× 5	× 4	× 3

- *STOP.*
- Check your answers on page 333.
- Correct the problems you missed.
- Go on to Set 2.

Set 2

1. 394	2. 261	3. 240	4. 81	5. 21072
× 2	× 3	× 4	× 8	× 4

- *STOP.*
- Check your answers on page 333.
- Correct the problems you missed.
- Go on to Set 3 or 4.

Set 3

1. 121	2. 191	3. 160	4. 71	5. 103264
× 7	× 5	× 6	× 9	× 2

- *STOP.*
- Check your answers on page 333.
- Correct the problems you missed.
- Go on to Set 4.

Set 4

1. How many pennies could you get for the half-dollars?

2. A creeping charley must be watered three times a week. How many times a year (52 weeks) must it be watered?

3. A highrise apartment house is 21 floors high. It has six apartments on each floor. How many apartments does it have?

4. A brick wall is 20 bricks wide and seven bricks high. How many bricks did it take to make the wall?

5. Horses have four legs. How many legs do 32 horses have?

6. Find the volume of the box using $V = lwh$ for the volume V of a box of length l, width w, and height h.

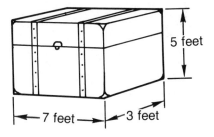

5 feet

7 feet   3 feet

- *STOP*

- Check your answers on page 333.

- Correct the problems you missed.

- Shade box 4 opposite "multiplication of whole numbers" on page xviii.

- If this was the last subskill you had to work on in this section, take the test on page 64.

- If you have other subskills to work on in this section, go on to the next one.

SUBSKILL 5: Single-Digit Multiplier with Exchanging of Ones and Tens.

Problem:

$$\begin{array}{r} 1\ 6\ 8 \\ \times\quad 4 \\ \hline \end{array}$$

Solution:
- Multiply top numbers by bottom number.

- Work from right to left.

- Exchange ten of a kind for one of next larger kind.

$$\begin{array}{r} ②③ \\ 1\ 6\ 8 \\ \times\quad 4 \\ \hline \boxed{6\ 7\ 2} \end{array}$$

Lesson:

$$\begin{array}{r} 1\ 6\ 8 \\ \times\quad 4 \\ \hline \end{array}$$

③2	Four groups of eight ones or 32 ones
②4 0	Four groups of six tens or 24 tens
4 0 0	Four groups of a hundred or four hundreds
6 7 2	Sum

Drill and Practice:

Set 1

1. 259	2. 114	3. 243	4. 97	5. 1146
× 3	× 8	× 4	× 8	× 6

Set 2

1. 128	2. 237	3. 162	4. 83	5. 12044
× 7	× 4	× 5	× 7	× 3

- *STOP.*
- Check your answers on page 333.
- Correct the problems you missed.
- Go on to Set 2.

- *STOP.*
- Check your answers on page 333.
- Correct the problems you missed.
- Go on to Set 3 or 4.

Set 3

1. 134 2. 198 3. 356 4. 56 5. 213367
   × 6   × 5   × 2   × 9   ×   2

- *STOP.*
- Check your answers on page 333.
- Correct the problems you missed.
- Go on to Set 4.

Set 4

1. Determine the cost of seven rolls of rope.

86¢
50-ft.
Sisal rope

2. Determine the cost of eight square feet of tile.

1ST QUALITY, CRYSTAL CLEAR
MIRROR WALL TILE
- ENHANCES BACKGROUND!
- ADDS DIMENSION TO ROOM!

GOLD VEIN PATTERN 89¢ SQ. FT.   12 x 12" Only **59**¢ SQ. FT.

3. Complete the sales slip.

No. 166- 6 Date_____ 19___

Name_____

Address_____

SOLD BY	CASH	C. O. D.	CHARGE	ON ACCT.	MDSE. RETD.	PAID OUT

QUAN.		DESCRIPTION	AMOUNT
34	1	3/8" WASHERS @ 4¢ EA	
118	2	1/4 × 1 CAR SCREWS @ 6¢ EA	
25	3	7/16" HEX NUTS @ 8¢ EA	
49	4	12×2 WOOD SCREWS @ 7¢ EA	
	5		
	6	TOTAL	
	7		
	8		
	9		
	10		
	11		
	12		

Customer's Order No. _____ Rec'd By _____

4. Lozenges come 12 to a roll. How many would you get in nine rolls?

5. Find the area of the rug using $A = lw$ for the area A of a rectangle of length l and width w.

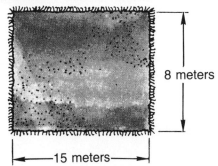

8 meters

15 meters

6. Every month you diet for one week and you lose five pounds. Then you gain it back again. How much weight do you lose and gain in
   (a) one year (12 months)?
   (b) 50 years?

- *STOP*

- Check your answers on page 333.

- Correct the problems you missed.

- Shade box 5 opposite "multiplication of whole numbers" on page xviii.

- If this was the last subskill you had to work on in this section, take the test on page 64.

- If you have other subskills to work on in this section, go on to the next one.

SUBSKILL 6: Single-Digit Multiplier with Exchanging of Ones, Tens, Hundreds, and Thousands

Problem: 1 2 9 7 6
        ×   6

Solution: • Multiply top numbers by bottom number.

• Work from right to left.

• Exchange ten of a kind for one of next larger kind.

Lesson: 1 2 9 7 6
        ×   6

           ③6   Six groups of six ones or 36 ones

        ④2 0   Six groups of seven tens or 42 tens

      ⑤4 0 0   Six groups of nine hundreds or 54 hundreds

    ①2 0 0 0   Six groups of two thousands or 12 thousands

    6 0 0 0 0   Six groups of a ten thousand or six ten thousands

    7 7 8 5 6   Sum

Drill and Practice:

Set 1

1. 23456 2. 12547 3. 16253 4. 217292
  ×   4   ×   5   ×   3   ×   2

- *STOP.*
- Check your answers on page 333.
- Correct the problems you missed.
- Go on to Set 2.

Set 2

1. 15978   2. 23389   3. 24242   4. 1242425
    ×   7   ×   4   ×   8   ×   3

- *STOP.*
- Check your answers on page 333.
- Correct the problems you missed.
- Go on to Set 3 or 4.

Set 3

1. 23965   2. 12354   3. 25462   4. 12618450
    ×   9   ×   6   ×   2   ×   5

- *STOP.*
- Check your answers on page 334.
- Correct the problems you missed.
- Go on to Set 4.

Set 4

1. A housewife washes dishes three times a day. How many times does she wash dishes in
    (a) one week (seven days)?
    (b) one month (30 days)?
    (c) one year (365 days)?

2. Bloat drinks four cans of soda pop a day. How many cans of soda pop does he drink in
    (a) one week (seven days)?
    (b) one month (30 days)?
    (c) one year (365 days)?

3. It takes about 325 pounds of water to produce one pound of paper. About how many pounds of water would it take to produce eight pounds of paper?

4. If you travel 415 miles a day for four days, how far will you travel?

5. If you put a nickel in a piggy bank every day, how much will you save in
    (a) one week (seven days)?
    (b) one month (30 days)?
    (c) one year (365 days)?

- *STOP*
- Check your answers on page 334.
- Correct the problems you missed.
- Shade box 6 opposite "multiplication of whole numbers" on page xviii.
- If this was the last subskill you had to work on in this section, take the test on page 64.
- If you have other subskillls to work on in this section, go on to the next one.

SUBSKILL 7: Two-Digit Multiplier

Problem:

    2 4 2 6
  ×   7 3

Solution:

- Multiply top numbers by each bottom number.

- Work from right to left.

- Exchange ten of a kind for one of next larger kind.

- Make "steps."

- Add.

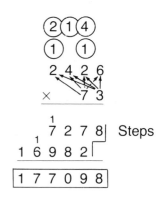

Lesson:

    2 4 2 6
  ×   7 3

①8	Three groups of six ones or 18 ones
6 0	Three groups of two tens or six tens
①2 0 0	Three groups of four hundreds or 12 hundreds
6 0 0 0	Three groups of two thousands or six thousands
④2 0	Seventy groups of six ones or 420 ones
①4 0 0	Seventy groups of two tens or 140 tens
②8 0 0 0	Seventy groups of four hundreds or 280 hundreds
1 4 0 0 0 0	Seventy groups of two thousands or 140 thousands
1 7 7 0 9 8	Sum

Drill and Practice:

Set 1

1. 4506   2. 3725   3. 406   4. 61   5. 68027
  ×   27   ×   81   × 92   ×35   ×   56

- *STOP.*
- Check your answers on page **334.**
- Correct the problems you missed.
- Go on to Set 2.

Set 2

1. 3250   2. 6083   3. 519   4. 74   5. 81123
  ×   45   ×   34   × 48   ×55   ×   43

- *STOP.*
- Check your answers on page **334.**
- Correct the problems you missed.
- Go on to Set 3 or 4.

Set 3

1. 5017 2. 9285 3. 444 4. 25 5. 45678
   × 76   × 46   × 99   ×12   ×   11

- *STOP.*
- Check your answers on page 334.
- Correct the problems you missed.
- Go on to Set 4.

Set 4

1. Count the beads.

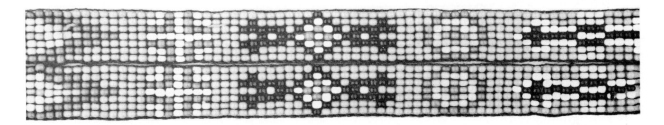

2. There are 12 inches in one foot. How many inches are in one mile (5280 feet)?

3. A tiger eats about 13 pounds of meat a day. About how much meat does a tiger eat in
     (a) one week (seven days)?
     (b) one month (30 days)?
     (c) one year (365 days)?

4. How much would it cost to rent the Karim V for 36 months?

LEASE A 1976 KARIM V
FOR 36 MOS.
$229
ON APPROVED CREDIT. # 450

5. You are working for a mail-order house and you have to mail 12,000 catalogues. The cost is 15 cents per catalogue. How much will you have to spend to mail them?

6. If you spend a quarter on junk food every day, how much do you spend on junk food in

   (a) one week (seven days)?
   (b) one month (30 days)?
   (c) one year (365 days)?

7. Solve the problems in Set 1 with the following lattice algorithm.

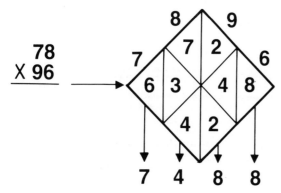

- *STOP*

- Check your answers on page 334.

- Correct the problems you missed.

- Shade box 7 opposite "multiplication of whole numbers" on page xviii.

- If this was the last subskill you had to work on in this section, take the test on page 64.

- If you have other subskills to work on in this section, go on to the next one.

SUBSKILL 8: Multiplier with Three or More Digits

Problem: 3 5 0 6
           ×   2 4 7

Solution:
- Multiply top numbers by each bottom number.

- Work from right to left.

- Exchange ten of a kind for one of next larger kind.

- Make "steps."

- Add.

① ①
② ②
③ ④

3 5 0 6
× 2 4 7
‾‾‾‾‾‾‾
  2 4 5 4 2
1 4 0 2 4
7 0 1 2
‾‾‾‾‾‾‾
8 6 5 9 8 2

Lesson:

$$\begin{array}{r} 3\ 5\ 0\ 6 \\ \times\ 2\ 4\ 7 \end{array}$$

④2	Seven groups of six ones or 42 ones
– – – –	Seven groups of zero tens or zero tens
③5 0 0	Seven groups of five hundreds or 35 hundreds
2 1 0 0 0	Seven groups of three thousands or 21 thousands
②4 0	Forty groups of six ones or 240 ones
– – – –	Forty groups of zero tens or zero tens
②0 0 0 0	Forty groups of five hundreds or 200 hundreds
1 2 0 0 0 0	Forty groups of three thousands or 120 thousands
①2 0 0	Two hundred groups of six ones or 1200 ones
– – – –	Two hundred groups of zero tens or zero tens
①0 0 0 0 0	Two hundred groups of five hundreds or 1000 hundreds
6 0 0 0 0 0	Two hundred groups of three thousands or 600 thousands
8 6 5 9 8 2	Sum

Drill and Practice:

Set 1

1. 2803   2. 3214   3. 487   4.   17   5. 68034
   × 242   × 523   ×345   ×555   × 5216

- *STOP.*
- Check your answers on page **334.**
- Correct the problems you missed.
- Go on to Set 2.

Set 2

1. 6104   2. 4242   3. 385   4.   35   5. 34055
   × 386   × 111   ×493   ×213   ×91348

- *STOP.*
- Check your answers on page **334.**
- Correct the problems you missed.
- Go on to Set 3 or 4.

Set 3

1. 4306 2. 5003 3. 406 4.   80 5. 4421103
   × 253   × 859   ×999   ×225   ×1231354

- *STOP.*
- Check your answers on page **334.**
- Correct the problems you missed.
- Go on to Set 4.

Set 4

1. The heartbeat of a jogger is about 72 times per minute. About how many times does the jogger's heart beat in
   (a) one hour (60 minutes)?
   (b) one day (24 hours)?
   (c) one month (30 days)?
   (d) one year (365 days)?

2. It takes about 525 pounds of water to grow one pound of potatoes. About how many pounds of water would it take to grow 895 pounds of potatoes?

3. According to the *Guinness Book of World Records,* the duration record for sitting in a tree is 61 days, 21 hours, and 56 minutes. How many seconds is this?

4. A farmer gets about 175 bushels of wheat per acre. How many bushels of wheat would the farmer get from 4593 acres?

5. Solve the problems in set 1 with the following lattice algorithm.

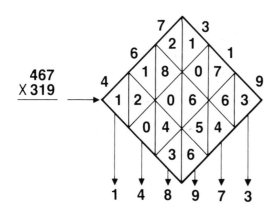

- *STOP*

- Check your answers on page 334.

- Correct the problems you missed.

- Shade box 8 opposite "multiplication of whole numbers" on page xviii.

- If this was the last subskill you had to work on in this section, take the test on page 64.

- If you have other subskills to work on in this section, go on to the next one.

SUBSKILL 9: Multiplier with Terminal Zeros

Problem:
```
  2 3 6 3 7
× 2 4 0 0 0
```

Solution:
- Bring down zeros.
- Multiply top numbers by each remaining bottom number.
- Work from right to left.
- Exchange ten of a kind for one of next larger kind.
- Make "steps."
- Add.

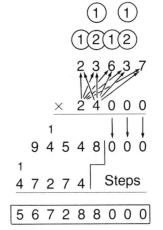

Lesson:

```
  2 3 6 3 7
× 2 4 0 0 0
```

②8 0 0 0	Four thousand groups of seven ones or 28,000 ones
①2 0 0 0 0	Four thousand groups of three tens or 12,000 tens
²②4 0 0 0 0 0	Four thousand groups of six hundreds or 24,000 hundreds
①2 0 0 0 0 0 0	Four thousand groups of three thousands or 12,000 thousands
8 0 0 0 0 0 0 0	Four thousand groups of two ten thousands or 8000 ten thousands
①4 0 0 0 0	Twenty thousand groups of seven ones or 140,000 ones
6 0 0 0 0 0	Twenty thousand groups of three tens or 60,000 tens
①2 0 0 0 0 0 0	Twenty thousand groups of six hundreds or 120,000 hundreds
6 0 0 0 0 0 0 0	Twenty thousand groups of three thousands or 60,000 thousands
¹4 0 0 0 0 0 0 0 0	Twenty thousand groups of two ten thousands or 40,000 ten thousands

```
5 6 7 2 8 8 0 0 0    Sum
```

Drill and Practice:

Set 1

1. 43521   2. 71439   3. 62231   4. 20038
   ×50000   × 700   × 3500   × 10

- *STOP.*
- Check your answers on page **334.**
- Correct the problems you missed.
- Go on to Set 2.

Set 2

1. 83201   2. 30045   3. 54545   4. 42811
   ×20000   × 400   × 2700   × 60

- *STOP.*
- Check your answers on page 334.
- Correct the problems you missed.
- Go on to Set 3 or 4.

Set 3

1. 54002   2. 63222   3. 33333   4. 30712
   ×90000   × 500   × 1000   × 150

- *STOP.*
- Check your answers on page 334.
- Correct the problems you missed.
- Go on to Set 4.

Set 4

1. How many dollar bills could you get for 500 ten-dollar bills?

2. An antacid tablet comes ten to a roll. How many tablets would you get in 23 rolls?

3. Raisins come 50 or so to the box. About how many raisins would you eat if you were to eat a box of raisins every day for
   (a) one week (seven days)?
   (b) one month (30 days)?
   (c) one year (365 days)?

4. There are 60 seconds in one minute. How many seconds are in
   (a) one hour (60 minutes)?
   (b) one day (24 hours)?
   (c) one year (365 days)?

5. The average person uses about 500 pounds of water a day. About how much water does the average person use in
   (a) one week (seven days)?
   (b) one month (30 days)?
   (c) one year (365 days)?

6. How many pennies could you get for one roll of
   (a) nickels (40 nickels)?
   (b) dimes (50 dimes)?
   (c) quarters (40 quarters)?
   (d) half-dollars (20 half-dollars)?

7. Your body replaces two million blood cells every second. How many blood cells will it replace in the next
   (a) minute (60 seconds)?
   (b) hour (60 minutes)?
   (c) day (24 hours)?
   (d) year (365 days)?

- *STOP*

- Check your answers on page 334.

- Correct the problems you missed.

- Shade box 9 opposite "multiplication of whole numbers" on page xviii.

- If this was the last subskill you had to work on in this section, take the test on page 64.

- If you have other subskills to work on in this section, go on to the next one.

SUBSKILL 10: Multiplier with Non-Terminal Zeros

Problem:

```
    6 2 4 5
×   3 0 0 8
```

Solution:

- Multiply top numbers by each non-zero bottom number.

- Work from right to left.

- Exchange ten of a kind for one of next larger kind.

- Bring down zeros.

- Make "steps."

- Add.

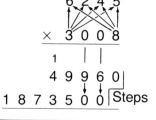

```
          6 2 4 5
        × 3 0 0 8
        1   | |
          4 9 9 6 0|
      1 8 7 3 5 0 0|Steps
      ─────────────────
      1 8 7 8 4 9 6 0
```

Lesson:

```
          6 2 4 5
        × 3 0 0 8
        ─────────────
              ④0        Eight groups of five ones or 40 ones
            ③2 0        Eight groups of four tens or 32 tens
          ①6 0 0        Eight groups of two hundreds or 16 hundreds
          1
          4 8 0 0 0     Eight groups of six thousands or 48 thousands
        ①5 0 0 0        Three thousand groups of five ones or 15,000 ones
      ①2 0 0 0 0        Three thousand groups of four tens or 12,000 tens
      6 0 0 0 0 0       Three thousand groups of two hundreds or 6000 hundreds
    1 8 0 0 0 0 0 0     Three thousand groups of six thousands or 18,000
                        thousands
    ─────────────────
    1 8 7 8 4 9 6 0     Sum
```

Drill and Practice:

Set 1

```
1.  3117      2.  4059      3.  4231      4.  50731
   ×2005         ×5002         × 203         ×30004
```

- *STOP.*
- Check your answers on page 334.
- Correct the problems you missed.
- Go on to Set 2.

Set 2

1. 7309	2. 3217	3. 4760	4. 230893
×4001	×1001	× 505	×200301

- *STOP.*
- Check your answers on page **334.**
- Correct the problems you missed.
- Go on to Set 3 or 4.

Set 3

1. 4567	2. 5020	3. 6900	4. 4590021
×9007	×3006	× 405	×5002004

- *STOP.*
- Check your answers on page **334.**
- Correct the problems you missed.
- Go on to Set 4.

Set 4

1. A stadium contains 105 rows of 307 seats each. How many seats does it contain?

2. An apple orchard consists of 209 rows of apple trees. Each row produces about 14,000 apples. How many apples does the orchard produce?

3. One thousand fifty men and women purchased an average of $807 worth of stock each. How much did they spend?

4. Two hundred and five men and 201 women received an average dividend of $407. How much did they receive all total?

- *STOP*
- Check your answers on page **334.**
- Correct the problems you missed.
- Shade box 10 opposite "multiplication of whole numbers" on page xviii.
- Take the test on page **64.**

Inventory Post Test for
Multiplication of Whole Numbers

1. $6 \times 4 = ?$

2. 21	3. 37	4. 271	5. 162	6. 16384	7. 4538	8. 4703	9. 37359	10. 4512
× 3	× 2	× 3	× 5	× 6	× 27	× 418	×27000	×3002

- *STOP*

- Check your answers with the instructor.

- As before, work through the subskills in this section which correspond to the problems you missed, except work the *even* drill-and-practice problems.

- Take the test on page **65**.

SKILL
Division of Whole Numbers

Inventory Pretest for
Division of Whole Numbers

1. $14 \div 5 = ?$ 2 rem. 4

2. $7 \overline{)86}$ 12 r2

3. $6 \overline{)452}$ 75 r 2

4. $4 \overline{)5126}$ 131 r2

5. $5 \overline{)25308}$ 5061 r3

6. $39 \overline{)846}$

7. $48 \overline{)9723}$

8. $801 \overline{)65902}$

9. Determine $510 \div 24$ and write the remainder as a fraction. Simplify if you know how.

10. Determine $317 \div 7$ to three decimal places.

- *STOP*

- Check your answers on page 334.

- Shade the boxes opposite "division of whole numbers" on page xviii which correspond to the problems you got right.

- If you got all of them right, take the test on page 91.

- If you missed some of them, start working on the subskills in this section which correspond to the ones you missed.

- For each subskill, look at the example, study the solution, think about the lesson, and work the *odd* drill-and-practice problems.

SUBSKILL 1: Division Facts

Problem: 14 ÷ 3 = ? *Solution:* • Memorize division facts in Table 6.1. Row number is dividend. Column number is divisor. 14 ÷ 3 = 4R2

Table 6.1 Division Facts (= undefined, R = remainder)*

÷	0	1	2	3	4	5	6	7	8	9	10	11	12	13	14	15 ...
0	*	0	0	0	0	0	0	0	0	0	0	0	0	0	0	0
1	*	1														
2	*	2	1													
3	*	3	1R1	1												
4	*	4	2	1R1	1											
5	*	5	2R1	1R2	1R1	1										
6	*	6	3	2	1R2	1R1	1									
7	*	7	3R1	2R1	1R3	1R2	1R1	1								
8	*	8	4	2R2	2	1R3	1R2	1R1	1							
9	*	9	4R1	3	2R1	1R4	1R3	1R2	1R1	1						
10	*	10	5	3R1	2R2	2	1R4	1R3	1R2	1R1	1					
11	*	11	5R1	3R2	2R3	2R1	1R5	1R4	1R3	1R2	1R1	1				
12	*	12	6	4	3	2R2	2	1R5	1R4	1R3	1R2	1R1	1			
13	*	13	6R1	4R1	3R1	2R3	2R1	1R6	1R5	1R4	1R3	1R2	1R1	1		
14	*	14	7	4R2	3R2	2R4	2R2	2	1R6	1R5	1R4	1R3	1R2	1R1	1	
15	*	15	7R1	5	3R3	3	2R3	2R1	1R7	1R6	1R5	1R4	1R3	1R2	1R1	1

Lesson: One ten and four ones grouped by threes.

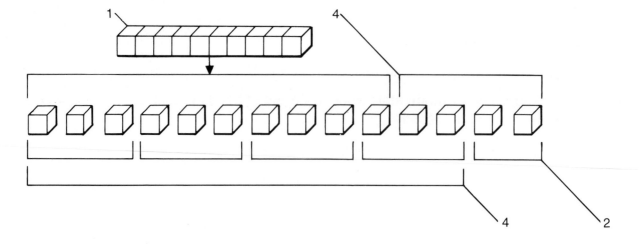

Drill and Practice:

Set 1

    1. $12 \div 4 = ?$ 2. $8 \div 3 = ?$

3. $5\overline{)10}$ 4. $2\overline{)11}$ 5. $9\overline{)16}$

- *STOP.*
- Check your answers on page **334**.
- Correct the problems you missed.
- Go on to Set 2.

Set 3

    1. $15 \div 3 = ?$ 2. $9 \div 2 = ?$

3. $0\overline{)14}$ 4. $14\overline{)0}$ 5. $3\overline{)18}$

- *STOP.*
- Check your answers on page **334**.
- Correct the problems you missed.
- Go on to Set 4.

Set 2

    1. $14 \div 2 = ?$ 2. $7 \div 4 = ?$

3. $6\overline{)13}$ 4. $7\overline{)15}$ 5. $1\overline{)17}$

- *STOP.*
- Check your answers on page **334**.
- Correct the problems you missed.
- Go on to Set 3 or 4.

Set 4

1. Count the groups of ten bottle caps each.

2. Write a division sentence for the eggs.

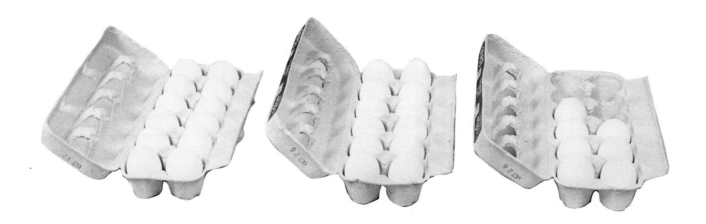

3. How many (a) nickels (b) dimes could you get for the pennies?

4. You have some quarters. When you arrange them in groups of two, three, or four, you always have one left over. What is the least number of quarters you could have?

5. You are dividing by seven. What remainders are possible?

- *STOP*
- Check your answers on page 334.
- Correct the problems you missed.
- Shade box 1 opposite "division of whole numbers" on page xviii.
- If this was the only subskill you had to work on in this section, take the test on page 89.
- If you have other subskills to work on in this section, go on to the next one.

SUBSKILL 2: Single-Digit Divisor, Two-Digit Dividend

Problem: 4) 9 3   Solution:
- Divide.
- Multiply.
- Subtract.
- Make sure difference is less than divisor.
- Bring down next number.
- Repeat until there are no more numbers to bring down.
- Designate remainder with R.

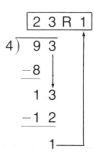

Lesson: Nine tens and three ones grouped by fours.

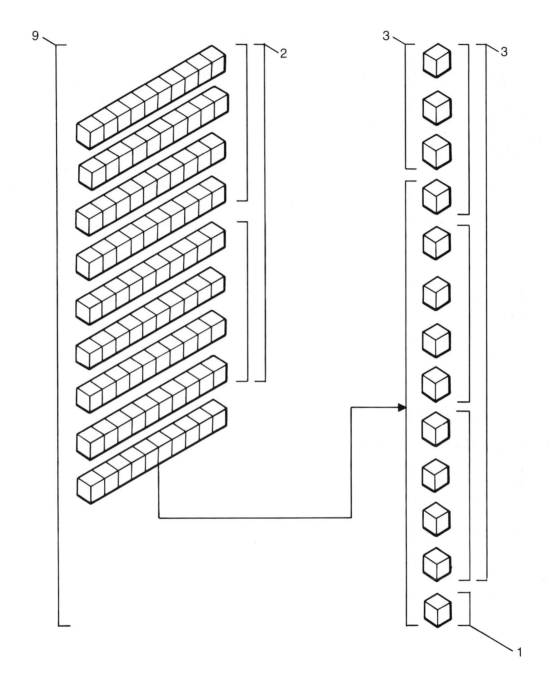

Drill and Practice:

Set 1

      1. $3 \overline{)\ 76}$ 2. $4 \overline{)\ 55}$

3. $7 \overline{)\ 91}$ 4. $8 \overline{)\ 32}$ 5. $9 \overline{)\ 70}$

- *STOP.*
- Check your answers on page **334**.
- Correct the problems you missed.
- Go on to Set 2.

Set 2

        1. $2 \overline{)\ 25}$ 2. $5 \overline{)\ 57}$

3. $6 \overline{)\ 80}$ 4. $7 \overline{)\ 53}$ 5. $8 \overline{)\ 19}$

- *STOP.*
- Check your answers on page 334.
- Correct the problems you missed.
- Go on to Set 3 or 4.

Set 3

        1. $5 \overline{)\ 82}$ 2. $1 \overline{)\ 17}$

3. $3 \overline{)\ 35}$ 4. $6 \overline{)\ 40}$ 5. $9 \overline{)\ 65}$

- *STOP.*
- Check your answers on page 334.
- Correct the problems you missed.
- Go on to Set 4.

Set 4

1. A traveling salesman has to spend every other weekend away from home. How many weekends a year (52 weeks) is that?

2. How many six-packs of cola would you have to buy to provide each of 86 people with a bottle of cola?.

3. Hot dog buns are sold eight to a package. How many packages of hot dog buns would you have to buy to make 108 hot dogs?

4. You just traveled 296 miles on eight gallons of gas. How many miles did you get per gallon?

5. Some small rectangles are two inches long and one inch wide. A large rectangle is eight inches long and four inches wide. How many of the small rectangles would fit inside the large rectangle?

- *STOP*

- Check your answers on page 334.

- Correct the problems you missed.

- Shade box 2 opposite "division of whole numbers" on page xviii.

- If this was the last subskill you had to work on in this section, take the test on page 89.

- If you have other subskills to work on in this section, go on to the next one.

SUBSKILL 3: Single-Digit Divisor, Three-Digit Dividend

Problem: 3) 4 3 5   *Solution:*

- Divide.

- Multiply.

- Subtract.

- Make sure difference is less than divisor.

- Bring down next number.

- Repeat until there are no more numbers to bring down.

- Designate remainder with R.

$$
\begin{array}{r}
1\ 4\ 5 \\
3\ )\overline{4\ 3\ 5} \\
-3 \\
\hline
1\ 3 \\
-1\ 2 \\
\hline
1\ 5 \\
-1\ 5 \\
\hline
\end{array}
$$

Lesson: Four hundreds, three tens, and five ones grouped by threes.

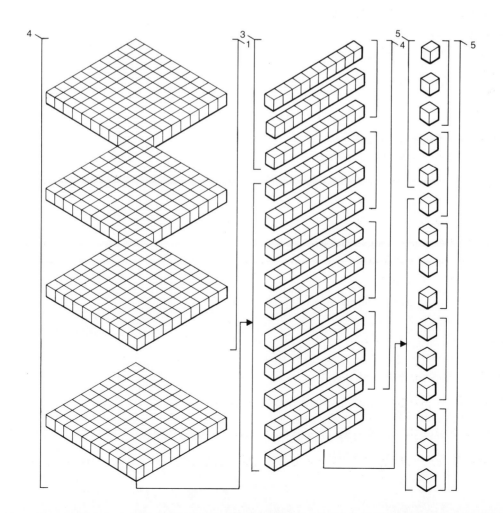

Drill and Practice:

Set 1

1. $3\overline{)735}$ 2. $4\overline{)571}$ 3. $7\overline{)854}$

4. $9\overline{)108}$ 5. $8\overline{)691}$

- *STOP.*
- Check your answers on page 334.
- Correct the problems you missed.
- Go on to Set 2.

Set 2

1. $2\overline{)553}$ 2. $5\overline{)613}$ 3. $6\overline{)666}$

4. $8\overline{)256}$ 5. $3\overline{)274}$

- *STOP.*
- Check your answers on page 335.
- Correct the problems you missed.
- Go on to Set 3 or 4.

Set 3

1. $5\overline{)560}$ 2. $1\overline{)418}$ 3. $3\overline{)231}$

4. $9\overline{)891}$ 5. $7\overline{)174}$

- *STOP.*
- Check your answers on page 335.
- Correct the problems you missed.
- Go on to Set 4.

Set 4

1. One yard is three feet. What is the most number of yards in 1250 feet?

2. One gallon is four quarts. How many gallons are 516 quarts?

3. How many two-inch strips of tape can be made from a 525-inch roll of tape?

4. A fence is strung along ten equally spaced fence posts. The fence is 999 feet long. How far apart are the fence posts?

- *STOP*

- Check your answers on page 335.

- Correct the problems you missed.

- Shade box 3 opposite "division of whole numbers" on page xviii.

- If this was the last subskill you had to work on in this section, take the test on page 89.

- If you have other subskills to work on in this section, go on to the next one.

SUBSKILL 4: Single-Digit Divisor,
No Zeros in
Quotient

Problem: 6) 8 1 0 8   *Solution:*

- Divide.

- Multiply.

- Subtract.

- Make sure difference is less than divisor.

- Bring down next number.

- Repeat until there are no more numbers to bring down.

- Designate remainder with R.

```
          1 3 5 1 R 2
       6 ) 8 1 0 8
         −6
           2 1
          −1 8
             3 0
            −3 0
               8
              −6
               2
```

Lesson:

```
          1 3 5 1 R 2
       6 ) 8 1 0 8
         −6 0 0 0        Eight thousands to be grouped by sixes
                         One group of six thousands or six thousands
           2 1 0 0       Twenty-one hundreds to be grouped by sixes
          −1 8 0 0       Three groups of six hundreds or 18 hundreds
             3 0 0       Thirty tens to be grouped by sixes
            −3 0 0       Five groups of six tens or 30 tens
                 8       Eight ones to be grouped by sixes
                −6       One group of six ones or six ones
                 2       Number of ones remaining
```

Drill and Practice:

Set 1

1. $5 \overline{)\ 73}$ 2. $4 \overline{)\ 535}$ 3. $8 \overline{)\ 8920}$

4. $7 \overline{)\ 63852}$

- *STOP.*
- Check your answers on page 335.
- Correct the problems you missed.
- Go on to Set 2.

Set 2

1. $2 \overline{)\ 45}$ 2. $3 \overline{)\ 458}$ 3. $6 \overline{)\ 7278}$

4. $8 \overline{)\ 558923}$

- *STOP.*
- Check your answers on page 335.
- Correct the problems you missed.
- Go on to Set 3 or 4.

Set 3

1. $8 \overline{)\ 92}$ 2. $2 \overline{)\ 313}$ 3. $5 \overline{)\ 7805}$

4. $4 \overline{)\ 3488526}$

- *STOP.*
- Check your answers on page 335.
- Correct the problems you missed.
- Go on to Set 4.

Set 4

1. You buy a six-pack of soda pop for 96 cents. How much did you pay per soda pop?

2. One eight-inch stalk of celery contains five calories. How many stalks of celery would you have to eat to consume 1915 calories?

3. Three partners split $8946 evenly. How much did each one get?

4. You are at a hamburger place with your sweetheart. The two of you split one large hamburger, one small order of fries, and one vanilla shake. A large hamburger contains 557 calories, a small order of fries 215 calories, and and vanilla shake 322 calories. How many calories will each of you consume?

- *STOP*
- Check your answers on page 335.
- Correct the problems you missed.
- Shade box 4 opposite "division of whole numbers" on page xviii.
- If this was the last subskill you had to work on in this section, take the test on page 89.
- If you have other subskills to work on in this section, go on to the next one.

SUBSKILL 5: Single-Digit Divisor, Zeros in Quotient

Problem: 8) 1 0 4 5 7 9   *Solution:*

- Divide.
- Multiply.
- Subtract.
- Make sure difference is less than divisor.
- Bring down next number.
- Repeat until there are no more numbers to bring down.
- Designate remainder with R.

```
              1 3 0 7 2 R 3
        8 ) 1 0 4 5 7 9
           −8
            2 4
           −2 4
                5
               −0
                5 7
               −5 6
                  1 9
                 −1 6
                    3
```

Lesson:

```
              1 3 0 7 2 R 3
        8 ) 1 0 4 5 7 9
           −8 0 0 0 0
            2 4 0 0 0
           −2 4 0 0 0
                5 0 0
               −0 0 0
                5 7 0
               −5 6 0
                  1 9
                 −1 6
                    3
```

Ten ten thousands to be grouped by eights
One group of eight ten thousands or eight ten thousands
Twenty-four thousands to be grouped by eights
Three groups of eight thousands or 24 thousands
Five hundreds to be grouped by eights
Zero groups of eight hundreds or zero hundreds
Fifty-seven tens to be grouped by eights
Seven groups of eight tens or 56 tens
Nineteen ones to be grouped by eights
Two groups of eight ones or 16 ones
Number of ones remaining

Drill and Practice:

Set 1

1. $2 \overline{)\ 613}$ 2. $5 \overline{)\ 2545}$ 3. $8 \overline{)\ 12038}$

4. $7 \overline{)\ 714356}$

- *STOP.*
- Check your answers on page 335.
- Correct the problems you missed.
- Go on to Set 2.

Set 2

1. $3 \overline{)\ 922}$ 2. $6 \overline{)\ 1824}$ 3. $9 \overline{)\ 58540}$

4. $4 \overline{)\ 8162031}$

- *STOP.*
- Check your answers on page 335.
- Correct the problems you missed.
- Go on to Set 3 or 4.

Set 3

1. $5 \overline{)\ 103}$ 2. $7 \overline{)\ 2149}$ 3. $6 \overline{)\ 13250}$

4. $2 \overline{)\ 40012101}$

- *STOP.*
- Check your answers on page 335.
- Correct the problems you missed.
- Go on to Set 4.

Set 4

1. You are driving a race car on a three-mile track. You have 318 miles to go. How many laps is that?

2. One small radish contains two calories. How many radishes would you have to eat to consume 614 calories?

3. A family of four is at a pizza parlor. They split a 15-inch pepperoni pizza. The pizza contains 2412 calories. How many calories does each member of the family consume?

4. You are planning a trip. Your destination is 2025 miles away by car. You wish to get there in five days. How many miles must you average each day?

- *STOP*

- Check your answers on page 335.

- Correct the problems you missed.

- Shade box 5 opposite "division of whole numbers" on page xviii.

- If this was the last subskill you had to work on in this section, take the test on page 89.

- If you have other subskills to work on in this section, go on to the next one.

SUBSKILL 6: Two-Digit Divisor, No Zeros in Quotient

Problem: 3 2) 8 3 5   *Solution:*

- Divide.

- Multiply.

- Subtract.

- Make sure difference is less than divisor.

- Bring down next number.

- Repeat until there are no more numbers to bring down.

- Designate remainder with R.

```
        2 6 R 3
   3 2 ) 8 3 5
        -6 4
          1 9 5
         -1 9 2
              3
```

Lesson:

```
          2 6 R 3
   3 2 ) 8 3 5      Eighty tens to be grouped by thirty-twos
       -6 4 0       Two groups of 32 tens or 64 tens
         1 9 5      One hundred and ninety-five ones to be grouped by thirty-twos
        -1 9 2      Six groups of 32 ones or 192 ones
             3      Number of ones remaining
```

Drill and Practice:

Set 1

1. $26 \overline{)552}$ 2. $19 \overline{)824}$ 3. $45 \overline{)513}$

4. $72 \overline{)145}$

- *STOP.*
- Check your answers on page 335.
- Correct the problems you missed.
- Go on to Set 2.

Set 2

1. $30 \overline{)750}$ 2. $55 \overline{)660}$ 3. $55 \overline{)468}$

4. $15 \overline{)4905}$

- *STOP.*
- Check your answers on page 335.
- Correct the problems you missed.
- Go on to Set 3 or 4.

Set 3

1. $12 \overline{)513}$ 2. $41 \overline{)895}$ 3. $91 \overline{)895}$

4. $27 \overline{)31549}$

- *STOP.*
- Check your answers on page 335.
- Correct the problems you missed.
- Go on to Set 4.

Set 4

1. Glut had 50 cents. He bought as many 15-cent bags of peanuts as he could. How many did he buy?

2. You are driving at an average speed of 50 miles per hour. Your destination is 300 miles away. How many hours will it take you to get there?

3. What is the least number of cartons of eggs you would have to buy to get 100 eggs?

4. One foot is 12 inches. How many feet are 150 inches?

5. You just traveled 364 miles on 14 gallons of gas. How many miles did you get per gallon?

6. Some small boxes are two feet long, three feet wide, and four feet high. A large box is four feet long, six feet wide, and eight feet high. How many of the small boxes would fit inside the large box?

7. Solve the problems in Set 1 with the following partial products by tens algorithm.

```
2 4 ) 5 5 6 8   →   2 4 ) 5 5 6 8 | 1 0 0
                          2 4 0 0  |
                          3 1 6 8  | 1 0 0
                          2 4 0 0  |
                            7 6 8  |   1 0
                            2 4 0  |
                            5 2 8  |   1 0
                            2 4 0  |
                            2 8 8  |   1 0
                            2 4 0  |
                              4 8  |     1
                              2 4  |
                              2 4  |     1
                              2 4  |
                              0 0  | 2 3 2
```

- *STOP*
- Check your answers on page 335.
- Correct the problems you missed.
- Shade box 6 opposite "division of whole numbers" on page xviii.
- If this was the last subskill you had to work on in this section, take the test on page 89.
- If you have other subskills to work on in this section, go on to the next one.

SUBSKILL 7: Two-Digit Divisor, Zeros in Quotient

Problem: $36 \overline{)7542}$ *Solution:*

- Divide.
- Multiply.
- Subtract.
- Make sure difference is less than divisor.
- Bring down next number.
- Repeat until there are no more numbers to bring down.
- Designate remainder with R.

$$
\begin{array}{r}
209\text{R}18 \\
36\overline{)7542} \\
-72 \\
\hline
34 \\
-0 \\
\hline
342 \\
-324 \\
\hline
18
\end{array}
$$

Lesson:

$$
\begin{array}{r}
209\text{R}18 \\
36\overline{)7542} \\
-7200 \\
\hline
340 \\
-00 \\
\hline
342 \\
-324 \\
\hline
18
\end{array}
$$

Seventy-five hundreds to be grouped by thirty-sixes

Two groups of 36 hundreds or 72 hundreds

Thirty-four tens to be grouped by thirty-sixes

Zero groups of 36 tens or zero tens

Three hundred and forty-two ones to be grouped by thirty-sixes

Nine groups of 36 ones or 324 ones

Number of ones remaining

Drill and Practice:

Set 1

1. $25 \overline{)5234}$

2. $50 \overline{)70000}$

3. $17 \overline{)353651}$

- *STOP.*
- Check your answers on page 335.
- Correct the problems you missed.
- Go on to Set 2.

Set 2

    1. 43) 4659

    2. 65) 13250

    3. 32) 6418088

- *STOP.*
- Check your answers on page 335.
- Correct the problems you missed.
- Go on to Set 3 or 4.

Set 3

    1. 19) 5847

    2. 95) 29147

    3. 71) 14484359

- *STOP.*
- Check your answers on page 335.
- Correct the problems you missed.
- Go on to Set 4.

Set 4

1. One four-inch dill pickle contains 18 calories. How many dill pickles would you have to eat to consume 1890 calories?

2. You are working for an advertising firm and you have to stuff 27,000 circulars into envelopes 30 to an envelope. How many envelopes will you need?

3. A feather box is one foot long, eight inches wide, and six inches high. It weighs 12 ounces. A coin box is one foot long, eight inches wide, and six inches high. It weighs 3436 ounces. How many of the feather boxes will fit inside the coin box?

4. You are estimating the distance around a pole. You take a piece of string and wrap it around the pole. The string is 5684 millimeters long. It goes around the pole 28 times. About how far around the pole is it?

- *STOP*
- Check your answers on page 335.
- Correct the problems you missed.
- Shade box 7 opposite "division of whole numbers" on page xviii.
- If this was the last subskill you had to work on in this section, take the test on page 89.
- If you have other subskills to work on in this section, go on to the next one.

SUBSKILL 8: Divisor with Three or More Digits

Problem: 1 2 7) 2 6 0 5 9 *Solution:*

- Divide.
- Multiply.
- Subtract.
- Make sure difference is less than divisor.
- Bring down next number.
- Repeat until there are no more numbers to bring down.
- Designate remainder with R.

$$
\begin{array}{r}
205\,\text{R}\,24 \\
127 \overline{)26059} \\
-254 \\
\hline
65 \\
-0 \\
\hline
659 \\
-635 \\
\hline
24
\end{array}
$$

Lesson:

$$
\begin{array}{r}
2\ 0\ 5\,\text{R}\,2\ 4 \\
1\ 2\ 7 \overline{)2\ 6\ 0\ 5\ 9} \\
-2\ 5\ 4\ 0\ 0 \\
\hline
6\ 5\ 0 \\
-0\ 0 \\
\hline
6\ 5\ 9 \\
-6\ 3\ 5 \\
\hline
2\ 4
\end{array}
$$

Two hundred and sixty hundreds to be grouped by one hundred twenty-sevens

Two groups of 127 hundreds or 254 hundreds

Sixty-five tens to be grouped by one hundred twenty-sevens

Zero groups of 127 tens or zero tens

Six hundred and fifty-nine ones to be grouped by one hundred twenty-sevens

Five groups of 127 ones or 635 ones

Number of ones remaining

Drill and Practice:

Set 1

     1. 254) 5103

     2. 377) 86720

     3. 2050) 9375601

- *STOP.*
- Check your answers on page 335.
- Correct the problems you missed.
- Go on to Set 2.

Set 2

     1. 408) 8235

     2. 511) 63493

     3. 15632) 8883217

- *STOP.*
- Check your answers on page 335.
- Correct the problems you missed.
- Go on to Set 3 or 4.

Set 3

     1. 325) 6500

     2. 980) 49372

     3. 386405) 7935002

- *STOP.*
- Check your answers on page 335.
- Correct the problems you missed.
- Go on to Set 4.

Set 4

1. A passenger jet is averaging 540 miles per hour. How many hours will it take it to fly 2160 miles?

2. A ream of paper contains 500 sheets of paper. How many reams of paper would you have to buy to run off 40,000 copies of an announcement?

3. There are 366 possible birthdays. There are about 220 million people in the United States. What is the least number of people in the United States that could have the same birthday?

4. A fast food chain has sold more than 20 billion two-inch thick hamburgers, that is, more than 40 billion inches of hamburgers.
    (a) How many feet of hamburgers to the nearest foot is 40 billion inches of hamburgers if 12 inches make one foot?
    (b) How many miles of hamburgers to the nearest mile is 40 billion inches of hamburgers if 5280 feet make one mile?

*   *STOP*

*   Check your answers on page 335.

*   Correct the problems you missed.

*   Shade box 8 opposite "division of whole numbers" on page xviii.

*   If this was the last subskill you had to work on in this section, take the test on page 89.

*   If you have other subskills to work on in this section, go on to the next one.

SUBSKILL 9: Fractional Remainder

Problem: Determine $1015 \div 28$ and write the remainder as a fraction. Simplify if you know how.

$$36\tfrac{7}{28} \text{ which simplifies to } 36\tfrac{1}{4}$$

$$28{\overline{\smash{\big)}\,1015}}$$
$$-84$$
$$175$$
$$-168$$
$$7$$

Solution:
*   Divide as usual.
*   Put remainder over divisor.
*   Simplify if you know how.

Lesson:

$$36\tfrac{7}{28} \text{ which simplifies to } 36\tfrac{1}{4}$$
$$28{\overline{\smash{\big)}\,1015}}$$

-840	One hundred and one tens to be grouped by twenty-eights
175	*Three* groups of 28 tens or 84 tens
-168	One hundred and seventy-five ones to be grouped by twenty-eights
7	*Six* groups of 28 ones or 168 ones
	Number of ones remaining with respect to a group of 28 ones

Drill and Practice:

Set 1

Divide and write the remainders as fractions. Simplify if you know how.

1. $18 \div 4 = ?$ 2. $60 \div 25 = ?$

3. $815 \div 37 = ?$ 4. $1000 \div 124 = ?$

- *STOP.*
- Check your answers on page 335.
- Correct the problems you missed.
- Go on to Set 2.

Set 2

Divide and write the remainders as fractions. Simplify if you know how.

1. $50 \div 8 = ?$ 2. $80 \div 12 = ?$

3. $513 \div 48 = ?$ 4. $5231 \div 259 = ?$

- *STOP.*
- Check your answers on page 335.
- Correct the problems you missed.
- Go on to Set 3 or 4.

Set 3

Divide and write the remainders as fractions. Simplify if you know how.

1. $80 \div 9 = ?$ 2. $95 \div 10 = ?$

3. $480 \div 23 = ?$ 4. $2943 \div 307 = ?$

- *STOP.*
- Check your answers on page 335.
- Correct the problems you missed.
- Go on to Set 4.

Set 4

1. One foot is 12 inches. How many feet are 100 inches?

2. According to the *Guinness Book of World Records*, the length of the longest moustache ever grown was 102 inches. How many feet was it?

e pound is 16 ounces. How many pounds are 152 ounces?

4. A bowling ball is traveling at four meters per second. How many seconds will it take it to travel the length of an 18-meter bowling alley?

5. You are jogging around a city block. You know that four times around the block is one mile. How far is 26 times around the block?

- *STOP*

- Check your answers on page 335.

- Correct the problems you missed.

- Shade box 9 opposite "division of whole numbers" on page xviii.

- If this was the last subskill you had to work on in this section, take the test on page 89.

- If you have other subskills to work on in this section, go on to the next one.

SUBSKILL 10: Decimal Remainder

Problem: Determine 451 ÷ 7 to three decimal places.

Solution: • Add decimal point and one zero to dividend if dividing to one decimal place, two zeros if dividing to two decimal places, three zeros if dividing to three decimal places, and so on.

• Divide as usual.

• Put decimal point in quotient directly above decimal point in dividend.

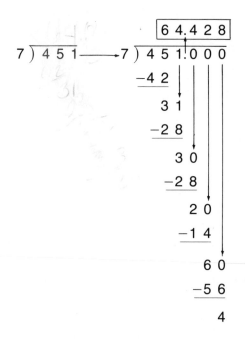

4

Lesson:

```
        6 4 . 4 2 8
 7 ) 4 5 1 . 0 0 0     Forty-five tens to be grouped by sevens
   −4 2 0 . 0 0 0      Six groups of seven tens or 42 tens
      3 1 . 0 0 0      Thirty-one ones to be grouped by sevens
     −2 8 . 0 0 0      Four groups of seven ones or 28 ones
        3 . 0 0 0      Thirty tenths to be grouped by sevens
       −2 . 8 0 0      Four groups of seven tenths or 28 tenths
          . 2 0 0      Twenty hundredths to be grouped by sevens
         −. 1 4 0      Two groups of seven hundredths or 14 hundredths
          . 0 6 0      Sixty thousandths to be grouped by sevens
         −. 0 5 6      Eight groups of seven thousandths or 56 thousandths
          . 0 0 4
```

Drill and Practice:

Set 1

Determine to three decimal places.

1. $642 \div 7 = ?$ 2. $28 \div 3 = ?$

3. $8491 \div 25 = ?$ 4. $5721 \div 83 = ?$

- • STOP.
- • Check your answers on page 335.
- • Correct the problems you missed.
- • Go on to Set 2.

Set 2

Determine to two decimal places.

1. $527 \div 8 = ?$ 2. $72 \div 5 = ?$

3. $6527 \div 40 = ?$ 4. $4930 \div 23 = ?$

- • STOP.
- • Check your answers on page 335.
- • Correct the problems you missed.
- • Go on to Set 3 or 4.

Set 3

Determine to one decimal place.

1. $826 \div 9 = ?$ 2. $92 \div 6 = ?$

3. $5689 \div 33 = ?$ 4. $1784 \div 19 = ?$

- *STOP.*
- Check your answers on page 335.
- Correct the problems you missed.
- Go on to Set 4.

Set 4

1. A passenger jet is flying at an altitude of 28,300 feet. How high is this in miles to two decimal places if there are 5280 feet in one mile?

2. The ocean depths have been explored to a depth of 35,802 feet. How deep is this in miles to two decimal places if there are 5280 feet in one mile?

3. You are standing on a street corner giving away one-dollar bills at the rate of one bill per second.

    (a) How many minutes to one decimal place will it take you to give away one thousand dollars if there are 60 seconds in one minute?

    (b). How many work weeks to two decimal places will it take you to give away one million dollars if there are 60 seconds in one minute, 60 minutes in one hour, eight hours in one work day, and five work days in one work week?

    (c) How many work years to three decimal places will it take you to give away one billion dollars if there are 60 seconds in one minute, 60 minutes in one hour, eight hours in one work day, five work days in one work week, and 48 work weeks in one work year?

4. You are riding a horse around a 325-meter track. How many times to two decimal places will you have to ride around the track to ride five kilometers (5000 meters)?

- *STOP*
- Check your answers on page 335.
- Correct the problems you missed.
- Shade box 10 opposite "division of whole numbers" on page xviii.
- Take the test on page 89.

Inventory Post Test for
Division of Whole Numbers

1. $9 \div 4 = ?$ 2. $6 \overline{)\, 50}$ 3. $5 \overline{)\, 716}$ 4. $3 \overline{)\, 5147}$

5. $8 \overline{)\, 96436}$ 6. $46 \overline{)\, 583}$ 7. $58 \overline{)\, 6154}$ 8. $320 \overline{)\, 64249}$

9. Determine $552 \div 36$ and write the remainder as a fraction. Simplify if you know how.

10. Determine $171 \div 28$ to three decimal places.

- *STOP*
- Check your answers with the instructor.
- As before, work through the subskills in this section which correspond to the problems you missed, except work the *even* drill-and-practice problems.
- Take the test on page 91.

General Survey Tests for Whole Numbers and Fractions

General Survey Post Test
for
Whole Numbers

1. 7 + 5 = ? 12

2. 31
   +17
   ‾‾‾
    48

3. 49
   +26
   ‾‾‾
    75

4. 492
   +358
   ‾‾‾‾
    850

5. 17622
    20482
   +31733
   ‾‾‾‾‾‾
    69837

6. 13 − 6 = ? 7

7. 56
   −24
   ‾‾‾
    32

8. 83
   −35
   ‾‾‾
    48

9. 653
   −276
   ‾‾‾‾
    377

10. 40010
    −14342
   ‾‾‾‾‾‾
     25768

11. 4 × 7 = ? 28

12. 38
    × 2
   ‾‾‾‾
    76

13. 38
    × 7

14. 3807
    × 49

15. 1579
    ×3400

16. 13 ÷ 4 = ? 3 r 1

17. 6) 82   13 r 4
        6
        ‾‾
        22
        18

18. 8) 439   54 r 7
        40
        ‾‾
        39
        32

19. 29) 6053   2
         58
         ‾‾‾
         253

20. Divide 42 into 636 and write the remainder as a fraction. Simplify if you know how.

- *STOP*
- Check your answers with the instructor.
- Enter the number correct and today's date in the spaces provided on page **xx**.
- Figure your growth and take pleasure in it.
- If you got 18 or more right, take the test on page **92**.
- If you got less than 18 right, take the inventory pretests for whole numbers again beginning with the one on page **3**.
- As before, work through the subskills which correspond to the problems you miss.

General Survey Pretest
for
Fractions

1. Which is divided into fourths?

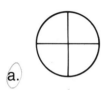

a.   b.   c.

2. Which illustrates four-eighths or $\frac{4}{8}$?

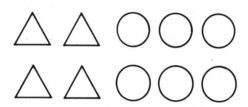

a.   b.   c.

3. Two triangles for every three circles: What ratio makes this comparison?

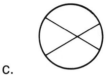

△ △ ○ ○ ○

△ △ ○ ○ ○

4. For each fraction in row A, find one or more equivalent fractions in row B.

Row A: $\frac{2}{3}$ $\frac{8}{18}$ $\frac{1}{2}$

Row B: $\frac{4}{9}$ $\frac{10}{15}$ $\frac{4}{6}$ $\frac{8}{16}$

5. For each improper fraction or mixed number in row A, find an equivalent improper fraction or mixed number in row B.

Row A: $4\frac{1}{9}$ $\frac{11}{5}$ $\frac{7}{5}$ $1\frac{4}{9}$

Row B: $1\frac{2}{5}$ $\frac{37}{9}$ $2\frac{1}{5}$ $\frac{13}{9}$

6. Which are equivalent to one?

a. $\frac{8}{8}$ b. $\frac{417}{471}$ c. $\frac{1111}{11111}$ d. $\frac{31721}{31721}$ e. $\frac{23}{24}$

7. Express $\frac{2}{3}$, $\frac{1}{5}$, and $\frac{5}{12}$ in terms of their LCD or least common denominator.

8. Find the GCF or greatest common factor of 12 and 20.

9. $\frac{1}{8} + \frac{5}{8} = ?$

10. $\frac{1}{4} + \frac{5}{6} = ?$

11. $3\frac{1}{2} + 4\frac{3}{5} = ?$

12. $\frac{7}{12} - \frac{1}{12} = ?$

13. $\frac{3}{8} - \frac{1}{6} = ?$

14. $7\frac{1}{3} - 4\frac{3}{4} = ?$

15. $\frac{5}{12} \times \frac{9}{10} = ?$

16. $6 \times \frac{2}{3} = ?$

17. $2\frac{5}{8} \times 5\frac{5}{7} = ?$

18. $\frac{5}{9} \div \frac{5}{12} = ?$

19. $5\frac{1}{4} \div 7 = ?$

20. $2\frac{1}{6} \div 2\frac{8}{9} = ?$

- *STOP*
- Check your answers on page 335.
- Enter the number correct and today's date in the spaces provided on page xx.
- If you got 18 or more right, take the test on page 203.
- If you got less than 18 right, take the test on page 95.

SKILL
Fractions: Basic Concepts

Inventory Pretest for Fractions:
Basic Concepts

1. Which is divided into fourths?

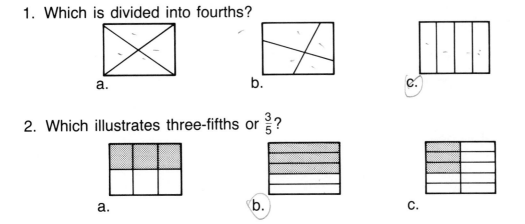

    a.   b.   c.

2. Which illustrates three-fifths or $\frac{3}{5}$?

    a.   b.   c.

3. What fractions are illustrated by points *A, B,* and *C*?

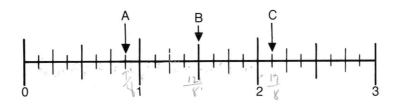

4. Four out of nine squares are shaded. What ratio makes this comparison?

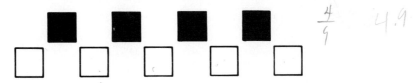

$\frac{4}{9}$ 4:9

5. Three triangles for every four circles: What ratio makes this comparison?

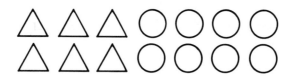

6. Solve for N: $\frac{4}{5} = \frac{N}{30}$

7. For each fraction in row A, find one or more equivalent fractions in row B.

Row A: $\frac{1}{3}$ $\frac{6}{15}$ $\frac{5}{6}$

Row B: $\frac{2}{5}$ $\frac{10}{12}$ $\frac{12}{30}$ $\frac{6}{18}$

8. For each improper fraction or mixed number in row A, find an equivalent improper fraction or mixed number in row B.

Row A: $\frac{11}{8}$ $3\frac{1}{5}$ $\frac{25}{8}$ $1\frac{3}{5}$

Row B: $\frac{16}{5}$ $1\frac{3}{8}$ $\frac{8}{5}$ $3\frac{1}{8}$

9. Which are equivalent to one?

a. $\frac{3}{3}$ b. $\frac{402}{420}$ c. $\frac{5382}{5382}$ d. $\frac{28}{29}$ e. $\frac{16}{16}$

10. $\frac{5}{6} \times 1 = ?$

11. $\frac{3}{4} \times \frac{6}{6} = ?$

12. Which are factors of eight?

a. .4   b. $\frac{1}{2}$ c. 1   d. 2   e. 3   f. 4   g. 8   h. 16

13. Find the GCF or greatest common factor of 18 and 48.

14. Simplify $\frac{55}{25}$.

15. Which are prime?

a. 2   b. 3   c. 4   d. 7   e. 8   f. 39   g. 201   h. 4041

16. Write the prime factorization of 24.

17. Find the LCM or least common multiple of two, three, and five.

18. Express $\frac{1}{3}$, $\frac{3}{5}$, and $\frac{5}{6}$ in terms of their LCD or least common denominator.

19. Invert $\frac{3}{4}$.

● *STOP*

● Check your answers on page 336.

● Shade the boxes opposite "fractions: basic concepts" on page xviii which correspond to the problems you got right.

● If you got all of them right, take the test on page 139.

● If you missed some of them, start working on the subskills in this section which correspond to the ones you missed.

● For each subskill, look at the example, study the solution, think about the lesson, and work the *odd* drill-and-practice problems.

SUBSKILL 1: Fractional Units

Problem: Which is divided into thirds?

a.   b.   c.

Solution: [b] Fractional units are *identical* in size and shape.

Lesson:

Halves: or   but not

Thirds: or   but not

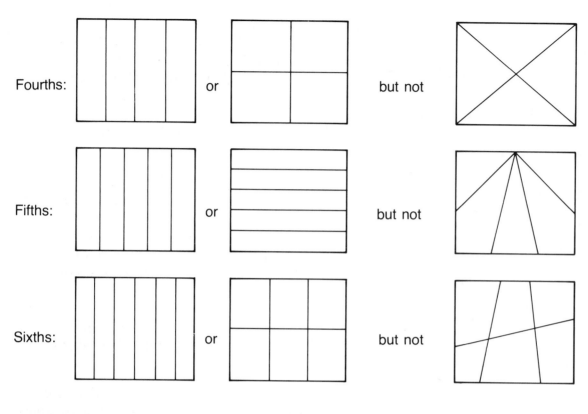

Fourths: or but not

Fifths: or but not

Sixths: or but not

Drill and Practice:

Set 1

1. Which is divided into thirds?

a.   b.   c.

2. Which is divided into fifths?

a. b. 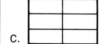 c.

3. Divide the square into eighths.

- *STOP.*
- Check your answers on page 336.
- Correct the problems you missed.
- Go on to Set 2.

Set 2

1. Which is divided into halves?

a.   b.   c.

2. Which is divided into tenths?

a. b. c.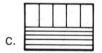

3. Divide the rectangle into fifths.

- *STOP.*
- Check your answers on page 336.
- Correct the problems you missed.
- Go on to Set 3 or 4.

Set 3

1. Which is divided into fourths?

a.　　　　b.　　　　c.

2. Which is divided into sixths?

a.　　　　b.　　　　c.

3. Divide the circle into fourths.

- *STOP.*
- Check your answers on page 336.
- Correct the problems you missed.
- Go on to Set 4.

Set 4

1. Which have been divided into eighths?

a.　　　　b.

c.

d.

e.

2. What fraction of a
   (a) foot (12 inches) is an inch?
   (b) yard (three feet) is a foot?
   (c) pound (16 ounces) is an ounce?
   (d) pint (two cups) is a cup?
   (e) quart (two pints) is a pint?
   (f) gallon (four quarts) is a quart?

3. What fraction of a
   (a) meter (100 centimeters) is a centimeter?
   (b) liter (1000 milliliters) is a milliliter?
   (c) kilogram (1000 grams) is a gram?
   (d) kilometer (1000 meters) is a meter?

4. The United States consists of 50 states. Is each state 1/50 of the United States?

5. One cubic centimeter is 1/1000 of a cubic decimeter. One cubic decimeter occupies one liter. How much does one cubic centimeter occupy?

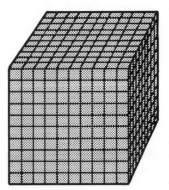
One cubic centimeter

6. One milliliter is 1/1000 of a liter. One liter of water weighs one kilogram. How much does one milliliter of water weigh?

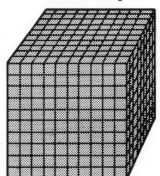
One Milliliter

- *STOP*
- Check your answers on page 336
- Correct the problems you missed.
- Shade box 1 opposite "fractions: basic concepts" on page xviii.
- If this was the only subskill you had to work on in this section, take the test on page 136.
- If you have other subskills to work on in this section, go on to the next one.

SUBSKILL 2: Fractions as Combinations of Fractional Units

Problem: Which illustrates three-fourths or $\frac{3}{4}$?

a. b. c.

Solution: [c] $\frac{a}{b}$ means *a* of *b* fractional units.

Lesson:

One-half
or
$\frac{1}{2}$:

Two-halves
or
$\frac{2}{2}$:

One-third
or
$\frac{1}{3}$:

Two-thirds
or
$\frac{2}{3}$:

Three-thirds
or
$\frac{3}{3}$:

One-fourth
or
$\frac{1}{4}$:

Two-fourths
or
$\frac{2}{4}$:

Three-fourths
or
$\frac{3}{4}$:

Four-fourths
or
$\frac{4}{4}$:

One-fifth
or
$\frac{1}{5}$:

Two-fifths
or
$\frac{2}{5}$:

Three-fifths
or
$\frac{3}{5}$:

Four-fifths
or
$\frac{4}{5}$:

Five-fifths
or
$\frac{5}{5}$:

Drill and Practice:

Set 1

1. Which illustrates three-fourths?

  a.   b.   c.

2. Which illustrates $\frac{1}{2}$?

  a.   b.   c.

3. Illustrate $\frac{5}{6}$ with the hexagon.

- *STOP.*
- Check your answers on page 336.
- Correct the problems you missed.
- Go on to Set 2.

Set 2

1. Which illustrates two-thirds?

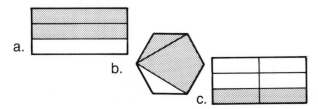
a.   b.   c.

2. Which illustrates $\frac{3}{6}$?

  a.   b.   c.

3. Illustrate $\frac{3}{8}$ with the square.

- *STOP.*
- Check your answers on page 336.
- Correct the problems you missed.
- Go on to Set 3 or 4.

Set 3

1. Which illustrates seven-tenths?

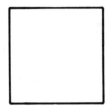
a.

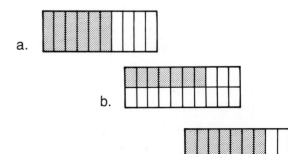
b.

c.

2. Which illustrates $\frac{1}{3}$?

a.   b.   c.

3. Illustrate $\frac{2}{4}$ with the circle.

- *STOP.*
- Check your answers on page 336.
- Correct the problems you missed.
- Go on to Set 4.

Set 4

1. Which illustrates $\frac{3}{8}$?

a.   b.

2. What fraction of a foot (12 inches) are
   (a) two inches?   (c) five inches?
   (b) seven inches?   (d) 11 inches?

3. What fraction of a pound (16 ounces) are
   (a) three ounces?   (c) seven ounces?
   (b) 11 ounces?   (d) 15 ounces?

4. What fraction of a gallon (four quarts) are three quarts?

5. What fraction of a
   (a) meter (100 centimeters) are 23 centimeters?
   (b) liter (1000 milliliters) are 957 milliliters?
   (c) kilogram (1000 grams) are nine grams?
   (d) kilometer (1000 meters) are 483 meters?

6. What fraction of the letters in the word *love* are vowels?

7. Find the riddle and its answer.
   Riddle:
       The first $\frac{1}{2}$ of the word *whatever.*
       The middle $\frac{3}{5}$ of the word *chase.*
       The first $\frac{1}{2}$ of the word *fivefold.*
       The last $\frac{1}{2}$ of the word *buckeyes.*
       The middle $\frac{3}{5}$ of the word *handy.*
       The last $\frac{5}{7}$ of the word *arrests.*
       The last $\frac{1}{3}$ of the word *beacon.*
       The middle $\frac{1}{9}$ of the word *crabapple.*
       The first $\frac{5}{9}$ of the word *waterfall.*
       The last $\frac{3}{7}$ of the word *grabbed.*
   Answer:
       The middle $\frac{3}{5}$ of the word *other.*
       The first $\frac{11}{13}$ of the word *Mississippian.*
       The last $\frac{5}{6}$ of the word *driver.*

- *STOP*

- Check your answers on page 336.

- Correct the problems you missed.

- Shade box 2 opposite "fractions: basic concepts" on page xviii.

- If this was the last subskill you had to work on in this section, take the test on page 136.

- If you have other subskills to work on in this section, go on to the next one.

SUBSKILL 3: Fractions as Points on a Line

Problem: What fractions or mixed numbers are illustrated by points *A, B, C, D,* and *E*?

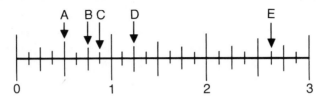

Solution: $\frac{a}{b}$ means *a* of *b* equidistant subdivisions of the unit length.

$A = \frac{4}{8} = \frac{2}{4} = \frac{1}{2}$

$B = \frac{6}{8} = \frac{3}{4}$

$C = \frac{7}{8}$

$D = \frac{10}{8} = \frac{5}{4} = 1\frac{1}{4}$

$E = \frac{21}{8} = 2\frac{5}{8}$

Lesson:

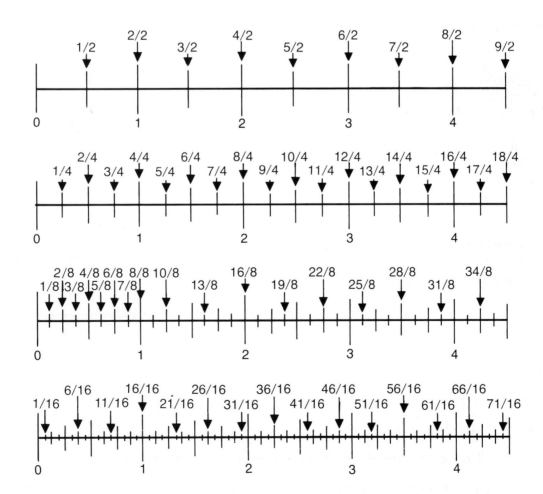

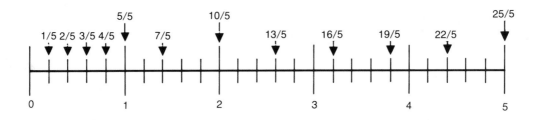

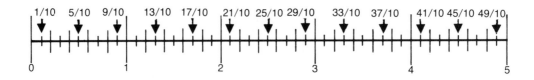

Drill and Practice:

Set 1

1. What fractions or mixed numbers are illustrated by points *A, B, C, D,* and *E?*

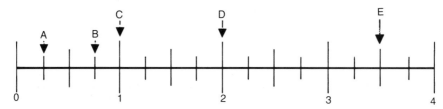

2. Which letter designates

   (a) $\frac{5}{4}$?   (b) $\frac{1}{2}$?   (c) $\frac{27}{8}$?   (d) $\frac{5}{2}$?   (e) $\frac{1}{8}$?

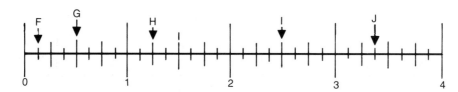

- *STOP.*
- Check your answers on page 336.
- Correct the problems you missed.
- Go on to Set 2.

Set 2

1. What fractions or mixed numbers are illustrated by points *A, B, C, D,* and *E?*

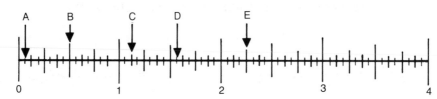

2. Which letter designates

    (a) $\frac{4}{5}$?   (b) $\frac{13}{5}$?   (c) $\frac{17}{5}$?   (d) $\frac{1}{5}$?   (e) $\frac{10}{5}$?

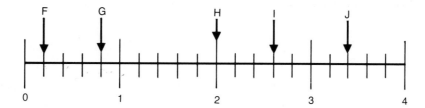

- *STOP.*
- Check your answers on page 337.
- Correct the problems you missed.
- Go on to Set 3 or 4.

Set 3

1. What fractions or mixed numbers are illustrated by points *A, B, C, D,* and *E*?

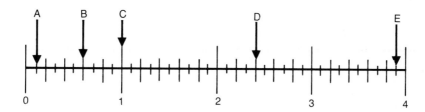

2. Which letter designates

    (a) $\frac{23}{10}$?   (b) $\frac{1}{20}$?   (c) $\frac{12}{10}$?   (d) $\frac{77}{20}$?   (e) $\frac{7}{10}$?

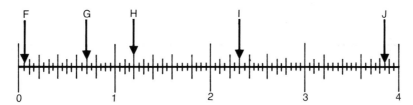

- *STOP.*
- Check your answers on page 337.
- Correct the problems you missed.
- Go on to Set 4.

Set 4

1. What fractions or mixed numbers are illustrated by the measurements?

(a)   (b)

2. What fractions or mixed numbers are illustrated by the measurements?

(a)

(b)

3. One meter = 1/10 of one dekameter = 1/100 of one hectometer = 1/1000 of one kilometer. How many meters equal
    (a) one dekameter?
    (b) one hectometer?
    (c) one kilometer?

4. One millimeter = 1/10 of one centimeter = 1/100 of one decimeter = 1/1000 of one meter. How many millimeters equal
    (a) one centimeter?
    (b) one decimeter?
    (c) one meter?

- *STOP*

- Check your answers on page 337.

- Correct the problems you missed.

- Shade box 3 opposite "fractions: basic concepts" on page xviii.

- If this was the last subskill you had to work on in this section, take the test on page 136.

- If you have other subskills to work on in this section, go on to the next one.

SUBSKILL 4: Fractions as Ratios of Part-to-Whole Comparisons

Problem: Six out of ten tires are white-walls. What ratio makes this comparison?

Solution: 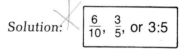

Lesson: Two out of five triangles are shaded. The ratio making this comparison is is $\frac{2}{5}$ or 2:5.

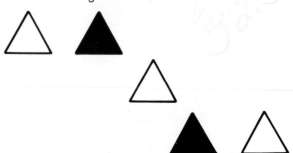

Three out of seven hexagons are unshaded. The ratio making this comparison is $\frac{3}{7}$ or 3:7.

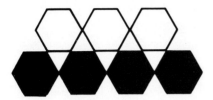

Five out of 11 rectangles are shaded. The ratio making this comparison is $\frac{5}{11}$ or 5:11.

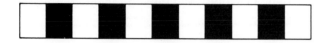

Six out of 20 regions are shaded. The ratio making this comparison is $\frac{6}{20}$, $\frac{3}{10}$, or 3:10.

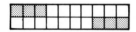

Thirty-six out of 100 regions are shaded. The ratio making this comparison is $\frac{36}{100}$, $\frac{9}{25}$, or 9:25.

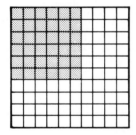

Drill and Practice:

Set 1

1. Four out of seven squares are shaded. What ratio makes this comparison?

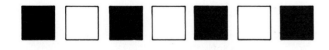

2. What ratio compares the number of shaded triangles to the number of triangles?

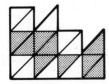

3. What ratio compares the number of circled dollar signs to the number of dollar signs?

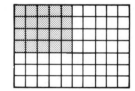

- *STOP.*
- Check your answers on page 337.
- Correct the problems you missed.
- Go on to Set 2.

Set 2

1. One out of six circles is unshaded. What ratio makes this comparison?

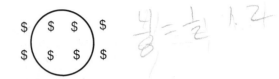

2. What ratio compares the number of shaded regions to the number of regions?

3. What ratio compares the number of s's to the number of letters in *Mississippi*?

- *STOP.*
- Check your answers on page 337.
- Correct the problems you missed.
- Go on to Set 3 or 4.

Set 3

1. Five out of nine triangles are upside down. What ratio makes this comparison?

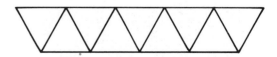

2. What ratio compares the number of un-shaded regions to the number of regions?

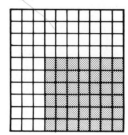

3. What ratio compares the number of big circles to the number of circles?

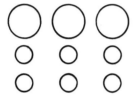

- *STOP.*
- Check your answers on page 337.
- Correct the problems you missed.
- Go on to Set 4.

- *STOP*

- Check your answers on page 337.

- Correct the problems you missed.

- Shade box 4 opposite "fractions: basic concepts" on page xviii.

- If this was the last subskill you had to work on in this section, take the test on page 136.

- If you have other subskills to work on in this section, go on to the next one.

Set 4

1. Four out of five toads want to help you with your mathematics. What ratio makes this comparison?

2. Most people work or go to school five days out of seven. What ratio makes this comparison?

3. About 24 out of 25 reusable bottles are actually reusable. What ratio makes this comparison?

4. Three out of four doctors recommend all kinds of things. What ratio makes this comparison?

5. You are a baseball player. On Saturday you go to bat three times. You get one hit. On Sunday you go to bat four times. You get two hits. What was your batting average for the weekend?

SUBSKILL 5: Fractions as Ratios of Part-to-Part Comparisons

Problem: Five triangles for every eight squares: What ratio makes this comparison?

△ △ △ △ △

☐ ☐ ☐ ☐
☐ ☐ ☐ ☐

Solution: $\boxed{\dfrac{5}{8} \text{ or } 5{:}8}$

Lesson: Three circles for every five squares: The ratio making this comparison is $\frac{3}{5}$ or 3:5.

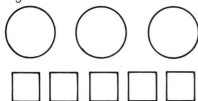

Four asterisks for every eight sharps: The ratio making this comparison is $\frac{4}{8}$, $\frac{1}{2}$, or 1:2.

```
 *  # #
 *  # #
 *  # #
 *  # #
```

Three shaded regions for every seven unshaded regions: The ratio making this comparison is $\frac{3}{7}$ or 3:7.

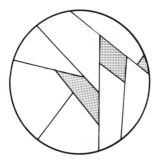

Drill and Practice:

Set 1

1. Two hexagons for every three circles: What ratio makes this comparison?

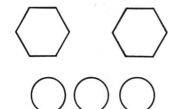

2. What ratio compares the number of squares to the number of triangles?

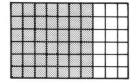

3. What ratio compares the number of shaded regions to the number of unshaded regions?

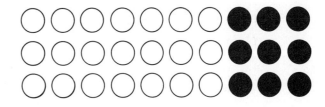

- *STOP.*
- Check your answers on page 337.
- Correct the problems you missed.
- Go on to Set 2.

Set 2

1. Seven unshaded circles for every three shaded circles: What ratio makes this comparison?

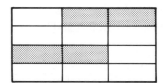

2. What ratio compares the number of shaded rectangles to the number of unshaded rectangles?

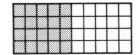

3. What ratio compares the number of shaded regions to the number of unshaded regions?

- *STOP.*
- Check your answers on page 337.
- Correct the problems you missed.
- Go on to Set 3 or 4.

Set 3

1. What ratio compares the number of s's to the number of letters other than s in *Mississippi?*

2. What ratio compares the number of large circles to the number of small circles?

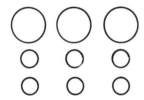

3. What ratio compares the number of shaded regions to the number of unshaded regions?

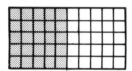

- *STOP*
- Check your answers on page 337.
- Correct the problems you missed.
- Shade box 5 opposite "fractions: basic concepts" on page xviii.
- If this was the last subskill you had to work on in this section, take the test on page 136.
- If you have other subskills to work on in this section, go on to the next one.

- *STOP.*
- Check your answers on page 337.
- Correct the problems you missed.
- Go on to Set 4.

Set 4

1. A car is traveling at 40 miles per hour. What ratio makes this comparison?

2. An infant's heart beats 130 times per minute. What ratio makes this comparison?

3. There are twice as many men as women at a party. What ratio makes this comparison?

4. A stitch in time saves nine. What ratio makes this comparison?

5. A man can lift 1½ times his weight. What ratio makes this comparison?

SUBSKILL 6: Solving Proportions

Problem: Solve for *N:* $\frac{3}{5} = \frac{12}{N}$

Solution:
- Cross multiply.
- Divide numbers on *both sides* by coefficient of unknown.

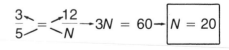

Lesson: Solving a proportion amounts to finding equal ratios.

$$\frac{3}{5} = \frac{12}{N} \quad \rightarrow \quad \frac{3}{5} = \frac{12}{20}$$

Drill and Practice:

Set 1

Solve for N.

1. $\dfrac{4}{7} = \dfrac{12}{N}$

2. $\dfrac{3}{8} = \dfrac{N}{16}$

3. $\dfrac{N}{2} = \dfrac{500}{1000}$

4. $\dfrac{5}{N} = \dfrac{20}{100}$

- *STOP.*
- Check your answers on page 337.
- Correct the problems you missed.
- Go on to Set 2.

Set 2

Solve for N.

1. $\dfrac{1}{3} = \dfrac{5}{N}$

2. $\dfrac{2}{5} = \dfrac{N}{60}$

3. $\dfrac{N}{4} = \dfrac{8}{12}$

4. $\dfrac{6}{N} = \dfrac{12}{15}$

- *STOP.*
- Check your answers on page 337.
- Correct the problems you missed.
- Go on to Set 3 or 4.

Set 3

Solve for N.

1. $\dfrac{45}{60} = \dfrac{9}{N}$

2. $\dfrac{40}{50} = \dfrac{N}{10}$

3. $\dfrac{N}{3} = \dfrac{4}{9}$

4. $\dfrac{6}{N} = \dfrac{11}{13}$

- *STOP.*
- Check your answers on page 337.
- Correct the problems you missed.
- Go on to Set 4.

Set 4

1. Four out of five toads want to help you with your mathematics. How many toads out of 100 want to help you with your mathematics?

2. Most people work or go to school five days out of seven. How many days out of (a) 14, (b) 28, (c) 91, and (d) 182 do most people work or go to school?

3. About 24 out of 25 reusable bottles are actually reusable. About how many reusable bottles out of 250 are actually reusable?

4. Three out of four doctors recommend all kinds of things. How many doctors out of 300 recommend all kinds of things?

5. A car is traveling at 40 miles per hour. How far will it travel in 12 hours?

6. An infant's heart beats 130 times per minute. How many times will the infant's heart beat in ten minutes?

7. There are 50 men at a party, and there are twice as many men as women at the party. How many women are at the party?

8. A stitch in time saves nine. How much will nine stitches save?

9. A man can lift 1½ times his weight. How much can the man lift if he weighs 160 pounds?

10. If it takes eight steps to walk five meters, how many steps will it take to walk

    (a) 20 meters?
    (b) 75 meters?
    (c) 120 meters?
    (d) 1310 meters?

11. Determine the cost of ten lasagna dinners.

13. Determine the cost of 15 tacos.

12. Determine the cost of 30 boxes of candy drops.

- *STOP*
- Check your answers on page 337.
- Correct the problems you missed.
- Shade box 6 opposite "fractions: basic concepts" on page xviii
- If this was the last subskill you had to work on in this section, take the test on page 136.
- If you have other subskills to work on in this section, go on to the next one.

SUBSKILL 7: Equivalent Forms of Proper Fractions

Problem: For each fraction in row A, find one or more equivalent fractions in row B.

Row A: $\dfrac{1}{2}$ $\dfrac{8}{12}$ $\dfrac{3}{4}$

Row B: $\dfrac{16}{32}$ $\dfrac{6}{9}$ $\dfrac{12}{16}$ $\dfrac{2}{3}$ $\dfrac{15}{20}$

Solution: Two fractions are equivalent if one can be obtained from the other by multiplying or dividing its numerator and denominator by the *same* number.

$$\boxed{\dfrac{1}{2} = \dfrac{16}{32}}$$

because

$$\dfrac{1 \times 16}{2 \times 16} = \dfrac{16}{32}$$

$$\boxed{\dfrac{8}{12} = \dfrac{6}{9} = \dfrac{2}{3}}$$

because

$$\dfrac{8}{12} = \dfrac{8 \div 4}{12 \div 4} = \dfrac{2}{3}$$

and

$$\dfrac{6}{9} = \dfrac{6 \div 3}{9 \div 3} = \dfrac{2}{3}$$

$$\boxed{\dfrac{3}{4} = \dfrac{12}{16} = \dfrac{15}{20}}$$

because

$$\dfrac{3}{4} = \dfrac{3 \times 4}{4 \times 4} = \dfrac{12}{16}$$

and

$$\dfrac{3}{4} = \dfrac{3 \times 5}{4 \times 5} = \dfrac{15}{20}$$

Lesson:

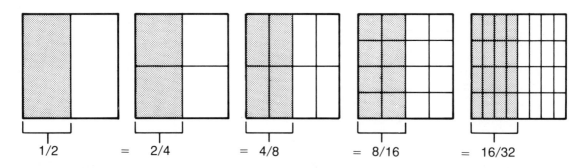

1/2   =   2/4   =   4/8   =   8/16   =   16/32

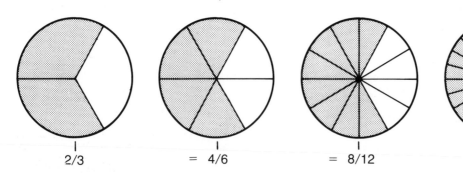

2/3   =   4/6   =   8/12   =   16/24

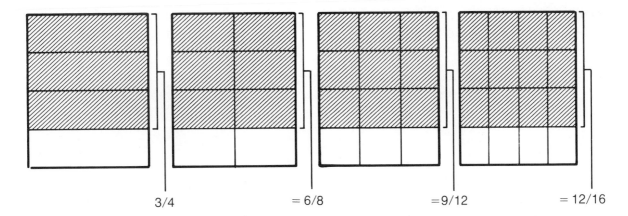

3/4   = 6/8   =9/12   = 12/16

Drill and Practice:

Set 1

1. For each fraction in row A, find one or more equivalent fractions in row B.

Row A: $\dfrac{1}{2}$ $\dfrac{2}{3}$ $\dfrac{9}{12}$ $\dfrac{4}{5}$

Row B: $\dfrac{10}{15}$ $\dfrac{4}{8}$ $\dfrac{3}{4}$ $\dfrac{8}{10}$ $\dfrac{3}{6}$ $\dfrac{5}{10}$ $\dfrac{16}{24}$

2. $\dfrac{1}{2} = \dfrac{7}{?}$

3. $\dfrac{4}{12} = \dfrac{1}{?}$

- *STOP.*
- Check your answers on page 337.
- Correct the problems you missed.
- Go on to Set 2.

Set 2

1. For each fraction in row A, find one or more equivalent fractions in row B.

Row A: $\dfrac{1}{2}$ $\dfrac{2}{6}$ $\dfrac{3}{4}$ $\dfrac{1}{5}$

Row B: $\dfrac{3}{15}$ $\dfrac{6}{8}$ $\dfrac{5}{15}$ $\dfrac{1}{3}$ $\dfrac{8}{16}$ $\dfrac{2}{4}$ $\dfrac{2}{10}$

2. $\dfrac{2}{3} = \dfrac{4}{?}$

3. $\dfrac{6}{24} = \dfrac{1}{?}$

- *STOP.*
- Check your answers on page 337.
- Correct the problems you missed.
- Go on to Set 3 or 4.

Set 3

1. For each fraction in row A, find one or more equivalent fractions in row B.

Row A: $\dfrac{1}{2}$ $\dfrac{1}{4}$ $\dfrac{10}{25}$ $\dfrac{5}{6}$

Row B: $\dfrac{15}{18}$ $\dfrac{4}{10}$ $\dfrac{2}{5}$ $\dfrac{2}{8}$ $\dfrac{12}{24}$ $\dfrac{3}{12}$ $\dfrac{10}{12}$

2. $\dfrac{3}{4} = \dfrac{?}{20}$

3. $\dfrac{24}{40} = \dfrac{?}{5}$

- *STOP.*
- Check your answers on page 337.
- Correct the problems you missed.
- Go on to Set 4.

Set 4

1. (a) How many ladyfingers?
   (b) How much of a package of ladyfingers?

2. (a) How many servings of gouda cheese?
   (b) How much of a ball of gouda cheese?

4. (a) How many full bottles of cola?
   (b) How much of a six-pack of cola?

3. (a) How many pieces of lemon cake?
   (b) How much lemon cake?

5. (a) How many shaded squares?
   (b) How much of the grid is shaded?

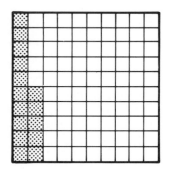

- *STOP*

- Check your answers on page 337.

- Correct the problems you missed.

- Shade box 7 opposite "fractions: basic concepts" on page xviii.

- If this was the last subskill you had to work on in this section, take the test on page 136.

- If you have other subskills to work on in this section, go on to the next one.

SUBSKILL 8: Equivalence of Improper Fractions and Mixed Numbers

Problem: For each improper fraction or mixed number in row A, find an equivalent improper fraction or mixed number in row B.

Row A: $\frac{5}{4}$ $1\frac{7}{8}$ $\frac{5}{2}$ $3\frac{5}{16}$ $\frac{15}{4}$ $4\frac{3}{8}$

Row B: $\frac{15}{8}$ $1\frac{1}{4}$ $\frac{35}{8}$ $2\frac{1}{2}$ $\frac{53}{16}$ $3\frac{3}{4}$

Solution: $\frac{a}{c}$ and $N\frac{b}{c}$

are equivalent if $a = (c \times N) + b$.

$$\boxed{\frac{5}{4} = 1\frac{1}{4}}$$

since $\quad 5 = (4 \times 1) + 1$

$$\boxed{1\frac{7}{8} = \frac{15}{8}}$$

since $\quad (8 \times 1) + 7 = 15$

$$\boxed{\frac{5}{2} = 2\frac{1}{2}}$$

since $5 = (2 \times 2) + 1$

$$\boxed{3\frac{5}{16} = \frac{53}{16}}$$

since $(16 \times 3) + 5 = 53$

$$\boxed{\frac{15}{4} = 3\frac{3}{4}}$$

since $15 = (4 \times 3) + 3$

$$\boxed{4\frac{3}{8} = \frac{35}{8}}$$

since $(8 \times 4) + 3 = 35$

Lesson:

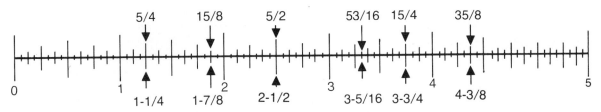

Drill and Practice:

Set 1

1. For each improper fraction or mixed number in row A, find an equivalent improper fraction or mixed number in row B.

   Row A: $1\frac{1}{8}$ $\frac{39}{16}$ $2\frac{1}{4}$ $\frac{3}{2}$ $3\frac{3}{10}$

   Row B: $1\frac{1}{2}$ $\frac{9}{4}$ $\frac{33}{10}$ $\frac{9}{8}$ $2\frac{7}{16}$

2. Convert to mixed numbers.

   (a) $\frac{7}{2}$ (b) $\frac{7}{4}$ (c) $\frac{11}{8}$

3. Convert to improper fractions.

   (a) $4\frac{1}{2}$ (b) $2\frac{3}{4}$ (c) $3\frac{1}{8}$

- *STOP.*
- Check your answers on page 337.
- Correct the problems you missed.
- Go on to Set 2.

Set 2

1. For each improper fraction or mixed number in row A, find an equivalent improper fraction or mixed number in row B.

   Row A: $1\frac{5}{8}$ $\frac{13}{4}$ $2\frac{5}{8}$ $\frac{11}{4}$ $2\frac{3}{5}$

   Row B: $2\frac{3}{4}$ $\frac{13}{5}$ $\frac{13}{8}$ $\frac{21}{8}$ $3\frac{1}{4}$

2. Convert to mixed numbers.

   (a) $\frac{15}{4}$ (b) $\frac{17}{8}$ (c) $\frac{17}{16}$

3. Convert to improper fractions.

   (a) $5\frac{1}{4}$ (b) $2\frac{3}{8}$ (c) $3\frac{3}{16}$

- *STOP.*
- Check your answers on page 338.
- Correct the problems you missed.
- Go on to Set 3 or 4.

Set 3

1. For each improper fraction or mixed number in row A, find an equivalent improper fraction or mixed number in row B.

   Row A: $2\frac{1}{16}$ $\frac{9}{5}$ $2\frac{3}{16}$ $\frac{11}{5}$ $2\frac{5}{16}$

   Row B: $\frac{37}{16}$ $2\frac{1}{5}$ $\frac{35}{16}$ $1\frac{4}{5}$ $\frac{33}{16}$

2. Convert to mixed numbers.

   (a) $\frac{23}{8}$ (b) $\frac{19}{16}$ (c) $\frac{27}{10}$

3. Convert to improper fractions.

(a) $3\frac{3}{8}$ (b) $4\frac{5}{16}$ (c) $9\frac{3}{10}$

- *STOP.*
- Check your answers on page 338.
- Correct the problems you missed.
- Go on to Set 4.

Set 4

1. (a) How many pieces of cake?
   (b) How many cakes?

2. (a) How many pieces of pumpkin pie?
   (b) How many pumpkin pies?

3. (a) How many cupcakes?
   (b) How many packages of cupcakes?

4. (a) How many pieces of candy?
   (b) How many boxes of candy?

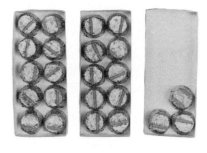

5. (a) How many bottles of Cola?
   (b) How many six-packs of Cola?

- *STOP*
- Check your answers on page 338.
- Correct the problems you missed.
- Shade box 8 opposite "fractions basic concepts" on page xviii.
- If this was the last subskill you had to work on in this section, take the test on page 136.
- If you have other subskills to work on in this section, go on to the next one.

SUBSKILL 9: Equivalent Forms of One

Problem: Which are equivalent to one?

  a. $\dfrac{2}{2}$ b. $\dfrac{15}{16}$ c. $\dfrac{4302}{4302}$

  d. $\dfrac{523}{532}$ e. $\dfrac{3}{3}$ f. $\dfrac{24}{24}$

Solution: $\boxed{\text{a, c, e, and f}}$ $\dfrac{a}{b}$ is equivalent to one whenever $a = b$.

Lesson:

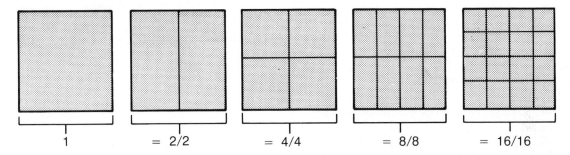

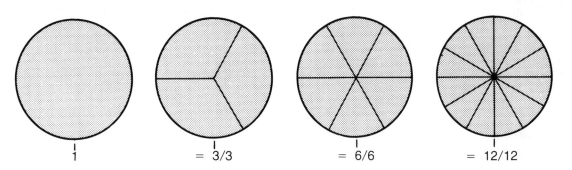

Drill and Practice:

Set 1

1. Which are equivalent to one?

  a. $\dfrac{4}{4}$ b. $\dfrac{20}{20}$ c. $\dfrac{1101}{1011}$

  d. $\dfrac{345}{345}$ e. $\dfrac{6}{6}$ f. $\dfrac{98}{99}$

2. $1 = \dfrac{9}{?}$

• *STOP.*
• Check your answers on page 338.
• Correct the problems you missed.
• Go on to Set 2.

Set 2

1. Which are equivalent to one?

  a. $\dfrac{8}{7}$ b. $\dfrac{12}{12}$ c. $\dfrac{2000}{2000}$

  d. $\dfrac{813}{318}$ e. $\dfrac{8}{8}$ f. $\dfrac{32}{32}$

2. $1 = \dfrac{?}{23}$

• *STOP.*
• Check your answers on page 338.
• Correct the problems you missed.
• Go on to Set 3 or 4.

Set 3

1. Which are equivalent to one?

a. $\dfrac{5}{5}$ b. $\dfrac{16}{16}$ c. $\dfrac{7777}{7778}$

d. $\dfrac{101}{101}$ e. $\dfrac{7}{7}$ f. $\dfrac{18}{81}$

2. $1. = \dfrac{111}{?}$

- *STOP.*
- Check your answers on page 338.
- Correct the problems you missed.
- Go on to Set 4.

Set 4

1. (a) How many sticks of strawberry popsicles?
   (b) How many strawberry popsicles?

2. (a) How many portions of cider?
   (b) How many jugs of cider?

3. (a) How many bottles of soda pop?
   (b) How many six-packs of soda pop?

4. (a) How many threads?
   (b) How many bolts?

5. What fraction of a
   (a) foot (12 inches) are 12 inches?

   (b) yard (three feet) are three feet?

   (c) pound (16 ounces) are 16 ounces?

   (d) pint (two cups) are two cups?

   (e) quart (two pints) are two pints?

   (f) gallon (four quarts) are four quarts?

6. What fraction of a
   (a) meter (100 centimeters) are 100 centimeters?

   (b) liter (1000 milliliters) are 1000 milliliters?

   (c) kilogram (1000 grams) are 1000 grams?

   (d) kilometer (1000 meters) are 1000 meters?

7. What do you have if you divide something into pieces that are identical in size and shape and keep all the pieces?

8. What is any non-zero number divided by itself?

9. Write 100 with six nines.

- *STOP*
- Check your answers on page 338.
- Correct the problems you missed.
- Shade box 9 opposite "fractions: basic concepts" on page xviii.
- If this was the last subskill you had to work on in this section, take the test on page 136.
- If you have other subskills to work on in this section, go on to the next one.

SUBSKILL 10: Multiplying Fractions by One

Problem: $\frac{2}{3} \times 1 = ?$

Solution: $\boxed{\frac{2}{3}}$ Multiplying a fraction by one leaves the fraction unchanged.

Lesson: $\frac{2}{3} \times 1 = \frac{2}{3} \times \frac{1}{1} = \frac{2 \times 1}{3 \times 1} = \frac{2}{3}$

Drill and Practice:

Set 1

1. $\frac{1}{2} \times 1 = ?$

2. $\frac{3}{4} \times 1 = ?$

3. $\frac{5}{6} \times 1 = ?$

4. $\frac{7}{8} \times 1 = ?$

- *STOP.*
- Check your answers on page 338.
- Correct the problems you missed.
- Go on to Set 2.

Set 2

1. $\frac{1}{3} \times 1 = ?$

2. $\frac{4}{7} \times 1 = ?$

3. $\frac{7}{10} \times 1 = ?$

4. $\frac{10}{13} \times 1 = ?$

- *STOP.*
- Check your answers on page 338.
- Correct the problems you missed.
- Go on to Set 3 or 4.

Set 3

1. $\frac{2}{5} \times 1 = ?$

2. $\frac{5}{8} \times 1 = ?$

3. $\frac{7}{12} \times 1 = ?$

4. $\frac{17}{20} \times 1 = ?$

- *STOP.*
- Check your answers on page 338.
- Correct the problems you missed.
- Go on to Set 4.

Set 4

1. What do you get when you multiply a fraction by one?

2. Zero is the easiest number to multiply with. You always get zero. What is the next easiest number to multiply with?

3. Why is one a very boring number to multiply with?

4. Why the emphasis on multiplying fractions
   by one?

- *STOP*

- Check your answers on page 338.

- Correct the problems you missed.

- Shade box 10 opposite "fractions: basic concepts" on page xviii.

- If this was the last subskill you had to work on in this section, take the test on page 136.

- If you have other subskills to work on in this section, go on to the next one.

SUBSKILL 11: Multiplying
Fractions by an
Equivalent Form of
One

Problem: $\dfrac{3}{4} \times \dfrac{5}{5} = ?$ Solution: • Multiply across. $\dfrac{3}{4} \times \dfrac{5}{5} = \dfrac{3 \times 5}{4 \times 5} = \boxed{\dfrac{15}{20}}$

Lesson: Multiplying a fraction by an equivalent form of one changes the appearance of the fraction but not the fraction itself.

$$\frac{3}{4} = \frac{3}{4} \times 1 = \frac{3}{4} \times \boxed{\frac{5}{5}} = \frac{3 \times 5}{4 \times 5} = \frac{15}{20}$$

Drill and Practice:

Set 1

1. $\dfrac{2}{3} \times \dfrac{4}{4} = ?$ 2. $\dfrac{1}{6} \times \dfrac{2}{2} = ?$

3. $\dfrac{5}{12} \times \dfrac{3}{3} = ?$ 4. $\dfrac{7}{8} \times \dfrac{10}{10} = ?$

- *STOP.*
- Check your answers on page 338.
- Correct the problems you missed.
- Go on to Set 2.

Set 2

1. $\dfrac{1}{2} \times \dfrac{6}{6} = ?$ 2. $\dfrac{3}{4} \times \dfrac{8}{8} = ?$

3. $\dfrac{4}{5} \times \dfrac{2}{2} = ?$ 4. $\dfrac{2}{3} \times \dfrac{9}{9} = ?$

- *STOP.*
- Check your answers on page 338.
- Correct the problems you missed.
- Go on to Set 3 or 4.

Set 3

1. $\dfrac{11}{12} \times \dfrac{5}{5} = ?$ 2. $\dfrac{10}{10} \times \dfrac{10}{10} = ?$

3. $\dfrac{5}{9} \times \dfrac{4}{4} = ?$ 4. $\dfrac{1}{2} \times \dfrac{3}{3} = ?$

- *STOP.*
- Check your answers on page 338.
- Correct the problems you missed.
- Go on to Set 4.

Set 4

1. How many equivalent forms of one are there?

2. What is magic about multiplying a fraction by an equivalent form of one?

3. How does multiplying a fraction by an equivalent form of one compare to multiplying the numerator and denominator of the fraction by the same number?

4. Why the emphasis on multiplying fractions by equivalent forms of one?

- *STOP*

- Check your answers on page 338.

- Correct the problems you missed.

- Shade box 11 opposite "fractions: basic concepts" on page xviii.

- If this was the last subskill you had to work on in this section, take the test on page 136.

- If you have other subskills to work on in this section, go on to the next one.

SUBSKILL 12: Factors

Problem: Which are factors of ten?

a. .2   b. $\frac{1}{2}$ c. 1   d. 2

e. 3   f. 5   g. 10   h. 20

Solution: [c, d, f, and g] A factor is a counting number like one, two, three, and so on that is an *exact* divisor of another counting number. (Two-tenths and ½ are *not* factors because they are not counting numbers, and three and 20 are *not* factors because they do not divide ten evenly.)

Lesson: The key to determining the factors of a number is to know that the exact divisors of the number include

two if it is an even number

three if the sum of its digits is divisible by three

four if its last two digits are divisible by four

five if it ends in zero or five

six if it is an even number and the sum of its digits is divisible by three

nine if the sum of its digits is divisible by nine

ten if it ends in zero

To illustrate:

The exact divisors of 258 include two because it is an even number, three because $2 + 5 + 8 = 15$ is divisible by three, and six because of both of the preceding.

The exact divisors of 3816 include two because it is an even number, three and nine because $3 + 8 + 1 + 6 = 18$ is divisible by three and nine, six because of both of the preceding, and four because 16 is divisible by four.

The exact divisors of 720 include two because it is an even number, three and nine because $7 + 2 + 0 = 9$ is divisible by three and nine, six because of both of the preceding, four because 20 is divisible by four, and five and ten because it ends in zero.

Drill and Practice:

Set 1

1. Which are factors of 12?

   a. .6   b. $\frac{2}{3}$ c. 1   d. 2   e. 3

   f. 4   g. 6   h. 12   i. 24   j. 48

2. Which is divisible by three?
   a. 121   b. 3846   c. 10820   d. 479033

3. Which are divisible by five?
   a. 440   b. 2346   c. 55052   d. 347215

4. Which are divisible by nine?
   a. 339   b. 1305   c. 11436   d. 402606

5. List all the factors of
   (a) 14   (b) 30   (c) 15   (d) 306

- *STOP.*
- Check your answers on page 338.
- Correct the problems you missed.
- Go on to Set 2.

Set 2

1. Which are factors of 18?

   a. .9   b. $\frac{1}{9}$ c. 1   d. 2   e. 3

   f. 6   g. 9   h. 18   i. 36   j. 72

2. Which are divisible by four?
   a. 122   b. 5048   c. 80202   d. 124304

3. Which are divisible by six?
   a. 432   b. 5312   c. 60138   d. 701530

4. Which are divisible by ten?
   a. 485   b. 9119   c. 34870   d. 405700

5. List all the factors of
   (a) 20   (b) 40   (c) 51   (d) 805

- *STOP.*
- Check your answers on page 338.
- Correct the problems you missed.
- Go on to Set 3 or 4.

Set 3

1. Which are factors of 25?

   a. .25   b. $\frac{1}{5}$ c. 1   d. 2   e. 3

   f. 5   g. 10   h. 25   i. 50   j. 100

2. Which are divisible by six?
   a. 408   b. 6192   c. 41514   d. 412133

3. Which are divisible by two?
   a. 654   b. 4036   c. 80253   d. 595110

4. Which are divisible by nine?
   a. 609   b. 4199   c. 22221   d. 489762

5. List all the factors of
   (a) 39   (b) 80   (c) 47   (d) 1001

- *STOP.*
- Check your answers on page 338.
- Correct the problems you missed.
- Go on to Set 4.

Set 4

1. Why the emphasis on factors?

- *STOP*

- Check your answers on page 338.

- Correct the problems you missed.

- Shade box 12 opposite "fractions: basic concepts" on page xviii.

- If this was the last subskill you had to work on in this section, take the test on page 136.

- If you have other subskills to work on in this section, go on to the next one.

SUBSKILL 13: The GCF or Greatest Common Factor

Problem: Find the GCF or greatest common factor of 24 and 60.

Solution: 12 The GCF of two or more numbers is the *largest* exact divisor of the numbers.

Lesson: To find the GCF of some numbers, just think of it. Failing that, make use of the words the acronym stands for *in reverse* as follows:

- List *factors* of each number.
- List factors *common* to numbers.
- Select *greatest* of factors common to numbers.

To illustrate:

The factors of 24 are <u>one</u>, <u>two</u>, <u>three</u>, <u>four</u>, <u>six</u>, eight, <u>12</u>, and 24, and the factors of 60 are <u>one</u>, <u>two</u>, <u>three</u>, <u>four</u>, five, <u>six</u>, ten, <u>12</u>, 15, 30, and 60.

The factors common to 24 and 60 are one, two, three, four, six, and 12 as underlined above.

The greatest of the factors common to 24 and 60 is 12. This is the GCF of the numbers.

Drill and Practice:

Set 1

Find the GCF or greatest common factor of

1. 6 and 8   2. 12 and 28   3. 18 and 24.

- *STOP.*
- Check your answers on page 338.
- Correct the problems you missed.
- Go on to Set 2.

Set 2

Find the GCF or greatest common factor of

1. 18 and 45   2. 20 and 30   3. 15 and 60

- *STOP.*
- Check your answers on page 338.
- Correct the problems you missed.
- Go on to Set 3 or 4.

Set 3

Find the GCF or greatest common factor of
1. 6 and 16   2. 8 and 24   3. 26 and 39

- *STOP.*
- Check your answers on page 339.
- Correct the problems you missed.
- Go on to Set 4.

Set 4

1. Why the emphasis on the GCF or greatest common factor?

- *STOP*

- Check your answers on page 339.

- Correct the problems you missed.

- Shade box 13 opposite "fractions: basic concepts" on page xviii.

- If this was the last subskill you had to work on in this section, take the test on page 136.

- If you have other subskills to work on in this section, go on to the next one.

SUBSKILL 14: Simplifying Fractions

Problem: Simplify $\dfrac{60}{36}$.

Solution: • Divide numerator and denominator by any common factor but preferably the GCF or greatest common factor.

   • Convert to mixed or whole number if numerator is greater than denominator.

So, knowing that the GCF of 60 and 36 is 12,

$$\dfrac{\overset{5}{\cancel{60}}}{\underset{3}{\cancel{36}}} = \boxed{1\,\dfrac{2}{3}}$$

Lesson: $\dfrac{60}{36} = \dfrac{5 \times 12}{3 \times 12} = \dfrac{5}{3} \times \dfrac{12}{12} = \dfrac{5}{3} \times 1 = \dfrac{5}{3} = 1\,\dfrac{2}{3}$

Drill and Practice:

Set 1

Simplify.

1. $\frac{12}{8}$ 2. $\frac{14}{21}$ 3. $\frac{28}{10}$ 4. $\frac{10}{28}$ 5. $\frac{12}{9}$

- *STOP.*
- Check your answers on page 339.
- Correct the problems you missed.
- Go on to Set 2.

Set 2

Simplify.

1. $\frac{90}{60}$ 2. $\frac{10}{25}$ 3. $\frac{8}{6}$ 4. $\frac{6}{8}$ 5. $\frac{120}{45}$

- *STOP.*
- Check your answers on page 339.
- Correct the problems you missed.
- Go on to Set 3 or 4.

Set 3

Simplify.

1. $\frac{48}{36}$ 2. $\frac{12}{20}$ 3. $\frac{21}{7}$ 4. $\frac{7}{21}$ 5. $\frac{30}{12}$

- *STOP.*
- Check your answers on page 339.
- Correct the problems you missed.
- Go on to Set 4.

Set 4

1. Convert to fractions of a foot (12 inches) and simplify.

   (a) two inches   (e) three inches
   (b) four inches   (f) six inches
   (c) eight inches   (g) nine inches
   (d) ten inches

2. Convert to fractions of a pound (16 ounces) and simplify.

   (a) two ounces   (e) four ounces
   (b) six ounces   (f) eight ounces
   (c) ten ounces   (g) 12 ounces
   (d) 14 ounces

3. Simplify.

   (a) ten millimeters
   (b) 25 centimeters
   (c) 50 centimeters
   (d) eight decimeters

4. Simplify.

   (a) 750 milliliters
   (b) 80 centiliters
   (c) five centiliters
   (d) five deciliters

5. Convert to fractions of a kilogram (1000 grams) and simplify.

   (a) 250 grams
   (b) five dekagrams
   (c) 75 dekagrams
   (d) eight hectograms

6. Convert to fractions of a kilometer (1000 meters) and simplify.

   (a) 500 meters
   (b) six dekameters
   (c) nine dekameters
   (d) five hectometers

- *STOP*

- Check your answers on page 339.

- Correct the problems you missed.

- Shade box 14 opposite "fractions: basic concepts" on page xviii.

- If this was the last subskill you had to work on in this section, take the test on page 136.

- If you have other subskills to work on in this section, go on to the next one.

SUBSKILL 15: Prime Numbers

Problem: Which are prime?

a. $\frac{3}{7}$ b. 1   c. 1.7   d. 2

e. 11   f. 12   g. 13   h. 15

i. 23   j. 91   k. 234   l. 740

Solution: d, e, g, and i   A prime number is a counting number like one, two, three, and so on that *cannot* be written as a product of counting numbers except as one times itself. (3/7 and 1.7 are *not* prime numbers because they are *not* counting numbers. One is *not* a prime number because the first prime number is two. And 12, 15, 91, 234, and 740 are *not* prime numbers because $12 = 2 \times 2 \times 3$, $15 = 3 \times 5$, $91 = 7 \times 13$, $234 = 2 \times 117$, and $740 = 2 \times 2 \times 5 \times 37$.)

Lesson: The classic method for determining prime numbers is the "sieve" method attributed to Eratosthenes. It amounts to listing the counting numbers from one to whatever in ten columns from one to ten as illustrated in Figure 8.1 and crossing out the multiples of two, three, five, seven, and so on as you come to them as illustrated in Figure 8.2. (The multiples of two were crossed out with a $\backslash$, the multiples of three with a /, the multiples of five with a $\int$, and the multiples of seven with a —. Note the patterns that ensued. The next multiples to be crossed out would be the multiples of 11.) The numbers that are left are prime numbers.

Figure 8.1

1	2	3	4	5	6	7	8	9	10
11	12	13	14	15	16	17	18	19	20
21	...								

Figure 8.2

1	2	3	4̶	5	6̶	7	8̶	9̶	1̶0̶
11	1̶2̶	13	1̶4̶	1̶5̶	1̶6̶	17	1̶8̶	19	2̶0̶
2̶1̶	2̶2̶	23	2̶4̶	2̶5̶	2̶6̶	2̶7̶	2̶8̶	29	3̶0̶
31	3̶2̶	3̶3̶	3̶4̶	3̶5̶	3̶6̶	37	3̶8̶	3̶9̶	4̶0̶
41	4̶2̶	43	4̶4̶	4̶5̶	4̶6̶	47	4̶8̶	4̶9̶	5̶0̶
5̶1̶	5̶2̶	53	5̶4̶	5̶5̶	5̶6̶	5̶7̶	5̶8̶	59	6̶0̶
61	6̶2̶	6̶3̶	6̶4̶	6̶5̶	6̶6̶	67	6̶8̶	6̶9̶	7̶0̶
71	7̶2̶	73	7̶4̶	7̶5̶	7̶6̶	7̶7̶	7̶8̶	79	8̶0̶
8̶1̶	8̶2̶	83	8̶4̶	8̶5̶	8̶6̶	8̶7̶	8̶8̶	89	9̶0̶
9̶1̶	9̶2̶	9̶3̶	9̶4̶	9̶5̶	9̶6̶	97	9̶8̶	9̶9̶	1̶0̶0̶

Drill and Practice:

Set 1

1. Which are prime?

a. $\frac{2}{3}$ b. 1 c. 2 d. 3.7

e. 4 f. 5 g. 6 h. 7

i. 8 j. 9 k. 314 l. 985

- *STOP.*
- Check your answers on page 339.
- Correct the problems you missed.
- Go on to Set 2.

Set 2

1. Which are prime?

a. $\frac{5}{11}$ b. 3 c. 1.0 d. 14

e. 16 f. 17 g. 18 h. 19

i. 20 j. 21 k. 432 l. 850

- *STOP.*
- Check your answers on page 339.
- Correct the problems you missed.
- Go on to Set 3 or 4.

Set 3

1. Which are prime?

a. $\frac{4}{9}$ b. 22 c. 23 d. 2.4

e. 25 f. 29 g. 37 h. 93

i. 101 j. 117 k. 204 l. 375

- *STOP.*
- Check your answers on page 339.
- Correct the problems you missed.
- Go on to Set 4.

Set 4

1. Why the emphasis on prime numbers?

- *STOP*

- Check your answers on page **339**.

- Correct the problems you missed.

- Shade box 15 opposite "fractions: basic concepts" on page xviii.

- If this was the last subskill you had to work on in this section, take the test on page **136**.

- If you have other subskills to work on in this section, go on to the next one.

SUBSKILL 16: Prime Factorization

Problem: Write the prime factorization of 30.

Solution: • Make factor tree with number as "base" of tree and prime factors of number as "roots" of tree.

• Arrange roots from smallest to largest and write as product.

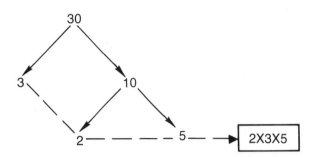

Lesson: The prime factorization of a number is the number written as a product of primes.

Drill and Practice:

Set 1

Write the prime factorization of

1. 18   2. 25   3. 36   4. 64   5. 6480

• *STOP.*
• Check your answers on page 339.
• Correct the problems you missed.
• Go on to Set 2.

Set 2

Write the prime factorization of

1. 20   2. 24   3. 50   4. 162   5. 97200

• *STOP.*
• Check your answers on page 339.
• Correct the problems you missed.
• Go on to Set 3 or 4.

Set 3

Write the prime factorization of

1. 39   2. 40   3. 108   4. 128   5. 1080

• *STOP.*
• Check your answers on page 339.
• Correct the problems you missed.
• Go on to Set 4.

Set 4

1. Why the emphasis on prime factorization?

- *STOP*

- Check your answers on page 339.

- Correct the problems you missed.

- Shade box 16 opposite "fractions: basic concepts" on page xviii.

- If this was the last subskill you had to work on in this section, take the test on page 136.

- If you have other subskills to work on in this section, go on to the next one.

SUBSKILL 17: The LCM or Least
Common Multiple

Problem: Find the LCM or least common multiple of four, six, and eight.

Solution: |24| The LCM of two or more numbers is the *smallest* number the numbers divide evenly.

Lesson: To find the LCM of some numbers, just think of it. Failing that, make use of the words the acronym stands for *in reverse* as follows:

- List *multiples* of each number.
- List multiples *common* to numbers.
- Select *least* of multiples common to numbers.

To illustrate:

The multiples of four are $4 \times 1 = 4$, $4 \times 2 = 8$, $4 \times 3 = 12$, $4 \times 4 = 16$, $4 \times 5 = 20$, $4 \times 6 = \underline{24}$, $4 \times 7 = 28$, $4 \times 8 = 32$, $4 \times 9 = 36$, $4 \times 10 = 40$, $4 \times 11 = 44$, $4 \times 12 = \underline{48}$, $4 \times 13 = 52$, $4 \times 14 = 56$, $4 \times 15 = 60$, $4 \times 16 = 64$, $4 \times 17 = 68$, $4 \times 18 = \underline{72}$, $4 \times 19 = 76$, $4 \times 20 = 80$, . . .

The multiples of six are $6 \times 1 = 6$, $6 \times 2 = 12$, $6 \times 3 = 18$, $6 \times 4 = \underline{24}$, $6 \times 5 = 30$, $6 \times 6 = 36$, $6 \times 7 = 42$, $6 \times 8 = \underline{48}$, $6 \times 9 = 54$, $6 \times 10 = 60$, $6 \times 11 = 66$, $6 \times 12 = \underline{72}$, $6 \times 13 = 78$, $6 \times 14 = 84$, $6 \times 15 = 90$, . . .

And the multiples of eight are $8 \times 1 = 8$, $8 \times 2 = 16$, $8 \times 3 = \underline{24}$, $8 \times 4 = 32$, $8 \times 5 = 40$, $8 \times 6 = \underline{48}$, $8 \times 7 = 56$, $8 \times 8 = 64$, $8 \times 9 = \underline{72}$, $8 \times 10 = 80$, $8 \times 11 = 88$, $8 \times 12 = 96$, $8 \times 13 = 104$, $8 \times 14 = 112$, . . .

The multiples common to four, six, and eight are 24, 48, 72, and so on indefinitely as underlined above.

The least of the multiples common to four, six, and eight is 24. This is the LCM of the numbers.

Drill and Practice:

Set 1

Find the LCM or least common multiple of

1. 4 and 6   2. 4 and 8   3. 4, 5, and 6

- *STOP.*
- Check your answers on page 339.
- Correct the problems you missed.
- Go on to Set 2.

Set 2

Find the LCM or least common multiple of

1. 6 and 8   2. 6 and 12   3. 3, 4, and 6

- *STOP.*
- Check your answers on page 339.
- Correct the problems you missed.
- Go on to Set 3 or 4.

Set 3

Find the LCM or least common multiple of

1. 2 and 3   2. 2 and 4   3. 2, 3, and 4

- *STOP.*
- Check your answers on page 339.
- Correct the problems you missed.
- Go on to Set 4.

Set 4

1. Why the emphasis on the LCM or least common multiple?

- *STOP*
- Check your answers on page **339.**
- Correct the problems you missed.
- Shade box 17 opposite "fractions: basic concepts" on page **xviii.**
- If this was the last subskill you had to work on in this section, take the test on page **136.**
- If you have other subskills to work on in this section, go on to the next one.

SUBSKILL 18: The LCD or Least Common Denominator

Problem: Express 2/3, 4/5, and 1/6 in terms of their LCD or least common denominator.

Solution: The LCD is 30, the LCM of three, five, and six. Knowing the LCD,

$$\frac{2}{3} = \frac{2}{3} \times 1 = \frac{2}{3} \times \frac{10}{10} = \frac{2 \times 10}{3 \times 10} = \boxed{\frac{20}{30}}$$

$$\frac{4}{5} = \frac{4}{5} \times 1 = \frac{4}{5} \times \frac{6}{6} = \frac{4 \times 6}{5 \times 6} = \boxed{\frac{24}{30}}$$

$$\frac{1}{6} = \frac{1}{6} \times 1 = \frac{1}{6} \times \frac{5}{5} = \frac{1 \times 5}{6 \times 5} = \boxed{\frac{5}{30}}$$

Lesson: The 10/10 form of one was chosen for 2/3 because ten times its denominator, three, is the LCD, 30. The 6/6 form of one was chosen for 4/5 because six times its denominator, five, is the LCD, 30. And the 5/5 form of one was chosen for 1/6 because five times its denominator, six, is the LCD, 30.

Drill and Practice:

Set 1

Express in terms of their LCD or least common denominator.

1. $\frac{2}{3}$ and $\frac{3}{4}$ 2. $\frac{1}{3}$ and $\frac{4}{5}$ 3. $\frac{1}{2}, \frac{2}{3},$ and $\frac{2}{5}$

- *STOP.*
- Check your answers on page 339.
- Correct the problems you missed.
- Go on to Set 2.

Set 2

Express in terms of their LCD or least common denominator.

1. $\frac{1}{4}$ and $\frac{3}{5}$ 2. $\frac{1}{4}$ and $\frac{5}{6}$ 3. $\frac{1}{6}, \frac{3}{10},$ and $\frac{4}{15}$

- *STOP.*
- Check your answers on page 339.
- Correct the problems you missed.
- Go on to Set 3 or 4.

Set 3

Express in terms of their LCD or least common denominator.

1. $\frac{1}{2}$ and $\frac{1}{3}$ 2. $\frac{1}{2}$ and $\frac{3}{7}$ 3. $\frac{1}{2}, \frac{3}{8},$ and $\frac{4}{9}$

- *STOP.*
- Check your answers on page 339.
- Correct the problems you missed.
- Go on to Set 4.

Set 4

1. Is the LCD or least common denominator the only number you can equate denominators with?

2. Why the emphasis on the LCD or least common denominator?

- *STOP*

- Check your answers on page 340

- Correct the problems you missed.

- Shade box 18 opposite "fractions: basic concepts" on page xviii.

- If this was the last subskill you had to work on in this section, take the test on page 136.

- If you have other subskills to work on in this section, go on to the next one.

SUBSKILL 19: Inverting

Problem: Invert $\frac{2}{3}$.

Solution: • Convert to fraction.

   • Make numerator a denominator.

   • Make denominator a numerator.

$$\frac{2}{3} \diagdown \boxed{\begin{array}{c} \leftarrow 3 \\ \leftarrow 2 \end{array}}$$

Lesson: Inverting a number gives the multiplicative *inverse* of the number, the number that times the original number equals one.

$$\frac{2}{3} \times \frac{3}{2} = \frac{2 \times 3}{3 \times 2} = \frac{6}{6} = 1$$

Drill and Practice:

Set 1

Invert.

1. $\frac{4}{5}$ 2. $\frac{1}{7}$ 3. 8   4. $3\frac{1}{2}$ 5. $4\frac{2}{7}$

- *STOP.*
- Check your answers on page 340.
- Correct the problems you missed.
- Go on to Set 2.

Set 2

Invert.

1. $\frac{3}{4}$ 2. $\frac{1}{2}$ 3. 10   4. $1\frac{5}{8}$ 5. $6\frac{2}{3}$

- *STOP.*
- Check your answers on page 340.
- Correct the problems you missed.
- Go on to Set 3 or 4.

Set 3

Invert.

1. $\frac{2}{3}$ 2. $\frac{1}{5}$ 3. 12   4. $2\frac{1}{9}$ 5. $5\frac{5}{6}$

- *STOP.*
- Check your answers on page 340.
- Correct the problems you missed.
- Go on to Set 4.

Set 4

1. Why the emphasis on inverting?

- *STOP*
- Check your answers on page 340.
- Correct the problems you missed.
- Shade box 19 opposite "fractions: basic concepts" on page xviii.
- Take the test on page 136.

Inventory Post Test for Fractions:
Basic Concepts

1. Which is divided into fourths?

a.

b.

c.

2. Which illustrates three-fourths or $\frac{3}{4}$?

a.

b.

c.

3. What fractions are illustrated by points *A*, *B*, and *C*?

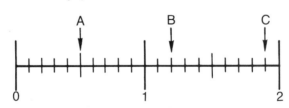

4. Four out of ten dollar signs are circled. What ratio makes this comparison?

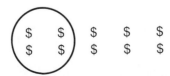

5. One small square for two large squares: What ratio makes this comparison?

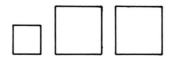

6. Solve for N: $\frac{3}{N} = \frac{9}{24}$

7. For each fraction in row A, find one or more equivalent fractions in row B.

Row A: $\qquad \frac{2}{3} \qquad \frac{6}{24} \qquad \frac{3}{5}$

Row B: $\quad \frac{1}{4} \qquad \frac{12}{20} \qquad \frac{6}{9} \qquad \frac{3}{12}$

8. For each improper fraction or mixed number in row A, find an equivalent improper fraction or mixed number in row B.

Row A: $\quad \frac{11}{2} \qquad 2\frac{1}{16} \qquad \frac{11}{3} \qquad 1\frac{2}{16}$

Row B: $\quad \frac{18}{16} \qquad 5\frac{1}{2} \qquad \frac{33}{16} \qquad 3\frac{2}{3}$

9. Which are equivalent to 1?

   a. $\frac{9}{8}$ 　　　 b. $\frac{312}{312}$ 　　　 c. $\frac{4178}{4178}$ 　　　 d. $\frac{99}{99}$ 　　　 e. $\frac{11}{12}$

10. $\frac{3}{8} \times 1 = ?$

11. $\frac{7}{12} \times \frac{4}{4} = ?$

12. Which are factors of 15?

   a. .3 　　 b. $\frac{1}{3}$ 　　 c. 1 　　 d. 2 　　 e. 3 　　 f. 5 　　 g. 15 　　 h. 30

13. Find the GCF or greatest common factor of 36 and 90.

14. Simplify $\frac{21}{18}$.

15. Which are prime?

     a. 2   b. 5   c. 6   d. 9   e. 10   f. 17   g. 43   h. 51

16. Write the prime factorization of 36.

17. Find the LCM or least common multiple of five, six, and eight.

18. Express $\frac{3}{4}$, $\frac{1}{5}$, and $\frac{7}{10}$ in terms of their LCD or least common denominator.

19. Invert $\frac{5}{7}$.

- *STOP*
- Check your answers with the instructor.
- As before, work through the subskills in this section which correspond to the problems you missed, except work the *even* drill-and-practice problems.
- Take the test on page 139.

SKILL
Addition of Fractions

Inventory Pretest for Addition of Fractions

1. $\dfrac{1}{12} + \dfrac{7}{12} = ?$ 2. $\dfrac{2}{3} + \dfrac{4}{5} = ?$ 3. $3\dfrac{5}{6} + 4\dfrac{1}{12} = ?$ 4. $2\dfrac{1}{2} + 3\dfrac{4}{5} = ?$

- *STOP*

- Check your answers on page 340.

- Shade the boxes opposite "addition of fractions" on page xviii which correspond to the problems you got right.

- If you got all of them right, take the test on page 153.

- If you missed some of them, start working on the subskills in this section which correspond to the ones you missed.

- For each subskill, look at the example, study the solution, think about the lesson, and work the *odd* drill-and-practice problems.

SUBSKILL 1: Addition of Fractions with Equal Denominators

Problem: $\dfrac{7}{8} + \dfrac{3}{8} = ?$ • Simplify.

Solution: • Add numerators.

• Put sum over common denominator.

$$\dfrac{7}{8} + \dfrac{3}{8} = \dfrac{7+3}{8} = \dfrac{10}{8} = \dfrac{5}{4} = \boxed{1\dfrac{1}{4}}$$

Lesson:

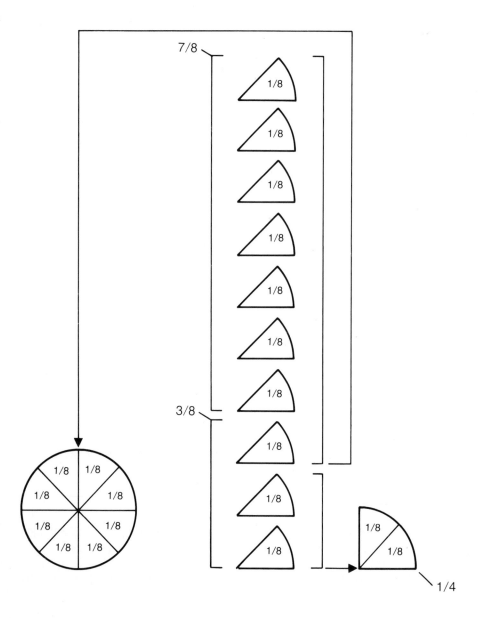

Drill and Practice:

Set 1

1. $\dfrac{5}{8} + \dfrac{7}{8} = ?$ 2. $\dfrac{4}{5} + \dfrac{3}{5} = ?$

3. $\dfrac{4}{6} + \dfrac{4}{6} = ?$ 4. $\dfrac{4}{12} + \dfrac{5}{12} + \dfrac{6}{12} = ?$

- *STOP.*
- Check your answers on page 340.
- Correct the problems you missed.
- Go on to Set 2.

Set 2

1. $\dfrac{3}{6} + \dfrac{4}{6} = ?$ 2. $\dfrac{3}{12} + \dfrac{8}{12} = ?$

3. $\dfrac{7}{10} + \dfrac{7}{10} = ?$ 4. $\dfrac{4}{9} + \dfrac{5}{9} + \dfrac{7}{9} = ?$

- *STOP.*
- Check your answers on page 340.
- Correct the problems you missed.
- Go on to Set 3 or 4.

Set 3

1. $\dfrac{2}{4} + \dfrac{3}{4} = ?$ 2. $\dfrac{8}{10} + \dfrac{5}{10} = ?$

3. $\dfrac{5}{7} + \dfrac{5}{7} = ?$ 4. $\dfrac{5}{18} + \dfrac{5}{18} + \dfrac{5}{18} = ?$

- *STOP.*
- Check your answers on page 340.
- Correct the problems you missed.
- Go on to Set 4.

Set 4

1. (a) How many pieces of cake?
    (b) How many cakes?

2. Write two addition sentences for the cherry pies.

 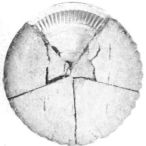

3. Write two addition sentences for the ruler.

4. Transportation and industry are responsible for 21/50 and 7/50 of the air pollution in the United States, respectively. How responsible are they together?

- *STOP*

- Check your answers on page 340.

- Correct the problems you missed.

- Shade box 1 opposite "addition of fractions" on page xviii.

- If this was the only subskill you had to work on in this section, take the test on page 152.

- If you have other subskills to work on in this section, go on to the next one.

SUBSKILL 2: Addition of Fractions with Unequal Denominators

Problem: $\dfrac{3}{4} + \dfrac{5}{6} = ?$ *Solution:*

- Find LCD or least common denominator.

$$\frac{3}{4} + \frac{5}{6} = \frac{3}{4} \times 1 + \frac{5}{6} \times 1 =$$

- Convert to equivalent fractions over LCD.

$$\frac{3}{4} \times \frac{3}{3} + \frac{5}{6} \times \frac{2}{2} =$$

- Add numerators.

- Put sum over LCD.

$$\frac{3 \times 3}{4 \times 3} + \frac{5 \times 2}{6 \times 2} =$$

- Simplify.

So, knowing that the LCD of 3/4 and 5/6 is 12,

$$\frac{9}{12} + \frac{10}{12} = \frac{9 + 10}{12} = \frac{19}{12} = \boxed{1\frac{7}{12}}$$

Lesson: The 3/3 and 2/2 forms of one were chosen for 3/4 and 5/6, respectively, because three times the denominator, four, of the one and two times the denominator, six, of the other equal the LCD, 12.

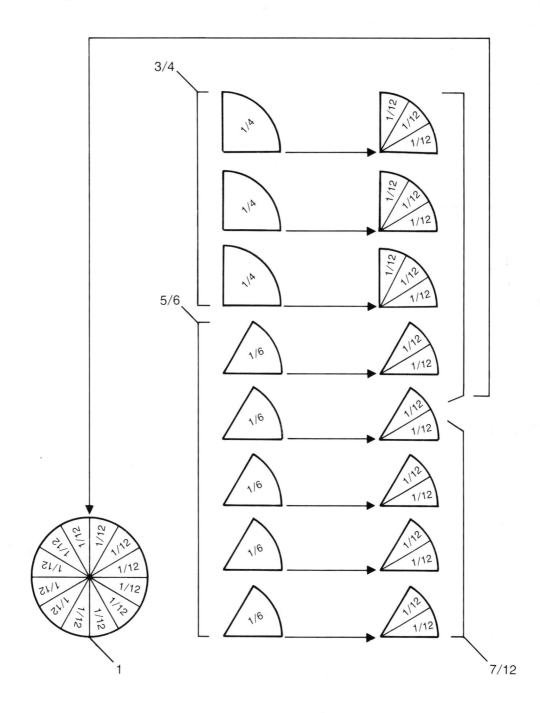

Drill and Practice:

Set 1

1. $\dfrac{2}{3} + \dfrac{3}{4} = ?$ 2. $\dfrac{1}{2} + \dfrac{1}{6} = ?$

3. $\dfrac{3}{5} + \dfrac{7}{10} = ?$ 4. $\dfrac{1}{2} + \dfrac{1}{3} + \dfrac{5}{6} = ?$

- *STOP.*
- Check your answers on page 000.
- Correct the problems you missed.
- Go on to Set 2.

Set 2

1. $\dfrac{1}{4} + \dfrac{7}{8} = ?$ 2. $\dfrac{1}{2} + \dfrac{1}{3} = ?$

3. $\dfrac{1}{4} + \dfrac{5}{6} = ?$ 4. $\dfrac{2}{3} + \dfrac{1}{6} + \dfrac{5}{12} = ?$

- *STOP.*
- Check your answers on page 340.
- Correct the problems you missed.
- Go on to Set 3 or 4.

Set 3

1. $\dfrac{1}{2} + \dfrac{3}{5} = ?$ 2. $\dfrac{1}{4} + \dfrac{1}{6} = ?$

3. $\dfrac{2}{3} + \dfrac{4}{5} = ?$ 4. $\dfrac{1}{2} + \dfrac{2}{3} + \dfrac{3}{5} = ?$

- *STOP.*
- Check your answers on page 340.
- Correct the problems you missed.
- Go on to Set 4.

Set 4

1. Write (a) an addition sentence with unequal denominators and (b) an addition sentence with equal denominators for the pumpkin pies.

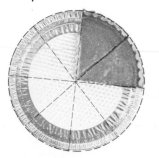 

2. Write (a) an addition sentence with unequal denominators and (b) an addition sentence with equal denominators for the rectangles.

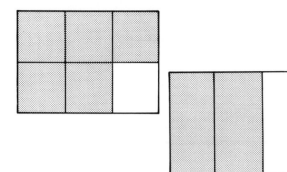

3. Write (a) an addition sentence with unequal denominators and (b) an addition sentence with equal denominators for the ruler.

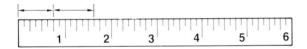

4. Solve the problems in Set 1 with the following cross multiplication technique.

$$\frac{3}{4} + \frac{5}{6} \quad \rightarrow \quad \frac{3}{4} + \frac{5}{6} =$$

$$\frac{18 + 20}{24} = \frac{38}{24} = \frac{19}{12} = \boxed{1\frac{7}{12}}$$

5. Industry and towns and cities are responsible for 3/5 and 1/4 of the water pollution in the United States, respectively. How responsible are they together?

- *STOP*
- Check your answers on page 340.
- Correct the problems you missed.
- Shade box 2 opposite "addition of fractions" on page xviii.
- If this was the last subskill you had to work on in this section, take the test on page 152.
- If you have other subskills to work on in this section, go on to the next one.

SUBSKILL 3: Addition of Fractions, Whole Numbers, and Mixed Numbers without Exchanging

Problem: $1\frac{1}{5} + 2\frac{3}{10} = ?$

Solution:
- Add fraction parts.
- Simplify.
- Add whole number parts.
- Combine sums.

So, knowing that the LCD of 1/5 and 3/10 is ten,

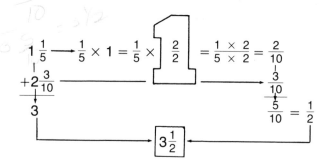

$$1\frac{1}{5} \longrightarrow \frac{1}{5} \times 1 = \frac{1}{5} \times \boxed{\frac{2}{2}} = \frac{1 \times 2}{5 \times 2} = \frac{2}{10}$$

$$+2\frac{3}{10} \qquad\qquad\qquad\qquad\qquad\qquad \frac{3}{10}$$

$$3 \qquad\qquad\qquad\qquad\qquad\qquad \frac{5}{10} = \frac{1}{2}$$

$$\boxed{3\frac{1}{2}}$$

Lesson: The 2/2 form of one was chosen for 1/5 because two times its denominator, five, equals the LCD, ten.

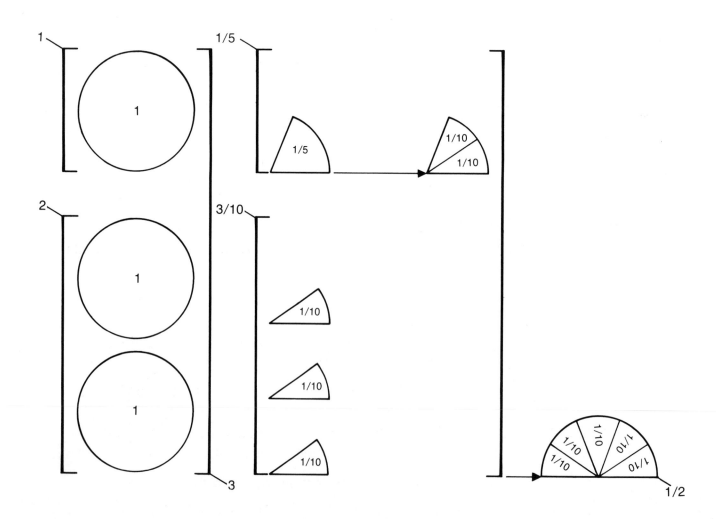

Drill and Practice:

Set 1

1. $3\frac{1}{3}$ 2. 4   3. $2\frac{1}{4} + 5\frac{2}{3} = ?$

   $+2\frac{1}{6}$ $+2\frac{1}{5}$ 4. $3\frac{1}{2} + \frac{1}{3} = ?$

- *STOP.*
- Check your answers on page 340.
- Correct the problems you missed.
- Go on to Set 2.

Set 2

1. $4\frac{2}{3}$ 2. $9\frac{1}{2}$ 3. $2\frac{3}{4} + 5\frac{1}{8} = ?$

   $+5\frac{2}{9}$ $+8$ 4. $3\frac{2}{5} + \frac{3}{10} = ?$

- *STOP.*
- Check your answers on page 340.
- Correct the problems you missed.
- Go on to Set 3 or 4.

Set 3

1. $5\frac{1}{6}$ 2. 7   3. $1\frac{2}{3} + 2\frac{1}{5} = ?$

   $+2\frac{4}{9}$ $+5\frac{3}{4}$ 4. $\frac{1}{2} + 9\frac{2}{5} = ?$

- *STOP.*
- Check your answers on page 340.
- Correct the problems you missed.
- Go on to Set 4.

Set 4

1. Write (a) an addition sentence with unequal denominators and (b) an addition sentence with
   equal denominators for the circles.

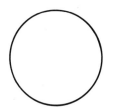 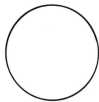  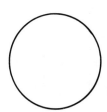 

2. Write (a) an addition sentence with unequal denominators and (b) an addition sentence with equal denominators for the squares.

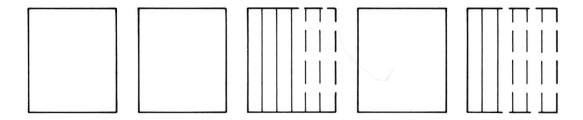

3. How long?

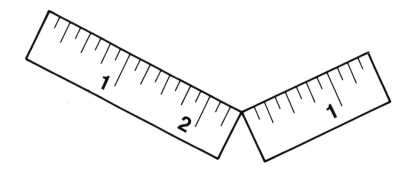

4. Find the perimeter of the triangle.

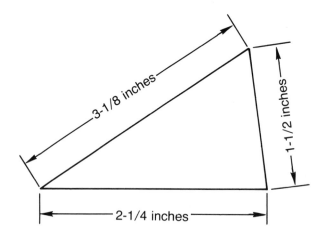

- *STOP*

- Check your answers on page 340.

- Correct the problems you missed.

- Shade box 3 opposite "addition of fractions" on page xviii.

- If this was the last subskill you had to work on in this section, take the test on page 152.

- If you have other subskills to work on in this section, go on to the next one.

SUBSKILL 4: Addition of Fractions, Whole Numbers, and Mixed Numbers with Exchanging

Problem: $2\frac{1}{2} + 1\frac{2}{3} = ?$

Solution:
- Add fraction parts.
- Simplify.
- Add whole number parts.
- Combine sums.

So, knowing that the LCD of 1/2 and 2/3 is six,

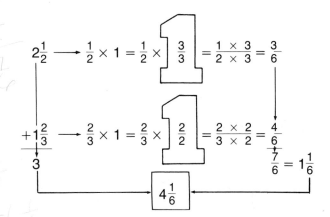

$2\frac{1}{2} \longrightarrow \frac{1}{2} \times 1 = \frac{1}{2} \times \boxed{\frac{3}{3}} = \frac{1 \times 3}{2 \times 3} = \frac{3}{6}$

$+1\frac{2}{3} \longrightarrow \frac{2}{3} \times 1 = \frac{2}{3} \times \boxed{\frac{2}{2}} = \frac{2 \times 2}{3 \times 2} = \frac{4}{6}$

$\quad\quad 3 \quad\quad\quad\quad\quad\quad\quad\quad\quad\quad\quad\quad \frac{7}{6} = 1\frac{1}{6}$

$\boxed{4\frac{1}{6}}$

Lesson: The 3/3 and 2/2 forms of one were chosen for 1/2 and 2/3, respectively, because three times the denominator, two, of the one and two times the denominator, three, of the other equals the LCD, six.

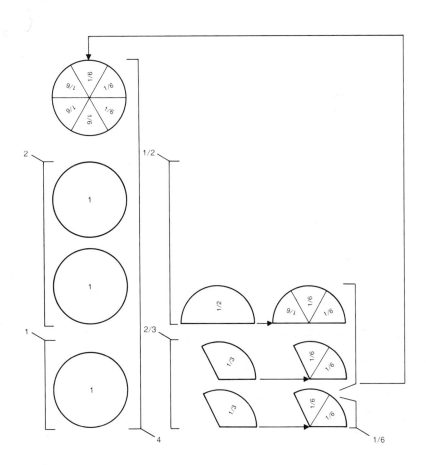

Drill and Practice:

Set 1

1. $2\frac{3}{4}$ 2. $\frac{1}{2}$ 3. $7\frac{2}{3} + 6\frac{1}{2} = ?$

   $+4\frac{5}{6}$ $+1\frac{5}{8}$ 4. $8\frac{3}{5} + \frac{7}{10} = ?$

- *STOP.*
- Check your answers on page 340.
- Correct the problems you missed.
- Go on to Set 2.

Set 2

1. $5\frac{2}{3}$ 2. $3\frac{1}{4}$ 3. $8\frac{4}{5} + 9\frac{3}{5} = ?$

   $+4\frac{5}{9}$ $+\frac{7}{8}$ 4. $9\frac{1}{2} + \frac{9}{10} = ?$

- *STOP.*
- Check your answers on page 340.
- Correct the problems you missed.
- Go on to Set 3 or 4.

Set 3

1. $4\frac{3}{4}$ 2. $\frac{2}{3}$ 3. $1\frac{3}{5} + 4\frac{5}{6} = ?$

   $+5\frac{4}{5}$ $+4\frac{7}{8}$ 4. $\frac{3}{10} + 6\frac{8}{9} = ?$

- *STOP.*
- Check your answers on page 340.
- Correct the problems you missed.
- Go on to Set 4.

Set 4

1. Write (a) an addition sentence with unequal denominators and (b) an addition sentence with equal denominators for the circles.

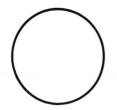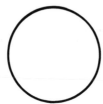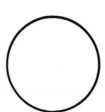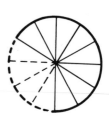

2. Write (a) an addition sentence with unequal denominators and (b) an addition sentence with equal denominators for the squares.

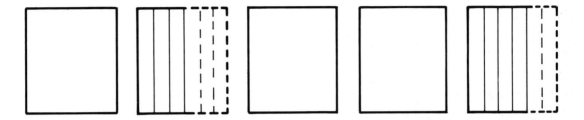

3. How long?

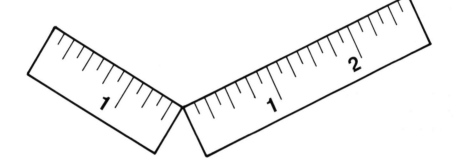

4. Find the perimeter of the rectangle.

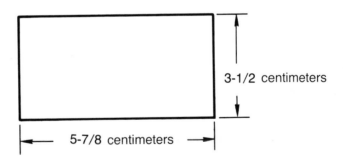

3-1/2 centimeters

5-7/8 centimeters

- *STOP*
- Check your answers on page 340.
- Correct the problems you missed.
- Shade box 4 opposite "addition of fractions" on page xviii.
- Take the test on page 152.

Inventory Post Test for
Addition of Fractions

1. $\frac{7}{8} + \frac{3}{8} = ?$ 2. $\frac{3}{4} + \frac{2}{3} = ?$ 3. $2\frac{1}{4} + 3\frac{1}{2} = ?$ 4. $3\frac{1}{3} + 2\frac{7}{10} = ?$

- *STOP*

- Check your answers with the instructor.

- As before, work through the subskills in this section which correspond to the problems you missed, except work the *even* drill-and-practice problems

- Take the test on page 153.

SKILL
Subtraction of Fractions

Inventory Pretest for
Subtraction of Fractions

1. $\dfrac{5}{10} - \dfrac{3}{10} = ?$ 2. $\dfrac{3}{8} - \dfrac{1}{5} = ?$ 3. $3\dfrac{2}{3} - 1\dfrac{1}{4} = ?$ 4. $5\dfrac{1}{2} - 2\dfrac{7}{8} = ?$

- *STOP*
- Check your answers on page 341.
- Shade the boxes opposite "subtraction of fractions" on page xviii which correspond to the problems you got right.
- If you got all of them right, take the test on page 167.
- If you missed some of them, start working on the subskills in this section which correspond to the ones you missed.
- For each subskill, look at the example, study the solution, think about the lesson, and work the *odd* drill-and-practice problems.

SUBSKILL 1: Subtraction of
Fractions with Equal
Denominators

Problem: $\dfrac{7}{8} - \dfrac{3}{8} = ?$

Solution:
- Subtract numerators.

- Put difference over common denominator.

- Simplify.

$$\frac{7}{8} - \frac{3}{8} = \frac{7-3}{8} = \frac{4}{8} = \boxed{\frac{1}{2}}$$

Lesson:

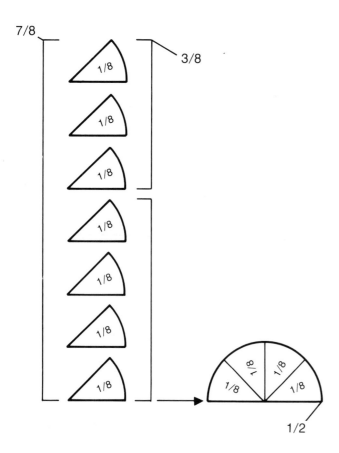

Drill and Practice:

Set 1

1. $\dfrac{7}{8} - \dfrac{5}{8} = ?$ 2. $\dfrac{8}{10} - \dfrac{3}{10} = ?$

3. $\dfrac{9}{12} - \dfrac{4}{12} = ?$ 4. $\dfrac{5}{6} - \dfrac{1}{6} = ?$

- *STOP.*
- Check your answers on page 341.
- Correct the problems you missed.
- Go on to Set 2.

Set 2

1. $\dfrac{2}{3} - \dfrac{1}{3} = ?$ 2. $\dfrac{3}{4} - \dfrac{1}{4} = ?$

3. $\dfrac{4}{5} - \dfrac{2}{5} = ?$ 4. $\dfrac{8}{9} - \dfrac{5}{9} = ?$

- *STOP.*
- Check your answers on page 341.
- Correct the problems you missed.
- Go on to Set 3 or 4.

Set 3

1. $\dfrac{9}{10} - \dfrac{5}{10} = ?$ 2. $\dfrac{8}{12} - \dfrac{6}{12} = ?$

3. $\dfrac{10}{15} - \dfrac{3}{15} = ?$ 4. $\dfrac{20}{24} - \dfrac{9}{24} = ?$

- *STOP.*
- Check your answers on page 341.
- Correct the problems you missed.
- Go on to Set 4.

Set 4

1. Write a subtraction sentence with equal de-nominators for the box of brownies.

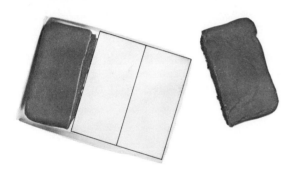

2. Write a subtraction sentence with equal de-nominators for the pound of butter.

3. Write two subtraction sentences with equal denominators for the ruler.

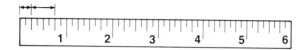

4. Transportation and industry are responsible for 21/50 and 7/50 of the air pollution in the United States, respectively. How much more responsible than industry is transportation?

- *STOP*

- Check your answers on page 341.

- Correct the problems you missed.

- Shade box 1 opposite "subtraction of fractions" on page xviii.

- If this was the only subskill you had to work on in this section, take the test on page 166.

- If you have other subskills to work on in this section, go on to the next one.

SUBSKILL 2: Subtraction of Fractions with Unequal Denominators

Problem: $\dfrac{2}{3} - \dfrac{1}{4} = ?$

Solution:
- Find LCD or least common denominator.
- Convert to equivalent fractions over LCD.

- Subtract numerators.
- Put difference over LCD.
- Simplify.

So, knowing that the LCD of 2/3 and 1/4 is 12,

$$\frac{2}{3} - \frac{1}{4} = \frac{2}{3} \times 1 - \frac{1}{4} \times 1 = \frac{2}{3} \times \boxed{\frac{4}{4}} - \frac{1}{4} \times \boxed{\frac{3}{3}} = \frac{2 \times 4}{3 \times 4} - \frac{1 \times 3}{4 \times 3} = \frac{8}{12} - \frac{3}{12} = \frac{8-3}{12} = \boxed{\frac{5}{12}}$$

Lesson: The 4/4 and 3/3 forms of one were chosen for 2/3 and 1/4, respectively, because four times the denominator, three, of the one and three times the denominator, four, of the other equal the LCD, 12.

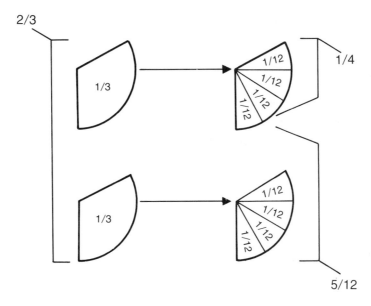

Drill and Practice:

Set 1

1. $\dfrac{1}{2} - \dfrac{1}{3} = ?$ 2. $\dfrac{9}{10} - \dfrac{1}{2} = ?$

3. $\dfrac{7}{10} - \dfrac{2}{5} = ?$ 4. $\dfrac{5}{6} - \dfrac{1}{2} = ?$

- *STOP.*
- Check your answers on page 341.
- Correct the problems you missed.
- Go on to Set 2.

Set 2

1. $\dfrac{7}{12} - \dfrac{1}{3} = ?$ 2. $\dfrac{3}{4} - \dfrac{1}{8} = ?$

3. $\dfrac{5}{6} - \dfrac{3}{4} = ?$ 4. $\dfrac{8}{9} - \dfrac{2}{3} = ?$

- *STOP.*
- Check your answers on page 341.
- Correct the problems you missed.
- Go on to Set 3 or 4.

Set 3

1. $\dfrac{4}{5} - \dfrac{1}{2} = ?$ 　　　　　 2. $\dfrac{3}{8} - \dfrac{1}{3} = ?$

3. $\dfrac{5}{6} - \dfrac{1}{3} = ?$ 　　　　　 4. $\dfrac{5}{9} - \dfrac{1}{6} =$

- *STOP.*
- Check your answers on page 341.
- Correct the problems you missed.
- Go on to Set 4.

Set 4

1. Write (a) a subtraction sentence with un-equal denominators and (b) a subtraction sentence with equal denominators for the lemon cake.

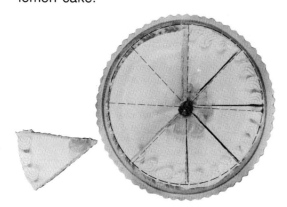

2. Write (a) a subtraction sentence with un-equal denominators and (b) a subtraction sentence with equal denominators for the pumpkin pie.

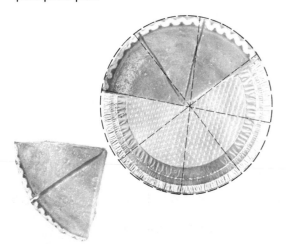

3. Write (a) a subtraction sentence with unequal denominators and (b) a subtraction sentence with equal denominators for the ruler.

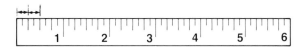

4. Solve the problems in Set 1 with the following cross multiplication technique.

$$\frac{5}{12} - \frac{3}{8} \longrightarrow \frac{5}{12} \underset{}{\overset{}{\underset{\longrightarrow}{\longleftarrow}}} \frac{3}{8} =$$

$$\frac{40 - 36}{96} = \frac{4}{96} = \boxed{\frac{1}{24}}$$

5. Industry and towns and cities are responsible for 3/5 and 1/4 of the water pollution in the United States, respectively. How much more responsible than towns and cities is industry?

- *STOP*

- Check your answers on page 341.

- Correct the problems you missed.

- Shade box 2 opposite "subtraction of fractions" on page xviii.

- If this was the last subskill you had to work on in this section, take the test on page 166.

- If you have other subskills to work on in this section, go on to the next one.

SUBSKILL 3: Subtraction of Fractions, Whole Numbers, and Mixed Numbers Without Exchanging

Problem: $3\frac{5}{6} - 2\frac{1}{2} = ?$

Solution:
- Subtract fraction parts.
- Simplify.
- Subtract whole number parts.
- Combine differences.

So, knowing that the LCD of 5/6 and 1/2 is six,

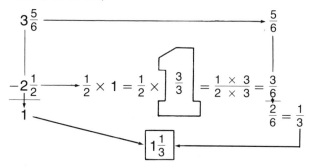

Lesson: The 3/3 form of one was chosen for the fraction 1/2 because three times its denominator, two, equals the LCD, six.

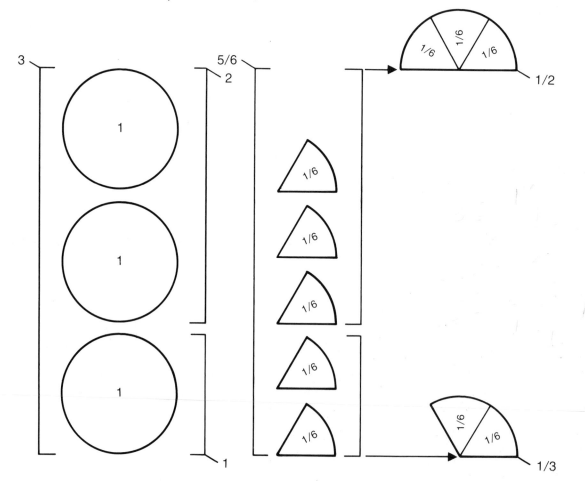

Drill and Practice:

Set 1

1. $5\frac{1}{2}$
   $-3\frac{1}{10}$

2. $2\frac{3}{4}$
   $-\frac{1}{6}$

3. $9\frac{11}{12} - 4\frac{1}{4} = ?$

4. $4\frac{2}{9} - 1 = ?$

- *STOP.*
- Check your answers on page 341.
- Correct the problems you missed.
- Go on to Set 2.

Set 2

1. $7\frac{1}{2}$
   $-5\frac{1}{4}$

2. $9\frac{7}{10}$
   $-\frac{1}{5}$

3. $8\frac{7}{8} - 3\frac{1}{2} = ?$

4. $5\frac{2}{3} - 2 = ?$

- *STOP.*
- Check your answers on page 341.
- Correct the problems you missed.
- Go on to Set 3 or 4.

Set 3

1. $8\frac{2}{3}$
   $-6\frac{1}{2}$

2. $9\frac{4}{5}$
   $-7\frac{1}{6}$

3. $4\frac{3}{8} - 1\frac{1}{10} = ?$

4. $5\frac{7}{9} - 5 = ?$

- *STOP.*
- Check your answers on page 341.
- Correct the problems you missed.
- Go on to Set 4.

Set 4

1. Write (a) a subtraction sentence with unequal denominators and (b) a subtraction sentence with equal denominators for the circles.

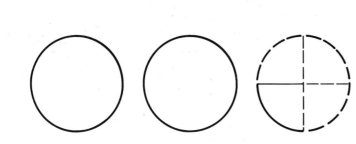
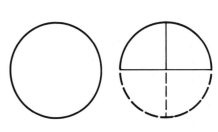

2. Write (a) a subtraction sentence with unequal denominators and (b) a subtraction
sentence with equal denominators for the
squares.

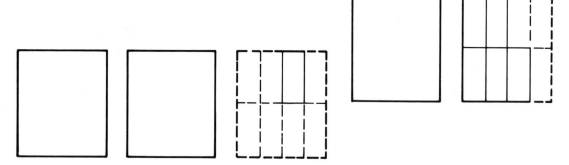

3. How much longer?

4. Jessica is five feet, 4¾ inches tall.
Bradlee is five feet, 2½ inches tall.
Jessica is how much taller than Bradlee?

- *STOP*
- Check your answers on page 341.
- Correct the problems you missed.
- Shade box 3 opposite "subtraction of fractions" on page xviii.
- If this was the last subskill you had to work on in this section, take the test on page 166.
- If you have other subskills to work on in this section, go on to the next one.

SUBSKILL 4: Subtraction of Fractions, Whole Numbers, and Mixed Numbers with Exchanging

Problem: $4\frac{1}{2} - 1\frac{4}{5} = ?$

Solution:
- Subtract fraction parts.

- Exchange a one if fraction part of minuend is greater than fraction part of subtrahend.

- Simplify.

- Subtract whole number parts.

- Combine differences.

So, knowing that the LCD of 1/2 and 4/5 is ten,

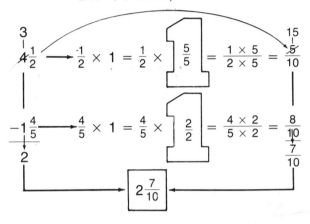

Lesson: The 5/5 and 2/2 forms of one were chosen for 1/2 and 4/5, respectively, because five times the denominator, two, of the one and two times the denominator, five, of the other equal the LCD, ten. The four was reduced to three to make for a one which was exchanged for 10/10 and added to 5/10.

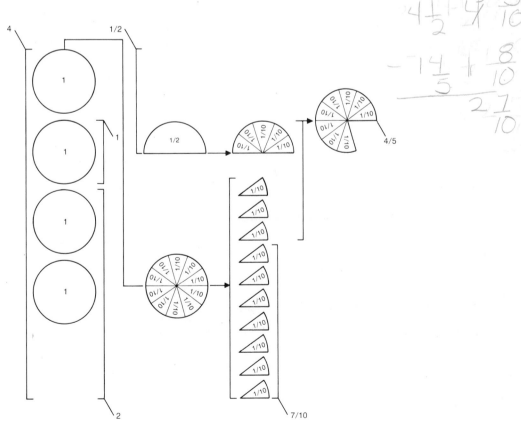

Drill and Practice:

Set 1

1. $4\frac{1}{3}$
   $-2\frac{3}{4}$

2. $9\frac{3}{10}$
   $-5\frac{4}{5}$

3. $3 - \frac{1}{6} = ?$

4. $5\frac{1}{2} - \frac{2}{3} = ?$

- *STOP.*
  Check your answers on page 341.
- Correct the problems you missed.
- Go on to Set 2.

Set 2

1. $3\frac{2}{5}$
   $-1\frac{1}{2}$

2. $5\frac{1}{4}$
   $-4\frac{7}{8}$

3. $7 - \frac{7}{10} = ?$

4. $8\frac{7}{12} - \frac{5}{6} = ?$

- *STOP.*
- Check your answers on page 341.
- Correct the problems you missed.
- Go on to Set 3 or 4.

Set 3

1. $4\frac{1}{6}$
   $-2\frac{4}{9}$

2. $9\frac{3}{8}$
   $-6\frac{2}{3}$

3. $1 - \frac{5}{24} = ?$

4. $7\frac{3}{4} - \frac{4}{5} = ?$

- *STOP.*
- Check your answers on page 341.
- Correct the problems you missed.
- Go on to Set 4.

Set 4

1. Write (a) a subtraction sentence with unequal denominators and (b) a subtraction sentence with equal denominators for the circles.

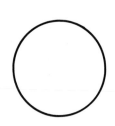

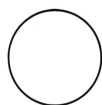

2. Write (a) a subtraction sentence with unequal denominators and (b) a subtraction sentence with equal denominators for the squares.

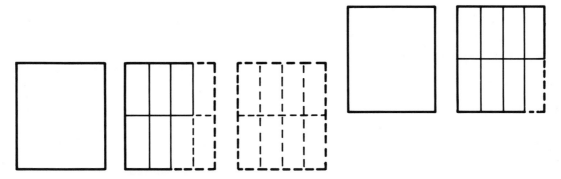

3. How much longer?

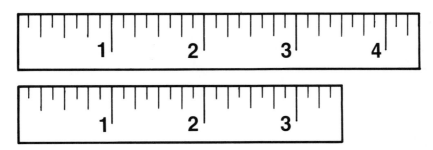

4. Kipp is five feet, 10¼ inches tall.
   Pax is five feet, 7¾ inches tall.
   Kipp is how much taller than Pax?

● *STOP*

● Check your answers on page 341.

● Correct the problems you missed.

● Shade box 4 opposite "subtraction of fractions" on page xviii.

● Take the test on page 166.

Inventory Post Test for
Subtraction of Fractions

1. $\dfrac{5}{6} - \dfrac{1}{6} = ?$ 2. $\dfrac{3}{4} - \dfrac{1}{3} = ?$ 3. $5\dfrac{3}{5} - 2\dfrac{1}{9} = ?$ 4. $6\dfrac{1}{4} - 1\dfrac{5}{12} = ?$

- *STOP*

- Check your answers with the instructor.

- As before, work through the subskills in this section which correspond to the problems you missed, except work the *even* drill-and-practice problems.

- Take the test on page 167.

SECTION 11

SKILL
Multiplication of Fractions

Inventory Pretest for
Multiplication of Fractions

1. $\dfrac{3}{4} \times \dfrac{8}{9} = ?$ *24⁄36*

2. $3 \times \dfrac{4}{9} = ?$ *12⁄9 = 9√12⁄9 = 14⁄4*

3. $\dfrac{2}{3} \times 3\dfrac{2}{3} = ?$

4. $3\dfrac{5}{8} \times 4 = ?$

5. $3\dfrac{5}{12} \times 4\dfrac{5}{6} = ?$

- *STOP*

- Check your answers on page 341.

- Shade the boxes opposite "multiplication of fractions" on page xix which correspond to the problems you got right.

- If you got all of them right, take the test on page 187.

- If you missed some of them, start working on the subskills in this section which correspond to the ones you missed.

- For each subskill, look at the example, study the solution, think about the lesson, and work the *odd* drill-and-practice problems.

SUBSKILL 1: Multiplication of Fractions

Problem: $\dfrac{2}{3} \times \dfrac{3}{4} = ?$ *6⁄12 = 1⁄2*

Solution:
- Multiply across.
- Simplify.

$$\dfrac{2}{3} \times \dfrac{3}{4} = \dfrac{2 \times 3}{3 \times 4} = \dfrac{6}{12} = \boxed{\dfrac{1}{2}}$$

Lesson: Two-thirds of a group of $\frac{3}{4}$.

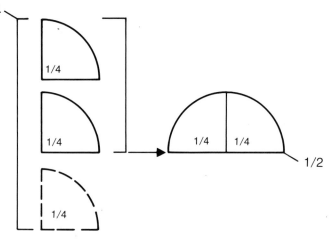

Drill and Practice:

Set 1

1. $\frac{1}{3} \times \frac{3}{6} = ?$ 2. $\frac{1}{2} \times \frac{4}{5} = ?$

3. $\frac{2}{3} \times \frac{3}{8} = ?$ 4. $\frac{3}{4} \times \frac{4}{3} = ?$

- *STOP.*
- Check your answers on page 341.
- Correct the problems you missed.
- Go on to Set 2.

Set 2

1. $\frac{4}{5} \times \frac{5}{6} = ?$ 2. $\frac{1}{2} \times \frac{8}{9} = ?$

3. $\frac{1}{4} \times \frac{12}{1} = ?$ 4. $\frac{2}{3} \times \frac{15}{10} = ?$

- *STOP.*
- Check your answers on page 341.
- Correct the problems you missed.
- Go on to Set 3 or 4.

Set 3

1. $\frac{4}{9} \times \frac{5}{12} = ?$ 2. $\frac{5}{6} \times \frac{7}{10} = ?$

3. $\frac{3}{5} \times \frac{10}{1} = ?$ 4. $\frac{1}{6} \times \frac{18}{3} = ?$

- *STOP.*
- Check your answers on page 341.
- Correct the problems you missed.
- Go on to Set 4.

Set 4

1. Write two multiplication sentences for the square.

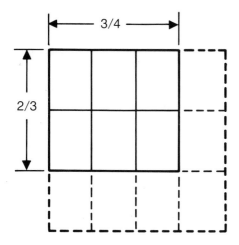

2. What fraction of the unit square is shaded?

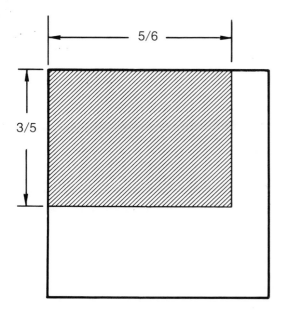

3. The radius of a circle is half the diameter of the circle. What is the radius of a circle of diameter 7/8?

4. Solve the problems in Set 1 with the following cancellation technique.

$$\frac{4}{5} \times \frac{5}{8} \longrightarrow \frac{\overset{1}{\cancel{4}}}{\underset{1}{\cancel{5}}} \times \frac{\overset{1}{\cancel{5}}}{\underset{2}{\cancel{8}}} = \frac{1 \times 1}{1 \times 2} = \boxed{\frac{1}{2}}$$

5. How many cups of evaporated skim milk would be needed to make two servings of strawberry whip?

Strawberry Whip

½ cup evaporated skim milk
2 cups fresh or frozen unsweetened
  strawberries
2 egg whites
2 packets granulated sugar substitute
  (equal to 4 teaspoons sugar)
6 strawberries, for garnish

Pour skim milk into small metal pan. Place in freezer until ice crystals form around the edge, about 30 minutes.

Meanwhile, place strawberries into blender container; cover and blend until smooth. In small bowl, beat egg whites until stiff. old puree into egg whites. Whip chilled milk until foamy. Add sweetner and continue beating until thick and fluffy; fold in strawberry mixture. Pour into 8 individual parfait glasses or dessert dishes. Serve immediately or refrigerate for 1 hour. Makes 6 servings. About 40 calories per serving.

- *STOP*

- Check your answers on page 341.

- Correct the problems you missed.

- Shade box 1 opposite "multiplication of fractions" on page xix.

- If this was the only subskill you had to work on in this section, take the test on page 185.

- If you have other subskills to work on in this section, go on to the next one.

SUBSKILL 2: Multiplication of
Fractions and Whole
Numbers

Problem: $2 \times \dfrac{5}{6} = ?$

Solution:
- Write whole number as fraction over one.

- Multiply across.

- Simplify.

$$2 \times \frac{5}{6} = \frac{2}{1} \times \frac{5}{6} = \frac{2 \times 5}{1 \times 6} = \frac{10}{6} = \frac{5}{3} = \boxed{1\frac{2}{3}}$$

Lesson: Two groups of $\dfrac{5}{6}$.

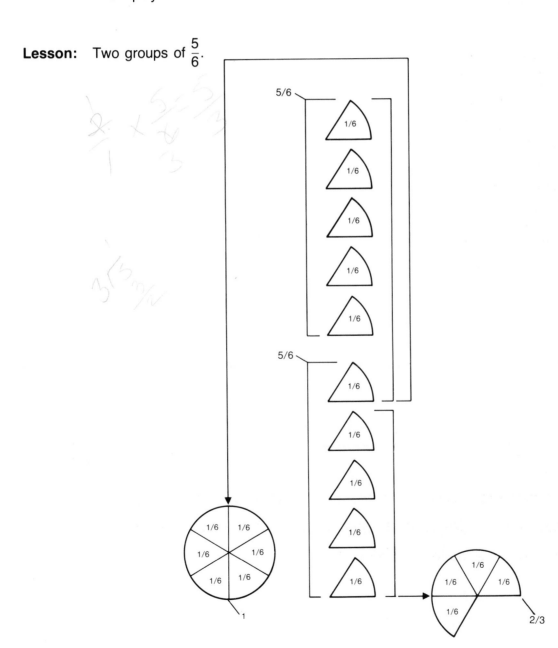

Drill and Practice:

Set 1

1. $3 \cdot \times \dfrac{1}{6} = ?$ 2. $\dfrac{3}{4} \times 2 = ?$

3. $4 \times \dfrac{3}{8} = ?$ 4. $\dfrac{1}{5} \times 5 = ?$

- *STOP.*
- Check your answers on page 342.
- Correct the problems you missed.
- Go on to Set 2.

Set 2

1. $3 \times \dfrac{2}{3} = ?$ 2. $\dfrac{7}{10} \times 2 = ?$

3. $4 \times \dfrac{5}{12} = ?$ 4. $\dfrac{1}{2} \times 2 = ?$

- *STOP.*
- Check your answers on page 342.
- Correct the problems you missed.
- Go on to Set 3 or 4.

Set 3

1. $3 \times \dfrac{5}{6} = ?$ 2. $\dfrac{7}{12} \times 8 = ?$

3. $9 \times \dfrac{2}{3} = ?$ 4. $\dfrac{1}{15} \times 15 = ?$

- *STOP.*
- Check your answers on page 342.
- Correct the problems you missed.
- Go on to Set 4.

Set 4

1. How many cups of milk?

2. A bag contains about 50 grapes. About how many grapes do you have to eat to eat a third of the bag?

3. A person weighs 1/6 as much on the moon. How much would a 120-pound person weigh on the moon?

4. Find the area of the triangle if the area of the shaded square is one.

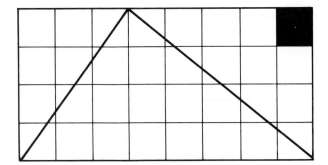

5. Find the area of the triangle using $A = \frac{1}{2}bh$ for the area A of a triangle of base b and height h.

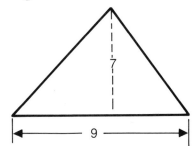

6. Using $C = 5/9 \ (F - 32)$ for converting from fahrenheit F to celsius C, convert to celsius:

   (a) 32°F (b) 104°F (c) 77°F (d) 212°F

7. To convert from kilometers to miles, multiply by 5/8. Convert to miles:

   (a) 40 km   (b) 520 km   (c) 120 km
   (d) 1000 km

8. A 120-pound woman burns up about 480 calories per hour when swimming. About how many calories would she burn up in ten minutes (1/6 of an hour) of swimming?

9. A 160-pound man burns up about 600 calories per hour when running. About how many calories would he burn up in five minutes (1/12 of an hour) of running?

10. How many teaspoons of lemon juice and salt would be needed to make ten to 15 vegetable sandwiches?

Vegetable Sandwiches

Small mixing bowl, fork
Measuring cups and spoons
Sharp knife
Table knife for cutting
1 small ripe avocado
1 scallion
½ teaspoon lemon juice
¼ teaspoon salt
1 or 2 tablespoons mayonnaise or sour cream
1 hard-cooked egg

Make these sandwiches with any whole-grained bread. Each recipe makes enough filling for two or three sandwiches.

Cut the avocado in half, pull off the skin and remove the seed. Put it in a mixing bowl, and mash it with a fork. Chop the scallion fine, and add it to the avocado. Add the lemon juice, salt and mayonnaise or sour cream, and mix well.

Chop the hard-cooked egg in rather large chunks, and add it to the avocado mixture. Stir it in lightly.

- *STOP*

- Check your answers on page 342.

- Correct the problems you missed.

- Shade box 2 opposite "multiplication of fractions" on page xix.

- If this was the last subskill you had to work on in this section, take the test on page 185.

- If you have other subskills to work on in this section, go on to the next one.

SUBSKILL 3: Multiplication of Fractions and Mixed Numbers

Problem: $3\frac{2}{3} \times \frac{3}{10} = ?$

Solution:
- Convert mixed number to improper fraction.

- Multiply across.

- Simplify.

$$3\frac{2}{3} \times \frac{3}{10} = \frac{11}{3} \times \frac{3}{10} = \frac{11 \times 3}{3 \times 10} = \frac{33}{30} = \frac{11}{10} = \boxed{1\frac{1}{10}}$$

Lesson: Three and two-thirds groups of $\frac{3}{10}$.

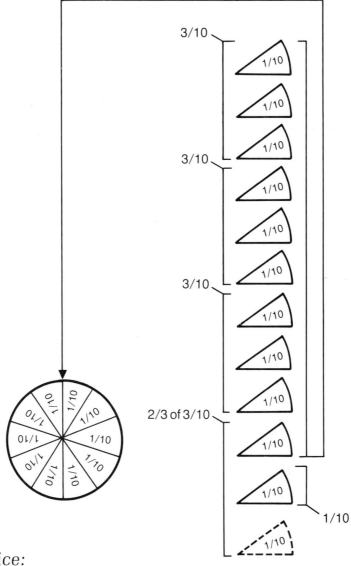

Drill and Practice:

Set 1

1. $\frac{1}{2} \times 1\frac{1}{3} = ?$ 2. $1\frac{1}{2} \times \frac{2}{3} = ?$

3. $\frac{3}{5} \times 1\frac{1}{4} = ?$ 4. $1\frac{1}{3} \times \frac{3}{4} = ?$

- *STOP.*
- Check your answers on page 342.
- Correct the problems you missed.
- Go on to Set 2.

Set 2

1. $\frac{2}{5} \times 1\frac{1}{9} = ?$ 2. $1\frac{4}{5} \times \frac{1}{3} = ?$

3. $\frac{1}{2} \times 1\frac{2}{3} = ?$ 4. $1\frac{2}{3} \times \frac{3}{4} = ?$

- *STOP.*
- Check your answers on page 342.
- Correct the problems you missed.
- Go on to Set 3 or 4.

Set 3

1. $\frac{1}{2} \times 4\frac{3}{5} = ?$ 2. $2\frac{1}{4} \times \frac{1}{3} = ?$

3. $\frac{1}{3} \times 8\frac{1}{12} = ?$ 4. $4\frac{4}{5} \times \frac{2}{3} = ?$

- *STOP.*
- Check your answers on page 342.
- Correct the problems you missed.
- Go on to Set 4.

Set 4

1. Write two multiplication sentences for the squares.

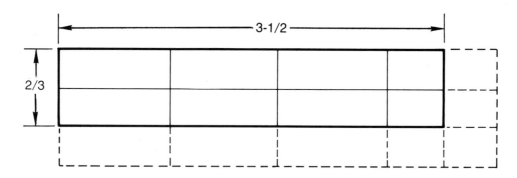

2. How much of the rectangle is shaded?

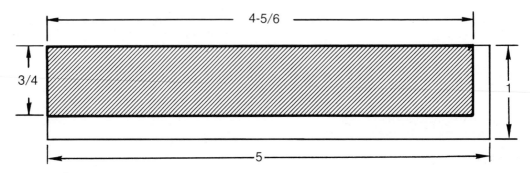

3. How many cups of soy sauce and teaspoons of ginger would be needed to make ten servings of barbecued shrimp.

Barbecued Shrimp

1 pound (about 24) uncooked medium-sized
  shrimp
¼ cup soy sauce
2 tablespoons tomato juice
1 tablespoon water
1 tablespoon cider vinegar
½ teaspoon ginger
Dash cayenne pepper
1 packet granulated sugar substitute (equal
  to 2 teaspoons sugar)
1 garlic clove, crushed

Peel and devein shrimp. On each of 4 skewers, thread 6 shrimp; place on broiler pan. In small saucepan, combine remaining ingredients and heat to boiling. Reduce heat and simmer 3 minutes, uncovered. Brush shrimp thoroughly with sauce. Broil 4 inches from heat for 2 minutes on each side or until tender. Baste frequently with sauce. (May be grilled over charcoal fire.) Makes 4 servings. About 110 calories per serving.

4. If you could run the mile in 6¾ minutes, how long would it take you to run 2/3 of a mile?

- *STOP*

- Check your answers on page 342.

- Correct the problems you missed.

- Shade box 3 opposite "multiplication of fractions" on page xix.

- If this was the last subskill you had to work on in this section, take the test on page 185.

- If you have other subskills to work on in this section, go on to the next one.

SUBSKILL 4: Multiplication of Mixed and Whole Numbers

Problem: $3 \times 1\frac{2}{3} = ?$

Solution:

- Convert mixed number to improper fraction.

- Write whole number as fraction over one.

- Multiply across.

- Simplify.

$$3 \times 1\frac{2}{3} = \frac{3}{1} \times \frac{5}{3} = \frac{3 \times 5}{1 \times 3} = \frac{15}{3} = \boxed{5}$$

Lesson: Three groups of $1\frac{2}{3}$.

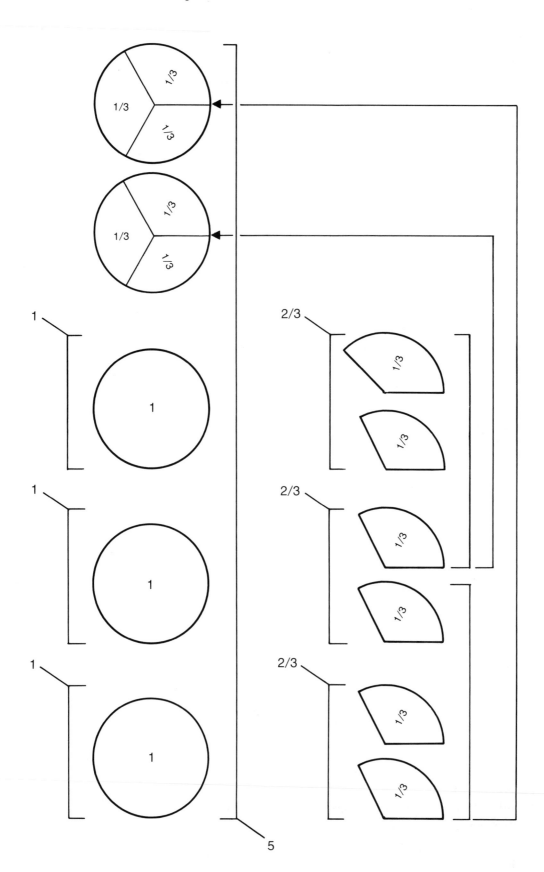

Drill and Practice:

Set 1

1. $4 \times 1\frac{1}{2} = ?$
2. $2 \times 3\frac{4}{5} = ?$

3. $2\frac{5}{12} \times 3 = ?$
4. $3\frac{3}{10} \times 5 = ?$

- *STOP.*
- Check your answers on page 342.
- Correct the problems you missed.
- Go on to Set 2.

Set 2

1. $2 \times 1\frac{3}{4} = ?$
2. $8 \times 2\frac{1}{6} = ?$

3. $3\frac{2}{5} \times 5 = ?$
4. $4\frac{2}{3} \times 2 = ?$

- *STOP.*
- Check your answers on page 342.
- Correct the problems you missed.
- Go on to Set 3 or 4.

Set 3

1. $4 \times 4\frac{11}{12} = ?$
2. $7 \times 3\frac{4}{5} = ?$

3. $6\frac{1}{3} \times 9 = ?$
4. $3\frac{1}{2} \times 10 = ?$

- *STOP.*
- Check your answers on page 342.
- Correct the problems you missed.
- Go on to Set 4.

Set 4

1. You worked 48 hours one week. You were paid $8 an hour for the first 40 hours and time-and-a-half for the remaining eight hours. How much were you paid?

2. How much would eight red quarry tiles cost?

3. How much would 32 vinyl asbestos tiles cost?

4. A thumb is about two centimeters wide. A dollar bill is 7½ thumbs long. About how long is the dollar bill in centimeters?

5. The average lifespan of a human being is 70 years. The average lifespan of a box turtle is $1\frac{3}{5}$ the average lifespan of a human being. What is the average lifespan of a box turtle?

6. A hummingbird weighs 1/10 of an ounce. It eats 6½ times its weight in food daily. How much would a 100-pound hummingbird eat?

7. Using $F = 1\frac{4}{5}C + 32$ for converting from celsius C to fahrenheit F, convert to fahrenheit:

   (a) 0°C   (b) 35°C   (c) 20°C   (d) 100°C

8. To convert from miles to kilometers, multiply by $1\frac{3}{5}$. Convert to kilometers:

(a) 5 miles (b) 500 miles (c) 100 miles

(d) 1000 miles

- *STOP*

- Check your answers on page 342.

- Correct the problems you missed.

- Shade box 4 opposite "multiplication of fractions" on page xix.

- If this was the last subskill you had to work on in this section, take the test on page 185.

- If you have other subskills to work on in this section, go on to the next one.

SUBSKILL 5: Multiplication of Mixed Numbers

Problem: $1\frac{1}{2} \times 2\frac{1}{5} = ?$

Solution: - Convert to improper fractions.

- Multiply across.

- Simplify.

$$1\frac{1}{2} \times 2\frac{1}{5} = \frac{3}{2} \times \frac{11}{5} = \frac{3 \times 11}{2 \times 5} = \frac{33}{10} = \boxed{3\frac{3}{10}}$$

Lesson: One and one-half groups of $2\frac{1}{5}$.

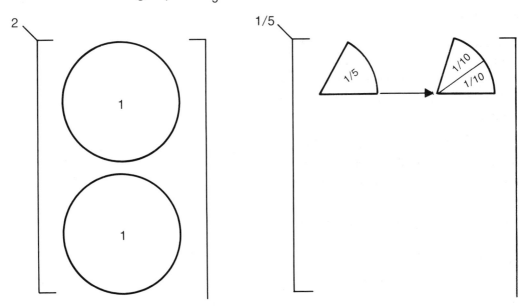

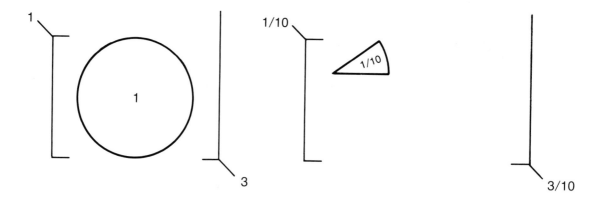

Drill and Practice:

Set 1

1. $1\frac{1}{3} \times 3\frac{1}{3} = ?$ 2. $1\frac{3}{4} \times 4\frac{4}{5} = ?$

3. $2\frac{1}{2} \times 4\frac{1}{3} = ?$ 4. $3\frac{1}{4} \times 1\frac{1}{2} = ?$

- *STOP.*
- Check your answers on page 342.
- Correct the problems you missed.
- Go on to Set 2.

Set 2

1. $1\frac{3}{5} \times 5\frac{5}{8} = ?$ 2. $2\frac{1}{4} \times 3\frac{2}{3} = ?$

3. $2\frac{5}{8} \times 4\frac{2}{3} = ?$ 4. $1\frac{2}{3} \times 2\frac{3}{5} = ?$

- *STOP.*
- Check your answers on page 342.
- Correct the problems you missed.
- Go on to Set 3 or 4.

Set 3

1. $5\frac{5}{6} \times 4\frac{3}{4} = ?$ 2. $3\frac{4}{5} \times 8\frac{1}{2} = ?$

3. $1\frac{2}{3} \times 6\frac{1}{5} = ?$ 4. $3\frac{5}{8} \times 4\frac{1}{2} = ?$

- *STOP.*
- Check your answers on page 342.
- Correct the problems you missed.
- Go on to Set 4.

Set 4

1. Write two multiplication sentences for the squares.

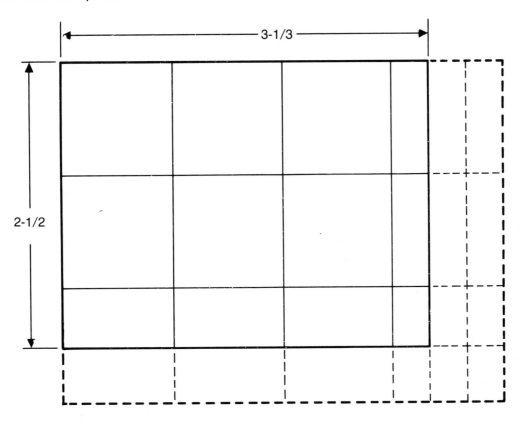

2. How much of the rectangle is shaded?

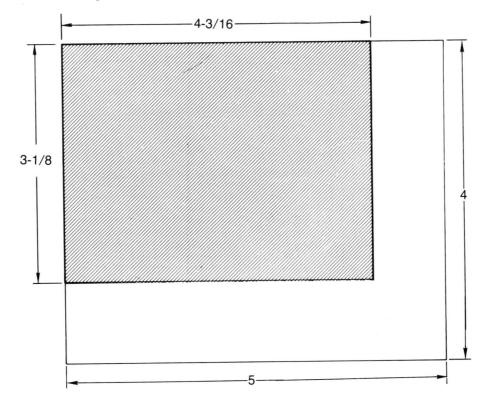

3. How many ounces of tuna fish would be needed to make 42 servings of tuna-stuffed mushrooms?

Tuna-Stuffed Mushrooms

24 large mushrooms
1 tablespoon dried onion flakes
1 tablespoon chopped parsley
2 tablespoons water
2 slices white bread
½ cup skim milk
¼ teaspoon garlic powder
Dash white pepper
1 can (3½ oz.) water packed tuna, drained and flaked
1 ounce (¼ cup) sharp Cheddar cheese, shredded
Paprika, for garnish

Clean mushrooms with damp cloth. Remove stems and set caps aside. Chop stems. In saucepan, combine stems, onion flakes, parsley and water. Cook until stems are tender, about 5 minutes.

In blender container, place bread and milk; purée for 30 seconds, until mixture is smooth. Add to mushroom mixture in saucepan and stir over low heat until thick. Add garlic powder, pepper, tuna and cheese. When cheese melts, stir; remove from heat and cool.

Preheat oven to 350°F. Fill mushroom caps with tuna mixture, arrange in baking pan. Sprinkle with paprika. Bake 15 to 20 minutes until filling is heated through. Serve hot. Makes 24 mushrooms. About 30 calories each.

4. If you could run the mile in 7½ minutes, how long would it take you to run 3½ miles?

- *STOP*

- Check your answers on page 342.

- Correct the problems you missed.

- Shade box 5 opposite "multiplication of fractions" on page xix.

- Take the test on page 185.

Inventory Post Test for
Multiplication of Fractions

1. $\frac{3}{10} \times \frac{5}{6} = ?$

2. $4 \times \frac{2}{3} = ?$

3. $\frac{3}{4} \times 2\frac{5}{12} = ?$

4. $2\frac{1}{5} \times 7 = ?$

5. $3\frac{5}{9} \times 2\frac{1}{4} = ?$

- *STOP*

- Check your answers with the instructor.

- As before, work through the subskills in this section which correspond to the problems you missed, except work the *even* drill-and-practice problems.

- Take the test on page 187.

SKILL
Division of Fractions

Inventory Pretest for Division of Fractions

1. $\dfrac{4}{9} \div \dfrac{3}{8} = ?$

2. $\dfrac{9}{10} \div 3 = ?$

3. $4\dfrac{2}{3} \div \dfrac{7}{8} = ?$

4. $3\dfrac{1}{4} \div 5 = ?$

5. $3\dfrac{1}{8} \div 4\dfrac{2}{5} = ?$

6. What is the reciprocal of $\dfrac{3}{7}$?

- *STOP*
- Check your answers on page 342.
- Shade the boxes opposite "division of fractions" on page xix which correspond to the problems you got right.
- If you got all of them right, take the test on page 201.
- If you missed some of them, start working on the subskills in this section which correspond to the ones you missed.
- For each subskill, look at the example, study the solution, think about the lesson, and work the *odd* drill-and-practice problems.

SUBSKILL 1: Division of Fractions

Problem: $\dfrac{5}{6} \div \dfrac{7}{12} = ?$

Yours is not to reason why, yours is but to invert [the divisor] and multiply.*

Solution: To divide fractions, recall the following rhyme:

*To reason why, see page 196.

$$\frac{5}{6} \div \frac{7}{12} = \frac{5}{6} \times \frac{12}{7} = \frac{5 \times 12}{6 \times 7} = \frac{60}{42} = \frac{10}{7} = \boxed{1\frac{3}{7}}$$

Lesson: Five-sixths grouped by $\frac{7}{12}$.

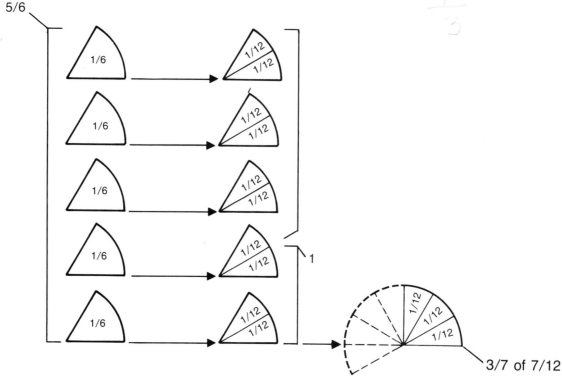

3/7 of 7/12

Drill and Practice:

Set 1

1. $\frac{2}{3} \div \frac{1}{3} = ?$ 2. $\frac{2}{3} \div \frac{1}{6} = ?$

3. $\frac{3}{4} \div \frac{5}{8} = ?$ 4. $\frac{3}{10} \div \frac{2}{5} = ?$

- *STOP.*
- Check your answers on page 342.
- Correct the problems you missed.
- Go on to Set 2.

Set 2

1. $\frac{3}{4} \div \frac{1}{4} = ?$ 2. $\frac{1}{2} \div \frac{1}{4} = ?$

3. $\frac{1}{4} \div \frac{1}{2} = ?$ 4. $\frac{9}{10} \div \frac{1}{2} = ?$

- *STOP.*
- Check your answers on page 342.
- Correct the problems you missed.
- Go on to Set 3 or 4.

Set 3

1. $\dfrac{1}{2} \div \dfrac{7}{10} = ?$　　　　2. $\dfrac{5}{6} \div \dfrac{2}{3} = ?$

3. $\dfrac{7}{8} \div \dfrac{1}{12} = ?$　　　　4. $\dfrac{3}{10} \div \dfrac{1}{3} = ?$

- *STOP.*
- Check your answers on page 342.
- Correct the problems you missed.
- Go on to Set 4.

Set 4

1. What times $\dfrac{5}{6}$ is $\dfrac{4}{9}$?

2. Transportation and industry are responsible for 21/50 and 7/50 of the air pollution in the United States, respectively. How many times more responsible than industry is transportation?

3. Industry and towns and cities are responsible for 3/5 and 1/4 of the water pollution in the United States, respectively. How many times more responsible than towns and cities is industry?

4. Solve the problems in Set 1 with the following cancellation technique.

$$\frac{4}{5} \div \frac{8}{5} = \frac{4}{5} \times \frac{5}{8} \rightarrow \frac{\overset{1}{\cancel{4}}}{\underset{1}{\cancel{5}}} \times \frac{\overset{1}{\cancel{5}}}{\underset{2}{\cancel{8}}} = \frac{1 \times 1}{1 \times 2} = \boxed{\frac{1}{2}}$$

- *STOP*

- Check your answers on page 342.

- Correct the problems you missed.

- Shade box 1 opposite "division of fractions" on page xix.

- If this was the only subskill you had to work on in this section, take the test on page 200.

- If you have other subskills to work on in this section, go on to the next one.

SUBSKILL 2: Division of Fractions
and Whole Numbers

Problem: $\dfrac{3}{4} \div 2 = ?$

Solution:
- Write whole number as fraction over one.

- Invert divisor.

- Multiply across.

- Simplify.

$$\dfrac{3}{4} \div 2 = \dfrac{3}{4} \div \dfrac{2}{1} = \dfrac{3}{4} \times \dfrac{1}{2} = \dfrac{3 \times 1}{4 \times 2} = \boxed{\dfrac{3}{8}}$$

Lesson: Three-fourths grouped by twos.

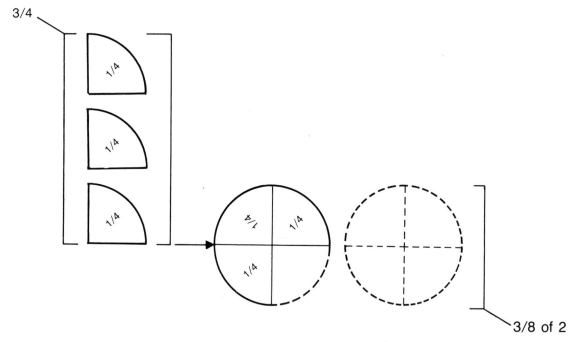

3/8 of 2

Drill and Practice:

Set 1

1. $\dfrac{4}{5} \div 2 = ?$ 2. $\dfrac{1}{3} \div 3 = ?$

3. $1 \div \dfrac{1}{4} = ?$ 4. $3 \div \dfrac{1}{2} = ?$

- *STOP.*
- Check your answers on page 342.
- Correct the problems you missed.
- Go on to Set 2.

Set 2

1. $\dfrac{2}{3} \div 2 = ?$ 2. $\dfrac{3}{4} \div 3 = ?$

3. $1 \div \dfrac{1}{2} = ?$ 4. $2 \div \dfrac{1}{5} = ?$

- *STOP.*
- Check your answers on page 343.
- Correct the problems you missed.
- Go on to Set 3 or 4.

Set 3

1. $\dfrac{3}{8} \div 5 = ?$ 2. $\dfrac{5}{12} \div 10 = ?$

3. $4 \div \dfrac{3}{10} = ?$ 4. $8 \div \dfrac{2}{3} = ?$

- *STOP.*
- Check your answers on page 343.
- Correct the problems you missed.
- Go on to Set 4.

Set 4

1. Write a division sentence for the pepperoni.

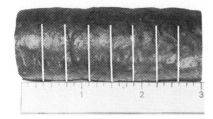

2. You have a 12-inch meatloaf. How many 3/4-inch slices can you cut?

3. How many times would you have to run around a 1/4-mile track to run five miles?

4. What times 4/9 is 20?

- *STOP*

- Check your answers on page 343.

- Correct the problems you missed.

- Shade box 2 opposite "division of fractions" on page xix.

- If this was the last subskill you had to work on in this section, take the test on page 200.

- If you have other subskills to work on in this section, go on to the next one.

SUBSKILL 3: Division of Fractions and Mixed Numbers

Problem: $1\frac{2}{3} \div \frac{5}{6} = ?$

Solution:
- Convert mixed number to improper fraction.
- Invert divisor.
- Multiply across.
- Simplify.

$$1\frac{2}{3} \div \frac{5}{6} = \frac{5}{3} \div \frac{5}{6} = \frac{5}{3} \times \frac{6}{5} = \frac{5 \times 6}{3 \times 5} = \frac{30}{15} = \boxed{2}$$

Lesson: One and two-thirds grouped by $\frac{5}{6}$.

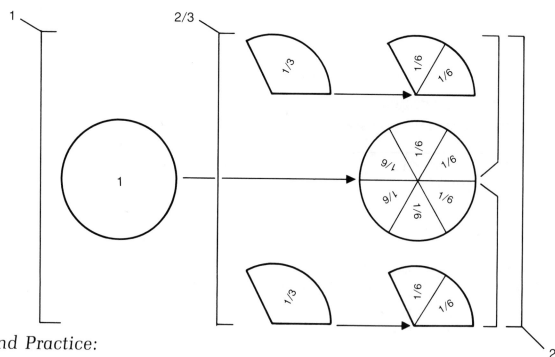

Drill and Practice:

Set 1

1. $1\frac{3}{4} \div \frac{1}{2} = ?$

2. $2\frac{2}{3} \div \frac{1}{3} = ?$

3. $1\frac{4}{5} \div \frac{1}{10} = ?$

4. $2\frac{1}{2} \div \frac{2}{3} = ?$

- *STOP.*
- Check your answers on page 343.
- Correct the problems you missed.
- Go on to Set 2.

Set 2

1. $1\frac{1}{2} \div \frac{1}{4} = ?$ 2. $2\frac{1}{3} \div \frac{5}{6} = ?$

3. $1\frac{3}{5} \div \frac{2}{5} = ?$ 4. $2\frac{2}{3} \div \frac{3}{4} = ?$

- *STOP.*
- Check your answers on page 343.
- Correct the problems you missed.
- Go on to Set 3 or 4.

Set 3

1. $4\frac{3}{5} \div \frac{5}{8} = ?$ 2. $\frac{7}{12} \div 3\frac{4}{5} = ?$

3. $2\frac{9}{10} \div \frac{3}{4} = ?$ 4. $\frac{2}{3} \div 3\frac{5}{6} = ?$

- *STOP.*
- Check your answers on page 343.
- Correct the problems you missed.
- Go on to Set 4.

Set 4

1. Write a division sentence for the pepperoni.

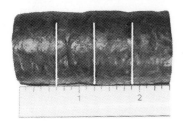

2. You have a 9⅓-inch sausage. How many 2/3-inch slices can you cut?

3. One revolution of a nut tightens it 3/16 of an inch. How many revolutions would tighten it 1½ inches?

4. What times 4/5 is 3½?

- *STOP*
- Check your answers on page 343.
- Correct the problems you missed.
- Shade box 3 opposite "division of fractions" on page xix.
- If this was the last subskill you had to work on in this section, take the test on page 200.
- If you have other subskills to work on in this section, go on to the next one.

SUBSKILL 4: Division of Mixed and Whole Numbers

Problem: $4\frac{1}{8} \div 3 = ?$

$$\frac{33}{8} \times \frac{3}{1} \qquad \frac{33}{8} \times \frac{1}{3} = \frac{11}{8}$$

Solution:

- Convert mixed number to improper fraction.

- Write whole number as fraction over one.

- Invert divisor.

- Multiply across.

- Simplify.

$$4\frac{1}{8} \div 3 = \frac{33}{8} \div \frac{3}{1} = \frac{33}{8} \times \frac{1}{3} =$$

$$\frac{33 \times 1}{8 \times 3} = \frac{33}{24} = \frac{11}{8} = \boxed{1\frac{3}{8}}$$

Lesson: Four and one-eighth grouped by threes.

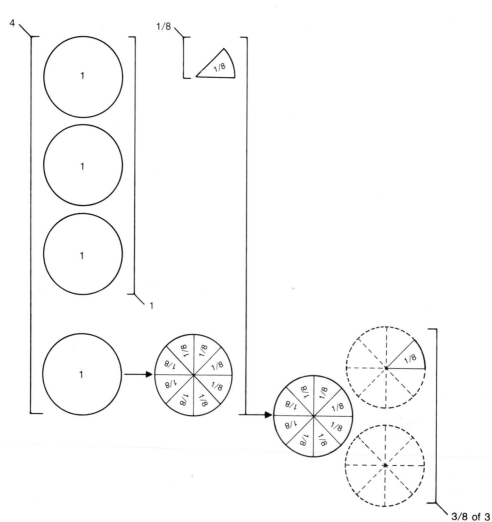

3/8 of 3

Drill and Practice:

Set 1

1. $2\frac{3}{4} \div 2 = ?$ 2. $5 \div 2\frac{1}{2} = ?$

3. $3\frac{5}{6} \div 2 = ?$ 4. $3 \div 1\frac{2}{3} = ?$

- *STOP.*
- Check your answers on page 343.
- Correct the problems you missed.
- Go on to Set 2.

Set 2

1. $3\frac{1}{4} \div 3 = ?$ 2. $5 \div 4\frac{1}{2} = ?$

3. $4\frac{1}{2} \div 5 = ?$ 4. $2 \div 1\frac{1}{2} = ?$

- *STOP.*
- Check your answers on page 343.
- Correct the problems you missed.
- Go on to Set 3 or 4.

Set 3

1. $5\frac{7}{8} \div 4 = ?$ 2. $4 \div 6\frac{5}{8} = ?$

3. $3\frac{1}{6} \div 2 = ?$ 4. $2 \div 3\frac{1}{6} = ?$

- *STOP.*
- Check your answers on page 343.
- Correct the problems you missed.
- Go on to Set 4.

Set 4

1. What times three is $7\frac{1}{2}$?

2. How would you split the cheese among 14 people?

3. A person needs about 2½ quarts of water a day to survive. How many quarts of water would a person need to survive 50 days?

4. How long in feet will the table top be if it is made from a board 10¾ feet long?

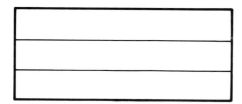

- • *STOP*

- • Check your answers on page 343.

- • Correct the problems you missed.

- • Shade box 4 opposite "division of fractions" on page xix.

- • If this was the last subskill you had to work on in this section, take the test on page 200.

- • If you have other subskills to work on in this section, go on to the next one.

SUBSKILL 5: Division of Mixed Numbers

Problem: $2\frac{3}{4} \div 4\frac{2}{5} = ?$

Solution:
- • Convert to improper fractions.

- • Invert divisor.

- • Multiply across.

- • Simplify.

$$2\frac{3}{4} \div 4\frac{2}{5} = \frac{11}{4} \div \frac{22}{5} = \frac{11}{4} \times \frac{5}{22} =$$

$$\frac{11 \times 5}{4 \times 22} = \frac{55}{88} = \boxed{\frac{5}{8}}$$

Lesson: The following explains why, in dividing fractions, we invert the divisor and multiply. The essence of the explanation is that in doing so we simplify the problem to one of dividing by one.

$$2\frac{3}{4} \div 4\frac{2}{5} = \frac{11}{4} \div \frac{22}{5} = \frac{\frac{11}{4}}{\frac{22}{5}} = \frac{\frac{11}{4}}{\frac{22}{5}} \times 1 = \frac{\frac{11}{4}}{\frac{22}{5}} \times \frac{\frac{5}{22}}{\frac{5}{22}}$$

$$\frac{\frac{11}{4} \times \frac{5}{22}}{\frac{22}{5} \times \frac{5}{22}} = \frac{\frac{11 \times 5}{4 \times 22}}{\frac{22 \times 5}{5 \times 22}} = \frac{\frac{55}{88}}{\frac{110}{110}} = \frac{\frac{55}{88}}{1} = \frac{55}{88} \div 1 = \frac{55}{88} = \frac{5}{8}$$

Drill and Practice:

Set 1

1. $3\frac{1}{6} \div 2\frac{4}{5} = ?$ 2. $5\frac{3}{8} \div 4\frac{1}{2} = ?$

3. $1\frac{5}{6} \div 2\frac{3}{4} = ?$ 4. $6\frac{2}{3} \div 3\frac{1}{9} = ?$

- *STOP.*
- Check your answers on page 343.
- Correct the problems you missed.
- Go on to Set 2.

Set 2

1. $2\frac{1}{12} \div 3\frac{1}{5} = ?$ 2. $3\frac{1}{8} \div 7\frac{2}{9} = ?$

3. $4\frac{7}{10} \div 6\frac{2}{5} = ?$ 4. $8\frac{4}{9} \div 2\frac{1}{6} = ?$

- *STOP.*
- Check your answers on page 343.
- Correct the problems you missed.
- Go on to Set 3 or 4.

Set 3

1. $3\frac{5}{8} \div 2\frac{5}{6} = ?$ 2. $5\frac{3}{4} \div 6\frac{1}{9} = ?$

3. $9\frac{1}{40} \div 2\frac{1}{2} = ?$ 4. $1\frac{4}{20} \div 2\frac{2}{15} = ?$

- *STOP.*
- Check your answers on page 343.
- Correct the problems you missed.
- Go on to Set 4.

Set 4

1. What times 3⅛ is 3¾?

2. A carpenter has an 8¾-foot 2×4. How many 1⅞-foot blocks can the carpenter cut?

3. How many 2¼-inch chain links in a 32-foot 5¼-inch chain?

4. You make a 22½-inch submarine sandwich. How many 4½-inch sections can you cut?

- *STOP*
- Check your answers on page 343.
- Correct the problems you missed.
- Shade box 5 opposite "division of fractions" on page xix.
- If this was the last subskill in this section you had to work on, take the test on page 200.
- If you have other subskills in this section to work on, go on to the next one.

SUBSKILL 6: Reciprocals

Problem: Form the reciprocal of $\frac{2}{3}$.

Solution: • Invert.

• Simplify.

$$\frac{2}{3} \diagbox \frac{3}{2} = \boxed{1\frac{1}{2}}$$

Lesson: The reciprocal of N is $\frac{1}{N}$ or $1 \div N$.

Thus the reciprocal of $\frac{2}{3}$ is $1 \div \frac{2}{3} = 1 \times \frac{3}{2} = \frac{3}{2}$.

Drill and Practice:

Set 1

Form the reciprocals.

1. $\frac{4}{5}$ 2. $\frac{1}{7}$ 3. 8   4. $3\frac{1}{2}$ 5. $4\frac{2}{7}$

- *STOP.*
- Check your answers on page 343.
- Correct the problems you missed.
- Go on to Set 2.

Set 2

Form the reciprocals.

1. $\frac{3}{4}$ 2. $\frac{1}{2}$ 3. 10   4. $1\frac{5}{8}$ 5. $6\frac{2}{3}$

- *STOP.*
- Check your answers on page 343.
- Correct the problems you missed.
- Go on to Set 3 or 4.

Set 3

Form the reciprocals.

1. $\frac{2}{3}$ 2. $\frac{1}{5}$ 3. 12   4. $2\frac{1}{9}$ 5. $5\frac{5}{6}$

- *STOP.*
- Check your answers on page 343.
- Correct the problems you missed.
- Go on to Set 4.

Set 4

1. What do you get when you push the nine button and the $1/N$ button on a pocket calculator?

2. What do you get when you multiply a number by its reciprocal?

3. How does the reciprocal of a number compare to the multiplicative inverse of the number?

4. What is the reciprocal of the reciprocal of a number?

5. What is the reciprocal of zero?

- *STOP*
- Check your answers on page 343.
- Correct the problems you missed.
- Shade box 6 opposite "division of fractions" on page xix.
- Take the test on page 200.

Inventory Post Test for
Division of Fractions

1. $\frac{5}{6} \div \frac{3}{10} = ?$ 2. $\frac{4}{5} \div 2 = ?$ 3. $3\frac{5}{9} \div \frac{3}{8} = ?$

4. $5\frac{1}{2} \div 3 = ?$ 5. $4\frac{5}{6} \div 1\frac{1}{12} = ?$ 6. What is the reciprocal of $\frac{5}{8}$?

- *STOP*

- Check your answers with the instructor.

- As before, work through the subskills in this section which correspond to the problems you missed, except work the *even* drill-and-practice problems.

- Take the test on page 201.

General Survey Tests for Fractions, Decimals, and Percents

General Survey Post Test
for
Fractions

1. Which is divided into sixths?

a. b. c.

2. Which illustrates five-eighths or $\frac{5}{8}$?

a. b. c.

3. Two small squares for every two large squares: What ratio makes this comparison?

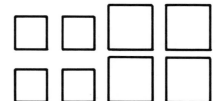

$\frac{2}{2} = 1$

4. For each fraction in row A, find one or more equivalent fractions in row B.

Row A: $\frac{2}{5}$ $\frac{8}{24}$ $\frac{3}{4}$

Row B: $\frac{1}{3}$ $\frac{12}{30}$ $\frac{16}{48}$ $\frac{12}{16}$

5. For each improper fraction or mixed number in row A, find an equivalent improper fraction or mixed number in row B.

$$\text{Row A:} \qquad 2\frac{1}{3} \qquad 1\frac{2}{3} \qquad \frac{11}{4} \qquad \frac{13}{4}$$

$$\text{Row B:} \qquad 2\frac{3}{4} \qquad 3\frac{1}{4} \qquad \frac{7}{3} \qquad \frac{5}{3}$$

6. Which are equivalent to one?

a. $\dfrac{4}{5}$ b. $\dfrac{328}{328}$ c. $\dfrac{77777}{77777}$ d. $\dfrac{41654}{46154}$ e. $\dfrac{6}{6}$

7. Express 4/5, 1/8, and 7/10 in terms of their LCD or least common denominator.

8. Find the GCF or greatest common factor of 18 and 30.

9. $\dfrac{1}{12} + \dfrac{5}{12} = ?$ 10. $\dfrac{1}{6} + \dfrac{7}{8} = ?$ 11. $4\dfrac{3}{4} + 1\dfrac{2}{5} = ?$

12. $\dfrac{7}{8} - \dfrac{5}{8} = ?$ 13. $\dfrac{7}{12} - \dfrac{3}{10} = ?$ 14. $6\dfrac{2}{3} - 1\dfrac{4}{5} = ?$

15. $\dfrac{3}{8} \times \dfrac{4}{9} = ?$ 16. $8 \times \dfrac{3}{4} = ?$ 17. $2\dfrac{1}{2} \times 3\dfrac{3}{5} = ?$

18. $\dfrac{4}{6} \div \dfrac{8}{9} = ?$ 19. $4\dfrac{4}{5} \div 8 = ?$ 20. $1\dfrac{1}{6} \div 2\dfrac{5}{8} = ?$

- *STOP*
- Check your answers with the instructor.
- Enter the number correct and today's date in the spaces provided on page XX.
- Figure your growth and take pleasure in it.
- If you got 18 or more right, take the test on page 203.
- If you got less than 18 right, take the inventory pretests for fractions again beginning with the one on page 95.
- As before, work through the subskills which correspond to the problems you miss.

General Survey Pretest
for
Decimals and Percents

1. Convert 12.225 to a mixed number.

2. Convert $8\frac{4}{7}$ to a decimal to the nearest tenth.

3. 47.083 + 21.6 + 15 + 34.27 = ?

4. 317.9 × 4.53 = ?

5. Determine 4.09 ÷ .017 to the nearest hundredth.

6. Convert $\frac{7}{11}$ to a percent.

7. Convert 416.05% to a decimal.

8. Five and one-half percent of 350 is what number?

9. What percent of 300 is 85?

10. Twenty-eight percent of what number is 50?

- *STOP*
- Check your answers on page 343.
- Enter the number correct and today's date in the spaces provided on page XX.
- If you got nine or more right, take the test on page 266.
- If you got less than nine right, take the test on page 203.

SKILL
Working with Decimals

Inventory Pretest for
Working with Decimals

1. Write the decimal.

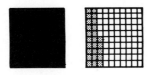

2. Write the verbal equivalent of 317.049.

3. Which exhibit unnecessary zeros?

   a. 300   b. 30.0   c. 3.00   d. .300   e. .030   f. .003

4. Which indicates the preciseness of the measurement of the distance from *A* to *B*?

   a. 7   b. .7   c. .70   d. .700

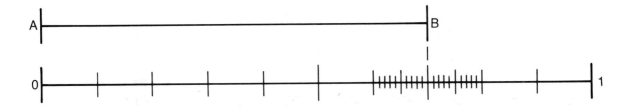

5. Convert 31.35 to a mixed number.

6. Round 7.172 to the nearest tenth.

7. Convert $12\frac{3}{7}$ to a decimal to the nearest thousandth.

8. $173.489 + 21.06 + 519 + 3.7 = ?$

9. $4038.5 - 619.382 = ?$

10. $408.9 \times 3.51 = ?$

11. Determine $6.17 \div .08$ to the nearest hundredth.

12. $15.025 \div 1000 = ?$

13. Convert $\frac{101}{110}$ to a repeating decimal.

14. Convert $.\overline{50} = .505050\ldots$ to a fraction.

- *STOP*

- Check your answers on page 343.

- Shade the boxes opposite "working with decimals" on page xix which correspond to the problems you got right.

- If you got all of them right, take the test on page 247.

- If you missed some of them, start working on the subskills in this section which correspond to the ones you missed.

- For each subskill, look at the example, study the solution, think about the lesson, and work the *odd* drill-and-practice problems.

SUBSKILL 1: Meaning of Decimal

Problem: Write the decimal.

Solution:
- Write whole number part.

- Put decimal point after whole number part.

- Regard fraction part as tenths, hundredths, thousandths, or the like.

- Write *numerator* of fraction part using one digit if tenths, two digits if hundredths, three digits if thousandths, and so on.

- If necessary, fill in with zeros to right of decimal point to get required number of digits.

> 3.08

Lesson: A decimal is an extension of our base-ten system of numeration. The digits to the *left* of a decimal point denote tens, hundreds, thousands, and so on in *ascending order,* and the digits to the *right* of a decimal point denote tenths, hundredths, thousandths, and so on in *descending* order.

Drill and Practice:

Set 1

1. Write the decimal.

2. Write the decimal.

3. Shade 1.3 of the squares.

4. Shade 2.45 of the squares.

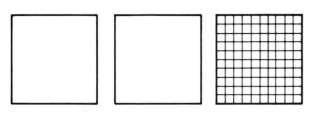

- *STOP.*
- Check your answers on page 343.
- Correct the problems you missed.
- Go on to Set 2.

Set 2

1. Write the decimal.

2. Write the decimal.

3. Shade 2.7 of the squares.

4. Shade 1.04 of the squares.

- *STOP.*
- Check your answers on page 344.
- Correct the problems you missed.
- Go on to Set 3 or 4.

Set 3

1. Write the decimal.

2. Write the decimal.

3. Shade 1.9 of the squares.

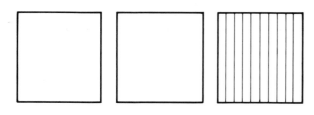

4. Shade 2.53 of the squares.

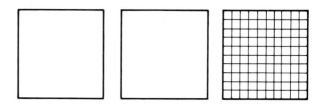

- *STOP.*
- Check your answers on page 344.
- Correct the problems you missed.
- Go on to Set 4.

Set 4

1. How many dollars, dimes, and pennies in $4.37?

2. How many meters, decimeters, centimeters, and millimeters in 3.045 meters?

3. Which is more, $1.10 or $1.01?

4. Which is longer, 1.01 meters or 1.001 meters?

5. Write the decimal for the indicated length in meters.

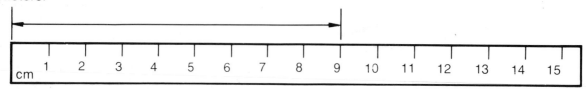

6. Indicate .12 meters.

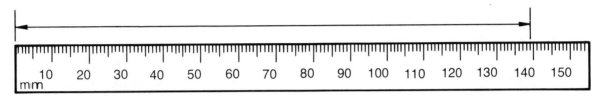

7. Write the decimal for the indicated length in meters.

8. Indicate .117 meters.

- *STOP*

- Check your answers on page 344.

- Correct the problems you missed.

- Shade box 1 opposite "working with decimals" on page xix.

- If this was the only subskill you had to work on in this section, take the test on page 244.

- If you have other subskills to work on in this section, go on to the next one.

SUBSKILL 2: Decimals and Their Verbal Equivalents

Problem: Write the verbal equivalent of 23.045.

Solution:
- Express digits to left of decimal point as whole number.

- Express decimal point as *and.*

- Express digits to right of decimal point as whole number of tenths, hundredths, thousandths, and so on, depending on position of last digit.

> Twenty-three and 45 thousandths

Lesson: .7 or seven-tenths
.06 or six-hundredths
.305 or 305 thousandths
4.9 or four and nine-tenths
5.17 or five and 17 hundredths
2.139 or two and 139 thousandths
91.4 or 91 and four-tenths
87.21 or 87 and 21 hundredths
23.045 or 23 and 45 thousandths
700.8 or 700 and eight-tenths
609.42 or 609 and 42 hundredths
928.003 or 928 and three-thousandths
1465.3907 or 1465 and 3907 ten-thousandths

Drill and Practice:

Set 1

1. Write the verbal equivalents of

    (a) .7   (b) .18   (c) 18.8   (d) 1.49

2. Give the decimals for
    (a) three-tenths

    (b) 117 and 33 thousandths

    (c) 58 hundredths

- *STOP.*
- Check your answers on page 344.
- Correct the problems you missed.
- Go on to Set 2.

Set 2

1. Write the verbal equivalents of

    (a) .9   (b) .203   (c) 203.6   (d) 3.456

2. Give the decimals for

    (a) one and eight-tenths

    (b) 203 and 75 hundredths

    (c) 35 and 136 thousandths

- *STOP.*
- Check your answers on page 344.
- Correct the problems you missed.
- Go on to Set 3 or 4.

Set 3

1. Write the verbal equivalents of

    (a) .36 (b) .408 (c) 1056.23 (d) 290.351

2. Give the decimals for

    (a) 20 and three-hundredths

    (b) 351 and eight-tenths

    (c) 42 and 402 thousandths

- *STOP.*
- Check your answers on page 344.
- Correct the problems you missed.
- Go on to Set 4.

Set 4

1. Finish writing the check.

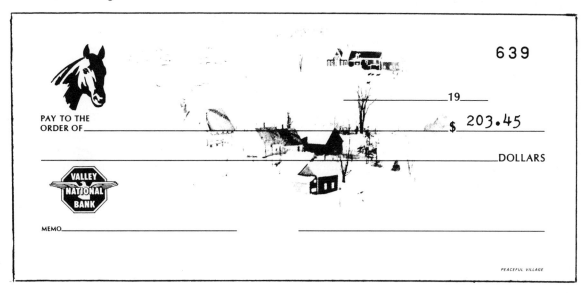

2. Finish writing the check.

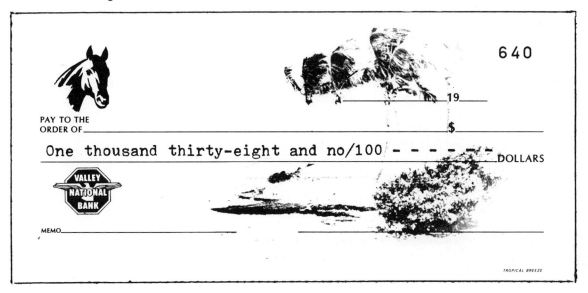

3. How would a meteorologist announce .07 inches of rainfall?

4. How would a surveyor record 25 thousandths of an inch?

- *STOP*

- Check your answers on page 344.

- Correct the problems you missed.

- Shade box 2 opposite "working with decimals" on page xix.

- If this was the last subskill you had to work on in this section, take the test on page 244.

- If you have other subskills to work on in this section, go on to the next one.

SUBSKILL 3: Unnecessary Zeros

Problem: Which exhibit unnecessary zeros?

    a. 500 b. 50.0 c. 5.00 d. .500

    e. .050 f. .005 g. \$.50 h. \$.05

    i. \$.500 j. \$5.00

Solution: | b, c, d, e, and i | Decimals with terminal zeros to the right of a decimal point exhibit unnecessary zeros unless the zeros indicate the preciseness of a measurement or zero dimes or pennies.

Lesson: 50.0 = 50 because fifty and zero tenths means the same as just fifty.

5.00 = 5 because five and zero hundredths means the same as just five.

.500 = .5 because $\frac{500}{1000} = \frac{5}{10}$.

.050 = .05 because $\frac{50}{1000} = \frac{5}{100}$.

\$.500 = \$.50 because five dimes, zero pennies, and zero mills (tenths of a penny) is the same amount of money as five dimes, zero pennies.

Note: Some nice people would say that a decimal like 0.5 with a single zero before the decimal point exhibits an unnecessary zero because the zero indicates nothing more than zero ones. Other nice people would say that the zero is necessary to emphasize the use of the decimal point. Both are correct. You pays your money, you takes your choice.

Drill and Practice:

Set 1

1. Which exhibit unnecessary zeros?

    a. 70   b. 7.0   c. .70   d. .07

    e. \$.70   f. \$.07

2. Which are equivalent to .370?

    a. .037 b. .307 c. .37 d. .3700

- *STOP.*
- Check your answers on page 344.
- Correct the problems you missed.
- Go on to Set 2.

Set 2

1. Which exhibit unnecessary zeros?

    a. 130   b. 13.0   c. 1.30   d. .130

    e. \$1.30   f. \$.130

2. Which are equivalent to 5.900?

    a. 5.009 b. 5.09 c. 5.90 d. 5.9

- *STOP.*
- Check your answers on page 344.
- Correct the problems you missed.
- Go on to Set 3 or 4.

Set 3

1. Which exhibit unnecessary zeros?

    a. 8   b. 8.0   c. 8.00   d. 8.000

    e. $8.00   f. $8.0

2. Which are equivalent to 43.50?

    a. 43.5 b. 43.500 c. 43.05 d. 43.005

- *STOP.*
- Check your answers on page 344.
- Correct the problems you missed.
- Go on to Set 4.

Set 4

1. Why the emphasis on unnecessary zeros?

- *STOP*

- Check your answers on page 344.

- Correct the problems you missed.

- Shade box 3 opposite "working with decimals" on page xix.

- If this was the last subskill you had to work on in this section, take the test on page 244.

- If you have other subskills to work on in this section, go on to the next one.

SUBSKILL 4: Measurements to the Nearest Tenths, Hundredths, and Thousandths

Problem: Which indicates the preciseness of the measurement of the distance from *A* to *C*?

    a. 8   b. .8   c. .80   d. .800

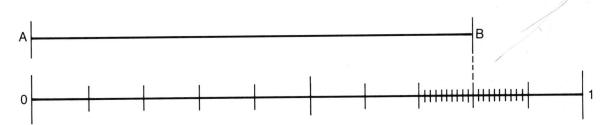

Solution: [c] The distance is graduated in tenths and tenths of tenths or hundredths.

Lesson: Terminal zeros to the right of a decimal point are retained if they indicate the preciseness of a measurement.

Drill and Practice:

Set 1

1. Which indicates the preciseness of the measurement of the distance from *A* to *B*?

a. .300   b. .30   c. .3   d. 3

2. What decimal indicates the preciseness of the measurement of the distance from *C* to *D*?

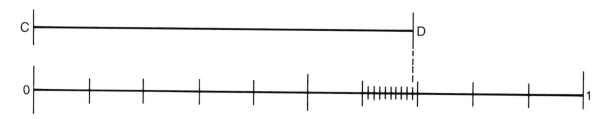

3. Which indicates the most precise measurement?

a. 7   b. 7.0   c. 7.00   d. 7.000

- *STOP.*
- Check your answers on page 344.
- Correct the problems you missed.
- Go on to Set 2.

Set 2

1. Which indicates the preciseness of the measurement of the distance from *A* to *B*?

a. .77   b. 7.7   c. .770   d. .077

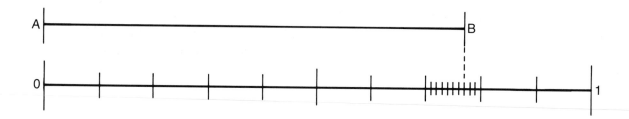

2. What decimal indicates the preciseness of the measurement of the distance from C to D?

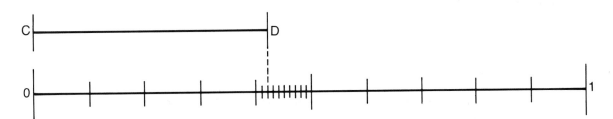

3. Which indicates the most precise measurement?

   a. 43   b. 4.3   c. 4.03   d. 4.003

- *STOP.*
- Check your answers on page 344.
- Correct the problems you missed.
- Go on to Set 3 or 4.

Set 3

1. Which indicates the preciseness of the measurement of the distance from A to B? (Note: the distance from A to B is less than .1.)

   a. 9   b. .90   c. .09   d. .090

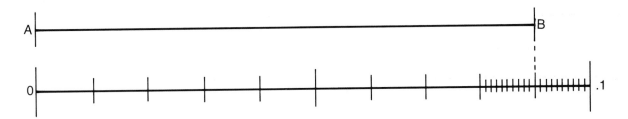

2. What decimal indicates the preciseness of the measurement of the distance from C to D? (Note: the distance from C to D is less than .1.)

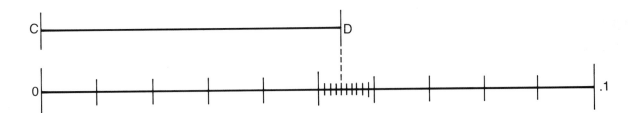

3. Which indicates the most precise measurement?

   a. 71   b. 7.1   c. .71   d. .071

- *STOP.*
- Check your answers on page 344.
- Correct the problems you missed.
- Go on to Set 4.

Set 4

1. Which measurements could have been made with a meter stick graduated in centimeters?

   a. 4.3 m b. 13 cm c. 2.72 m d. 3.125 m

   e. 20 mm

2. Which measurements could have been made with a meter stick graduated in millimeters?

   a. 2.305 m b. 3.7 cm c. 45 mm d. 7.5 mm

   e. 5.80 cm

3. How long is the following measurement?

   a. 3.6 m b. 3.56 m c. 3.560 m d. 3.561 m

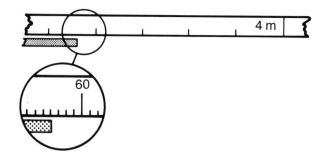

4. Which measurements could have been made with a micrometer calibrated in .01 millimeter increments?

   a. 4.03 mm   b. 4.30 mm   c. 7 mm

   d. 7.1 mm e. 9.037 mm f. 12.421 mm

- *STOP*

- Check your answers on page 344.

- Correct the problems you missed.

- Shade box 4 opposite "working with decimals" on page xix.

- If this was the last subskill you had to work on in this section, take the test on page 244.

- If you have other subskills to work on in this section, go on to the next one.

SUBSKILL 5: Converting Decimals to Fractions and Mixed Numbers

Problem: Convert .06 to a fraction.

Solution: • Sound out verbal equivalent of decimal.

.06 is sounded out as "six-hundredths," written as

$$\frac{6}{100},$$

- Write what is heard as fraction or mixed number.

- Simplify.

and simplified to $\boxed{\dfrac{3}{50}}$

Lesson: .7 or seven-tenths or $\frac{7}{10}$

.06 or six-hundredths or $\frac{6}{100} = \frac{3}{50}$

.305 or 305 thousandths or $\frac{305}{1000} = \frac{61}{200}$

4.9 or four and nine-tenths or $4\frac{9}{10}$

5.17 or five and 17 hundredths or $5\frac{17}{100}$

2.139 or two and 139 thousandths or $2\frac{139}{1000}$

91.4 or 91 and four-tenths or $91\frac{4}{10} = 91\frac{2}{5}$

87.20 or 87 and 20 hundredths or $87\frac{20}{100} = 87\frac{1}{5}$

23.045 or 23 and 45 thousandths or $23\frac{45}{1000} = 23\frac{9}{200}$

700.8 or 700 and eight-tenths or $700\frac{8}{10} = 700\frac{4}{5}$

609.42 or 609 and 42 hundredths or $609\frac{42}{100} = 609\frac{21}{50}$

928.003 or 928 and three-thousandths or $928\frac{3}{1000}$

1465.3907 or 1465 and 3907 ten-thousandths or $1465\frac{3907}{10000}$

Drill and Practice:

Set 1
Convert to fractions or mixed numbers.

1. .6   2. 5.7   3. 42.19   4. 103.408

- *STOP.*
- Check your answers on page 344.
- Correct the problems you missed.
- Go on to Set 2.

Set 2
Convert to fractions or mixed numbers.

1. .5   2. 3.20   3. 51.81   4. 342.125

- *STOP.*
- Check your answers on page 344.
- Correct the problems you missed.
- Go on to Set 3 or 4.

Set 3
Convert to fractions or mixed numbers.

1. .3   2. 1.25   3. 62.500   4. 909.312

- *STOP.*
- Check your answers on page 344.
- Correct the problems you missed.
- Go on to Set 4.

Set 4

1. Why the emphasis on converting decimals to fractions and mixed numbers?

- *STOP*

- Check your answers on page 344.

- Correct the problems you missed.

- Shade box 6 opposite "working with decimals" on page xix.

- If this was the last subskill you had to work on in this section, take the test on page 244.

- If you have other subskills to work on in this section, go on to the next one.

SUBSKILL 6: Rounding Decimals

Problem: Round 472.3564 to the nearest thousandth.

- Leave digit alone if digit to immediate right is less than five.

- Make zeros out of digits to right.

- Drop unnecessary zeros.

Solution: • Pinpoint digit.

- Increase digit by one if digit to immediate right is greater than or equal to five.

472.3564 ⟶ 472.356④ ⟶ 472.356 ⟶ 472.356

Lesson:

Decimal	Rounded to nearest thousand	Rounded to nearest hundred	Rounded to nearest ten	Rounded to nearest whole number
7035	7000	7000	7040	7035
4807.9	5000	4800	4810	4808
5460.37	5000	5500	5460	5460
807	1000	800	810	807
984.6	1000	1000	980	985
121.34		100	120	121
37			40	37
8.3			10	8
.6				1

Decimal	Rounded to nearest whole number	Rounded to nearest tenth	Rounded to nearest hundredth	Rounded to nearest thousandth
.7				1
.7	1	.7		
.06		.1	.06	
.305		.3	.31	.305
4.9	5	4.9		
5.17	5	5.2	5.17	
2.139	2	2.1	2.14	2.139
87.23	87	87.2	87.23	
928.003	928	928.0	928.00	928.003
1465.3907	1465	1465.4	1465.39	1465.391

Drill and Practice:

Set 1

1. Round .875 to the nearest
   (a) whole number
   (b) tenth
   (c) hundredth

2. Round 314.3629 to the nearest
   (a) hundred
   (b) whole number
   (c) hundredth
   (d) thousandth

- *STOP.*
- Check your answers on page 344.
- Correct the problems you missed.
- Go on to Set 2.

Set 2

1. Round 4.362 to the nearest
   (a) whole number
   (b) tenth
   (c) hundredth

2. Round 803.5276 to the nearest
   (a) thousand
   (b) ten
   (c) tenth
   (d) thousandth

- *STOP.*
- Check your answers on page 345.
- Correct the problems you missed.
- Go on to Set 3 or 4.

Set 3

1. Round .183 to the nearest
   (a) whole number
   (b) tenth
   (c) hundredth

2. Round 8125.65 to the nearest
   (a) thousand
   (b) hundred
   (c) whole number
   (d) tenth

- *STOP.*
- Check your answers on page 345.
- Correct the problems you missed.
- Go on to Set 4.

Set 4

1. The printout on a pocket calculator is 48.937498. It refers to money. What should you write down?

2. According to the *Guinness Book of World Records,* the world's biggest wiener was the one displayed in Central Park, New York City, on August 13, 1976. It weighed 1776 ounces. How many ounces to the nearest hundred ounces was that?

3. According to the *Guinness Book of World Records,* the world's deepest mine is the Western Deep Levels Mine in Carletonville, South Africa. It is 12,600 feet deep. How many feet to the nearest thousand feet is that?

4. According to the *Guinness Book of World Records,* the world's tallest monument is the stainless steel Gateway Arch in St. Louis, Missouri. It stands 630 feet tall. How many feet to the nearest hundred feet is that?

- *STOP*

- Check your answers on page 344.

- Correct the problems you missed.

- Shade box 6 opposite "working with decimals" on page xix.

- If this was the last subskill you had to work on in this section, take the test on page 244.

- If you have other subskills to work on in this section, go on to the next one.

SUBSKILL 7: Converting Fractions and Mixed Numbers to Decimals

Problem: Convert $\frac{3}{7}$ to a decimal to the nearest thousandth.

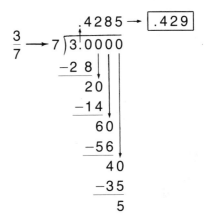

Solution:
- Add decimal point and two zeros to numerator if to nearest tenth, three zeros if to nearest hundredth, four zeros if to nearest thousandth, and so on.

- Divide denominator into numerator.

- Round to next to last digit.

Lesson: The fraction a/b can be thought of as $a \div b$.

Drill and Practice:

Set 1

Convert to decimals to the nearest thousandth.

1. $\frac{7}{25}$ 2. $3\frac{4}{5}$ 3. $\frac{4}{7}$ 4. $5\frac{3}{8}$

- *STOP.*
- Check your answers on page 345.
- Correct the problems you missed.
- Go on to Set 2.

Set 2

Convert to decimals to the nearest hundredth.

1. $\frac{9}{20}$ 2. $5\frac{1}{2}$ 3. $\frac{3}{11}$ 4. $1\frac{2}{3}$

- *STOP.*
- Check your answers on page 345.
- Correct the problems you missed.
- Go on to Set 3 or 4.

Set 3

Convert to decimals to the nearest tenth.

1. $\frac{43}{125}$ 2. $3\frac{19}{50}$ 3. $\frac{8}{13}$ 4. $15\frac{11}{12}$

- *STOP.*
- Check your answers on page 345.
- Correct the problems you missed.
- Go on to Set 4.

Set 4

1. Why the emphasis on converting fractions and mixed numbers to decimals?

- *STOP*

- Check your answers on page **345.**

- Correct the problems you missed.

- Shade box 7 opposite "working with decimals" on page **xix.**

- If this was the last subskill you had to work on in this section, take the test on page **244.**

- If you have other subskills to work on in this section, go on to the next one.

SUBSKILL 8: Adding Decimals

Problem: 848.235 + 12.04 + 173 + 2.9 = ?

Solution: • Line up decimal points.

 • Add.

 • Put decimal point in sum in line with other decimal points.

$$
\begin{array}{r}
①①① \\
8\ 4\ 8\ .\ 2\ 3\ 5 \\
1\ 2\ .\ 0\ 4 \\
1\ 7\ 3 \\
+\qquad 2\ .\ 9 \\
\hline
\boxed{1\ 0\ 3\ 6\ .\ 1\ 7\ 5}
\end{array}
$$

Lesson:

	Thousands	Hundreds	Tens	Ones	Tenths	Hundredths	Thousandths
	1←	1←	1←	1←			
		8	4	8	2	3	5
			1	2	0	4	
		1	7	3			
+				2	9		
		①	①	①	①		
	1	0	3	6	1	7	5

Drill and Practice:

Set 1

1. 308.6 + 42.71 + 1.983 = ?

2. 981.85 + 183 + 307.16 = ?

3. 1.86 + 2.543 = ?   4. 17.2   5. 168.6
                          32.73   48.7
                        + 5.96   307.9
                                      +408

- *STOP.*
- Check your answers on page 345.
- Correct the problems you missed.
- Go on to Set 2.

Set 2

1. 417.9 + 8.159 + 32.16 = ?

2. 503 + 417.22 + 100.18 = ?

3. 3.952 + .821 = ?   4. 21.3   5. 216.7
                          8.7   94.2
                        +51.92   316.3
                                     + 6.2

- *STOP.*
- Check your answers on page 345.
- Correct the problems you missed.
- Go on to Set 3 or 4.

Set 3

1. 5.9438 + 17.1 + 8.563 = ?
2. 3.1515 + 307.28 + 900 = ?
3. .9832 + 14.3 = ?

```
4.  13.27      5.     7.6
         5            18
    +28.2           407.9
                   +   3
```

- *STOP.*
- Check your answers on page 345.
- Correct the problems you missed.
- Go on to Set 4.

Set 4

1. What was the original cost of the carpeting?

Come in today, and save $3.00 on SoftCarpets. Now just $8.99

2. Figure the cost for one medium thin pork and pepperoni pizza and one large thick supreme cheese pizza.

Thin

The original, nationally-famous pizza. Specially formulated to have light, crisp crust, covered edge to edge with our unique and tangy sauce, Mozzarella cheese, and generous amounts of whatever toppings you desire.

TOPPINGS	SMALL (serves 1-2)	MED. (serves 2-3)	LARGE (serves 3-4)
Pizza Supreme	$2.90	$4.10	$5.50
Cheese, Pork, Mushrooms, Pepperoni, Onions, Green Peppers			
Pork/Pepperoni/ Mushroom	2.90	4.10	5.50
Mushroom/Pork/ Black Olive	2.90	4.10	5.50
Pepperoni/Mushroom/ Green Pepper	2.90	4.10	5.50
Pork and Mushroom	2.60	3.70	5.00
Beef and Onion	2.60	3.70	5.00
Pepperoni and Black Olive	2.60	3.70	5.00
Pork and Pepperoni	2.60	3.70	5.00
Pepperoni	2.30	3.30	4.50
Beef	2.30	3.30	4.50
Pork (Ground)	2.30	3.30	4.50
Italian Sausage	2.30	3.30	4.50
Ham	2.30	3.30	4.50
Mushroom	2.30	3.30	4.50
Black Olive	2.30	3.30	4.50
Green Pepper	2.00	2.90	4.00
Onion	2.00	2.90	4.00
Jalapeno	2.00	2.90	4.00
Green Chile	2.00	2.90	4.00
Deluxe Cheese	1.70	2.50	3.50

Thick

A special Pizza recipe for those who prefer a thicker crust and a chewy, cheesy, taste. Covered with a generous portion of Mozzarella cheese, delicate sauce, and a generous covering of your favorite topping.

TOPPINGS	SMALL (serves 1-2)	MED. (serves 2-3)	LARGE (serves 3-4)
Pizza Supreme	$3.30	$4.95	$6.55
Cheese, Pork, Mushrooms, Pepperoni, Onions, Green Peppers			
Pork/Pepperoni/ Mushroom	3.30	4.95	6.55
Mushroom/Pork/ Black Olive	3.30	4.95	6.55
Pepperoni/Mushroom/ Green Pepper	3.30	4.95	6.55
Pork and Mushroom	3.00	4.55	6.05
Beef and Onion	3.00	4.55	6.05
Pepperoni and Black Olive	3.00	4.55	6.05
Pork and Pepperoni	3.00	4.55	6.05
Pepperoni	2.70	4.15	5.55
Beef	2.70	4.15	5.55
Pork (Ground)	2.70	4.15	5.55
Italian Sausage	2.70	4.15	5.55
Ham	2.70	4.15	5.55
Mushroom	2.70	4.15	5.55
Black Olive	2.70	4.15	5.55
Green Pepper	2.40	3.75	5.05
Onion	2.40	3.75	5.05
Jalapeno	2.40	3.75	5.05
Green Chile	2.40	3.75	5.05
Deluxe Cheese	2.10	3.35	4.55

3. How much for one ice chest and one sleeping bag?

ICE CHEST

5⁹⁹

Lightweight & compact. Keeps food cold for hours. Molded carry handle.

3 LB. SLEEP BAG

7⁷⁷

Heavy nylon shell. Flannel lining. Full zipper and bag is washable.

4. Balance the check register.

CHECK NO.	DATE	CHECK ISSUED TO	AMOUNT OF CHECK		DATE OF DEP.	AMOUNT OF DEPOSIT		BALANCE	
						BALANCE BROUGHT FORWARD ➤		4855	95
612	7/24	A & P	62	37				62	37
								4793	58
613	7/27	SHELL OIL	85	02				85	02
								4708	56
		DEPOSIT			8/1	5493	48		

5. Complete the deposit slip.

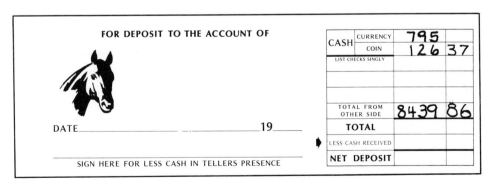

FOR DEPOSIT TO THE ACCOUNT OF

DATE_____ 19_____

SIGN HERE FOR LESS CASH IN TELLERS PRESENCE

CASH	CURRENCY	**795**	
	COIN	**126**	**37**
LIST CHECKS SINGLY			
TOTAL FROM OTHER SIDE		**8439**	**86**
TOTAL			
➤ LESS CASH RECEIVED			
NET DEPOSIT			

6. The following array of numbers is called a magic square. To see why, add the numbers in each row, each column, and along both diagonals.

2.3	2.4	1.9
1.8	2.2	2.6
2.5	2	2.1

7. How far is it across all four coins?

├── 2.4 cm ──┤├── 2.1 cm ──┤├── 1.9 cm ──┤├── 1.8 cm ──┤

8. Total the check.

#	ITEMS	1	2	3	4	5	$	C
	H' BURGERS	.35	.70	1.05	1.40	1.75		
	C' BURGERS	.40	.80	1.20	1.60	2.00		
I	DBL. HAM	.65	1.30	1.95	2.60	3.25		
	DBL. CHEESE	.75	1.50	2.25	3.00	3.75		
	Q H' BG	.75	1.50	2.25	3.00	3.75		
	Q C' BG	.85	1.70	2.55	3.40	4.25		
	FILET	.60	1.20	1.80	2.40	3.00		
3	BIG BURGERS	.85	1.70	2.55	3.40	4.25		
4	FRIES L.	.45	.90	1.35	1.80	2.25		
	FRIES S.	.30	.60	.90	1.20	1.50		
I	APPLE/CHERRY PIE	.30	.60	.90	1.20	1.50		
	COOKIES	.20	.40	.60	.80	1.00		
3	C - SHAKES	.45	.90	1.35	1.80	2.25		
	S - SHAKES	.45	.90	1.35	1.80	2.25		
	V - SHAKES	.45	.90	1.35	1.80	2.25		
	COLA SM.	.25	.50	.75	1.00	1.25		
	COLA M.	.30	.60	.90	1.20	1.50		
	COLA L.	.40	.80	1.20	1.60	2.00		
	ORANGE SM.	.25	.50	.75	1.00	1.25		
	ORANGE M.	.30	.60	.90	1.20	1.50		
	ORANGE L.	.40	.80	1.20	1.60	2.00		
	R' BEER SM.	.25	.50	.75	1.00	1.25		
	R' BEER M.	.30	.60	.90	1.20	1.50		
I	R'BEER L.	.40	.80	1.20	1.60	2.00		
	MILK	.25	.50	.75	1.00	1.25		
	O.J./HOT CHOC.	.25	.50	.75	1.00	1.25		
	COFFEE SM C/S	.25	.50	.75	1.00	1.25		
	SC. EGGS W/MUFFIN	.49	.98	1.47	1.96	2.45		
	EGG & MUFFIN	.85	1.70	2.55	3.40	4.25		
	SAUSAGE & EGGS	.99	1.98	2.97	3.96	4.95		
	MUFFINS	.25	.50	.75	1.00	1.25		
	H' CAKES & SAUS.	.90	1.80	2.70	3.60	4.50		
	HOT CAKES	.39	.78	1.17	1.56	1.95		
2	DONUTS	.20	.40	.60	.80	1.00		
I	BROWNIES	.35	.70	1.05	1.40	1.75		

☐ Qtr Dbl K M Pi O Ch Pl　　SUB

☐ Qtr Dbl K M Pi O Ch Pl　　TAX　　| 39

☐ M S L Pi O Ch Pl　　TOTAL

☐ Filet Ts Ch K M Pl

NAME_____

- *STOP*

- Check your answers on page 345.

- Correct the problems you missed.

- Shade box 8 opposite "working with decimals" on page xix.

- If this was the last subskill you had to work on in this section, take the test on page 244.

- If you have other subskills to work on in this section, go on to the next one.

SUBSKILL 9: Subtracting Decimals

Problem: 1382.9 − 715.453 = ?

Solution:
- Line up decimal points.

- Subtract.

- Fill in to right of decimal point with zeros.

- Put decimal point in difference in line with other decimal points.

⑨

```
 0 13 7 12  8 10 10
 1  3  8  2 . 9  0  0
−   7  1  5 . 4  5  3
 ┌─────────────────┐
 │ 6  6  7 . 4  4  7 │
 └─────────────────┘
```

Lesson:

Thousands	Hundreds	Tens	Ones	Tenths	Hundredths	Thousandths
0 / 1	13 / 3	7 / 8	12 / 2	8 / 9	9 / 10 / 0	10 / 0
−	7	1	5	4	5	3
	6	6	7	4	4	7

Drill and Practice:

Set 1

1. 4815.3 − 208.159 = ?

2. 232.14 − 106.281 = ?

3. 17.132 − 4.71 = ?

4. 8001.9
   −   17.823
   ———————

5.   23.4128
   −   1.5
   ———————

- *STOP.*
- Check your answers on page 345.
- Correct the problems you missed.
- Go on to Set 2.

Set 2

1. 23.582 − 17.6291 = ?

2. 8857 − 4660.3105 = ?

3. 183.1 − 66.92 = ?

4. 4125.873
   − 257.48
   ———————

5.   15.38
   − 10.4872
   ———————

- *STOP.*
- Check your answers on page 345.
- Correct the problems you missed.
- Go on to Set 3 or 4.

Set 3

1. 387.28 − 123.608 = ?

2. 300.9 − 273.8005 = ?

3. 48.375 − 27.9 = ?

4. 382.0055
   − 100.25
   ———————

5.   28.3504
   −   2.41
   ———————

- *STOP.*
- Check your answers on page 345.
- Correct the problems you missed.
- Go on to Set 4.

Set 4

1. Complete the deposit slip.

FOR DEPOSIT TO THE ACCOUNT OF			
	CASH	CURRENCY	327	
		COIN	28 48
	LIST CHECKS SINGLY		
	TOTAL FROM OTHER SIDE	807 96
DATE_____19____	TOTAL	1163 44
	LESS CASH RECEIVED	285 95
SIGN HERE FOR LESS CASH IN TELLERS PRESENCE	NET DEPOSIT	

2. Complete the receipt.

No. _____   19 ____

Received of   _____

_____ **Dollars**
                                                          100

Amt of Account	1432	85
Amt Paid	575	49
Balance Due		

$ _____   _____

3. Balance the check register.

CHECK NO	DATE	CHECK ISSUED TO	AMOUNT OF CHECK		DATE OF DEP	AMOUNT OF DEPOSIT		BALANCE	
			BALANCE BROUGHT FORWARD ➤					428	95
501	6/20	SAFEWAY	62	12				62	12
								366	83
502	7/1	PENNEYS	91	25				91	25
								275	58
503	7/3	MASTER CHARGE	85	95					

4. You drove around a city block. The odometer on your car read 48,027.6 when you left. It read 48,028.2 when you returned. How far around the block was it?

5. The land speed record in 1904 was 91.370 miles per hour held by Henry Ford. The land speed record in 1970 was 622.407 miles per hour held by Gary Gabelich. How much faster was Gabelich's speed than Ford's speed?

6. Figure the savings on the paint.

7. Figure the savings on the light adapter.

8. Figure the savings on the dress.

Long
Poly
Dress
$19.99

Reg. $25.98
Coral, yello,
jade, white,
blue. 8-16.

9. Figure the savings on the wedding special.

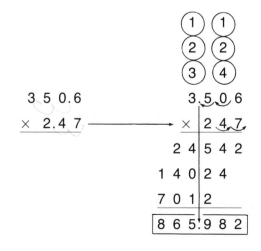

- *STOP*

- Check your answers on page 345.

- Correct the problems you missed.

- Shade box 9 opposite "working with decimals" on page xix.

- If this was the last subskill you had to work on in this section, take the test on page 244.

- If you have other subskills to work on in this section, go on to the next one.

SUBSKILL 10: Multiplying Decimals

Problem: $350.6 \times 2.47 = ?$

Solution:
- Move decimal point in multiplier to the *right* and discard.

  - Move decimal point in multiplicand to the *left* same number of places and retain.

  - Multiply.

  - Put decimal point in product directly beneath decimal point in multiplicand.

$$
\begin{array}{r}
3\ 5\ 0.6 \\
\times\ 2.4\ 7 \\
\end{array}
\longrightarrow
\begin{array}{r}
3.5\,0\ 6 \\
\times\ 2\ 4\ 7 \\
\hline
2\ 4\ 5\ 4\ 2 \\
1\ 4\ 0\ 2\ 4 \\
7\ 0\ 1\ 2 \\
\hline
8\ 6\ 5.9\ 8\ 2 \\
\end{array}
$$

Lesson: The decimal point in 2.47 was moved two places to the right to turn the number into a whole number. This had the effect of multiplying it by 100. The decimal point in 350.6 was moved two places to the left to compensate for what was done with the decimal point in 2.47. Thus the problem was left unchanged except for appearance because it was multiplied by 100/100 or one.

$$350.6 \times 2.47 = 350.6 \times 2.47 \times 1 = 350.6 \times 2.47 \times \frac{100}{100} =$$

$$350.6 \times 2.47 \times \frac{1 \times 100}{100 \times 1} = 350.6 \times 2.47 \times \frac{1}{100} \times \frac{100}{1} =$$

$$350.6 \times \frac{1}{100} \times 2.47 \times \frac{100}{1} = \frac{350.6 \times 1}{100} \times \frac{2.47 \times 100}{1} = \frac{350.6}{100} \times \frac{247}{1} = 3.506 \times 24$$

Drill and Practice:

Set 1

1. 432.9
   × 5.47

2. 512
   × .027

3. 61.4
   × .0019

4. 41.76
   × .0005

- *STOP.*
- Check your answers on page 345.
- Correct the problems you missed.
- Go on to Set 2.

Set 2

1. 781.6
   × 30.8

2. 618
   × .98

3. 2.03
   × .046

4. 3.205
   × .00417

- *STOP.*
- Check your answers on page 345.
- Correct the problems you missed.
- Go on to Set 3 or 4.

Set 3

1. 90.2
   × 431

2. 102
   × 3.7

3. .813
   × .48

4. .4001
   × .100101

- *STOP.*
- Check your answers on page 345.
- Correct the problems you missed.
- Go on to Set 4.

Set 4

1. The probability of *spinning* a tail on a relatively new penny is about .6. How many tails would you expect to get if you spun 50 such pennies?

2. To convert from inches to centimeters, multiply by 2.54. Convert to centimeters:

   (a) two inches   (d) six inches
   (b) ten inches   (e) one foot
   (c) one yard   (12 inches)
       (36 inches)   (f) 39.37 inches

3. Find the circumference of the circle using $\pi = 3.14$ and $C = \pi d$ for the circumference C of a circle of diameter d.

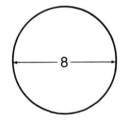

4. Figure the cost of four T-bone steaks weighing 6.35 pounds.

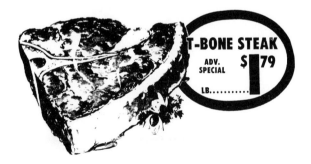

T-BONE STEAK
ADV. SPECIAL $1 79
LB..........

5. Figure the cost of 25 square yards of vinyl flooring.

12′ VINYL FLOORING
• FOAM CUSHIONED BACK!
• SHINY HI-GLOSS FINISH!
• MOST ROOMS SEAMLESS!
FROM 2 69 SQ. YD.

6. Figure your bill for renting a car for one day for 173 miles at 17 cents per mile plus $15.95 for the day.

7. Figure the bill for dinner for four people for two No. 1's, one No. 5, one No. 6, four orders of fries, one jalepeño pepper, one large order of cole slaw, two medium drinks, and two large drinks.

CHARLIE'S FRIED CHICKEN MENU

No. 1 Regular	.84		**No. 4 Large**	1.26
2 Large Pieces			3 Large Pieces	
No. 2 Regular	.94		**No. 5 Large**	1.41
2 Large Pieces—Dark			3 Large Pieces—Dark	
No. 3 Regular	.99		**No. 6 Large**	1.48
2 Large Pieces—White			3 Large Pieces—White	

Family Size	4.14	**Super Family Size**	6.19
10 Large Pieces		15 Large Pieces	
With French Fries for 3	4.96	With French Fries for 5	7.49

Dinner Pack	1.39	**Hot Fruit Pie**	.29
2 Large Pieces, French		**Pecan Pie**	.35
Fries, Jalapeño Pepper and		**Jalepeño Pepper**	.08
Cole Slaw		**Cole Slaw**	
Chicken Snack	.51	3 oz.	.29
1 Large Piece with Roll		12 oz.	.79
With French Fries	.75	**Drinks** .17–.27–.37	
French Fries	.29		

8. From the menu on the next page, figure the bill for dinner for six people for one No. 1, two No. 2's, two No. 6's, one No. 7, four small orders of slaw, two lemon tarts, one large drink, two regular drinks, and three cups of coffee.

Special Seafoods

NO. 1 2 Fish & Chips	1.69
NO. 2 2 Fish, Chips & Slaw	1.99
NO. 3 1 Fish & Chips	1.07
NO. 4 3 Fish & Chips	2.31
NO. 5 1 Fish & 3 Shrimp	1.94
NO. 6 3 Shrimp, 1 Fish & Chips	2.39
NO. 7 2 Chick & Chips	1.89
NO. 8 1 Chick & Chips	1.17
NO. 9 3 Chick & Chips	2.61
NO. 10 5 Shrimp & Chips	2.65
FISH FILET (ea)	.62
CHICKEN FILET (ea.)	.72

Side Orders

HUSH PUPPIES Made with Fresh Onions & Eggs	5 - .30 8 - .45
LEMON TART Crisp, Hot, Golden Crust w/Delicious Lemon Filling	.25
SLAW - Cup	.30
Pint	.89

Beverages

COLD DRINKS	
Large	.35
Regular	.25
COFFEE	.25
HOT TEA	.25
MILK	.25

- *STOP*
- Check your answers on page 345.
- Correct the problems you missed.
- Shade box 10 opposite "working with decimals" on page xix.
- If this was the last subskill you had to work on in this section, take the test on page 244.
- If you have other subskills to work on in this section, go on to the next one.

SUBSKILL 11: Dividing Decimals

Problem: Determine 4.51 ÷ .07 to the nearest hundredth.

Solution:

- Move decimal point in divisor to the *right* and discard.

- Move decimal point in dividend to the *right* same number of places and retain.

- Add two zeros to dividend if rounding to nearest tenth, three zeros if rounding to nearest hundredth, four zeros if rounding to nearest thousandth, and so on.

- Divide.

- Put decimal point in quotient directly above decimal point in dividend.

- Round to next to last digit.

$$64.428 \longrightarrow \boxed{64.43}$$

$$.07\,)\overline{4.51} \longrightarrow 7\,)\overline{451.000}$$

```
        6 4. 4 2 8 ──→ 64.43
  7 )4 5 1. 0 0 0
   -4 2
    3 1
   -2 8
      3 0
     -2 8
       2 0
      -1 4
        6 0
       -5 6
          4
```

Lesson: The decimal point in .07 was moved two places to the right to turn the number into a whole number. This had the effect of multiplying it by 100. And the decimal point in 4.51 was moved two places to the right to compensate for what was done with the decimal point in .07. Thus the problem was left unchanged except for appearance because it was multiplied by 100/100 or one.

$$4.51 \div .07 = \frac{4.51}{.07} = \frac{4.51}{.07} \times 1 = \frac{4.51}{.07} \times \frac{100}{100} = \frac{4.51 \times 100}{.07 \times 100} = \frac{451}{7}$$

Drill and Practice:

Set 1

Divide to the nearest hundredth.

1. 3.82 ÷ .05   2. .5902 ÷ .024

3. 2.59 ÷ .17   4. .08 ÷ 516

- *STOP.*
- Check your answers on page 345.
- Correct the problems you missed.
- Go on to Set 2.

Set 2

Divide to the nearest tenth.

1. 28.9 ÷ .09   2. 4.916 ÷ .03

3. 31.4 ÷ .82   4. 3.2 ÷ .2194

- *STOP.*
- Check your answers on page 345.
- Correct the problems you missed.
- Go on to Set 3 or 4.

Set 3

Divide to the nearest thousandth.

1. 326 ÷ .07   2. 38.15 ÷ .018

3. 218 ÷ .5   4. 41 ÷ .04012

- *STOP.*
- Check your answers on page 345.
- Correct the problems you missed.
- Go on to Set 4.

Set 4

1. You just traveled 357.4 miles on 16.7 gallons of gas. How many miles to the nearest tenth of a mile did you travel per gallon?

2. The raceway for the Indianapolis 500 is 2.5 miles around. How many laps to the nearest lap is 500 miles around?

3. Ray Harroun won the Indianapolis 500 in 1911 with an average speed of 74.59 miles per hour. Gordon Johncock won it in 1973 with an average speed of 159.014 miles per hour. How many times faster to the nearest hundredth was Johncock's average speed than Harroun's average speed?

4. A 1210-page phonebook is 3.5 centimeters thick. What is the thickness to the nearest thousandth of a centimeter of a page of the phonebook?

5. From the stacks of coins, figure the thickness to the nearest hundredth of a centimeter of (a) a penny and (b) a quarter.

9.2 cm   7.0 cm

- *STOP*

- Check your answers on page 345.

- Correct the problems you missed.

- Shade box 11 opposite "working with decimals" on page xix.

- If this was the last subskill you had to work on in this section, take the test on page 244.

- If you have other subskills to work on in this section, go on to the next one.

SUBSKILL 12: Multiplying or Dividing Decimals by Powers of Ten

Problem: 2.5 ÷ 100 = ?

Solution: • Move decimal point to the *right* as many places as there are zeros if *multiplying*.

• Move decimal point to the *left* as many places as there are zeros if *dividing*.

2.5 ÷ 100 = $\boxed{.025}$

Lesson:

$$
\begin{array}{r}
.025 \\
100\overline{)\,2.500} \\
\end{array}
$$

$100\overline{)\,2.500}$	Twenty-five tenths to be grouped by hundreds
$-.000$	*Zero* groups of 100 tenths or zero tenths
2.500	Two hundred fifty hundredths to be grouped by hundreds
-2.000	*Two* groups of 100 hundredths or 200 hundredths
$.500$	Five hundred thousandths to be grouped by hundreds
$-.500$	*Five* groups of 100 thousandths or 500 thousandths

Drill and Practice:

Set 1

1. $3.5 \div 1000 = ?$ 2. $4.3 \times 100 = ?$

3. $.47 \div 100 = ?$ 4. $.83 \times 1000 = ?$

5. $89.5 \div 10 = ?$ 6. $40.2 \times 10000 = ?$

- *STOP.*
- Check your answers on page 345.
- Correct the problems you missed.
- Go on to Set 2.

Set 2

1. $4.83 \times 10 = ?$ 2. $.056 \div 10000 = ?$

3. $7.95 \times 100 = ?$ 4. $.302 \div 1000 = ?$

5. $9.99 \times 1000 = ?$ 6. $4.06 \div 100 = ?$

- *STOP.*
- Check your answers on page 345.
- Correct the problems you missed.
- Go on to Set 3 or 4.

Set 3

1. $825.36 \div 1000000 = ?$

2. 408.06 × 10000000 = ?

3. .00621 ÷ 100000000 = ?

4. .00005 × 1000000000 = ?

5. 9900000000 ÷ 10000000000 = ?

6. 472 × 100000000000 = ?

- *STOP.*
- Check your answers on page 345.
- Correct the problems you missed.
- Go on to Set 4.

Set 4

1. One meter is ten decimeters is 100 centimeters is 1000 millimeters. How many meters are
   (a) 1628 decimeters?
   (b) 1628 centimeters?
   (c) 1628 millimeters?

2. One liter is ten deciliters is 100 centiliters is 1000 milliliters. How many liters are
   (a) 4716 deciliters?
   (b) 4716 centiliters
   (c) 4716 milliliters?

3. One kilogram is ten hectograms is 100 dekagrams is 1000 grams. How many kilograms are
   (a) 7304 hectograms?
   (b) 7304 dekagrams?
   (c) 7304 grams?

4. One kilometer is ten hectometers is 100 dekameters is 1000 meters. How many kilometers are
   (a) 2358 hectometers?
   (b) 2358 dekameters?
   (c) 2358 meters?

5. One meter is 100 centimeters. How many meters are 235 centimeters?

6. One liter is 1000 milliliters. How many liters are 8047 milliliters?

7. One kilogram is 1000 grams. How many kilograms are 729 grams?

8. One kilometer is 1000 meters. How many kilometers are 17,985 meters?

9. One meter is .1 dekameters is .01 hectometers is .001 kilometers. How many meters are
   (a) 105 dekameters?
   (b) 105 hectometers?
   (c) 105 kilometers?

10. One millimeter is .1 centimeters is .01 decimeters is .001 meters. How many millimeters are
    (a) 42 centimeters?
    (b) 42 decimeters?
    (c) 42 meters?

11. One milliliter is .1 centiliters is .01 deciliters is .001 liters. How many milliliters are
    (a) six centiliters?
    (b) six deciliters?
    (c) six liters?

12. One gram is .1 dekagrams is .01 hectograms is .001 kilograms. How many grams are
    (a) .9 dekagrams?
    (b) .9 hectograms?
    (c) .9 kilograms?

13. A waterflea is .025 centimeters long. How long would it appear magnified
    (a) ten times?
    (b) 100 times?
    (c) 1000 times?

- *STOP*

- Check your answers on page 345.

- Correct the problems you missed.

- Shade box 12 opposite "working with decimals" on page xix.

- If this was the last subskill you had to work on in this section, take the test on page 244.

- If you have other subskills to work on in this section, go on to the next one.

SUBSKILL 13: Converting
Fractions to
Repeating Decimals

Problem: Convert 419/990 to a repeating decimal.

Solution:
- Add decimal point and plenty of zeros to numerator.

- Divide denominator into numerator until quotient starts to repeat.

- Put bar over repeating part of quotient.

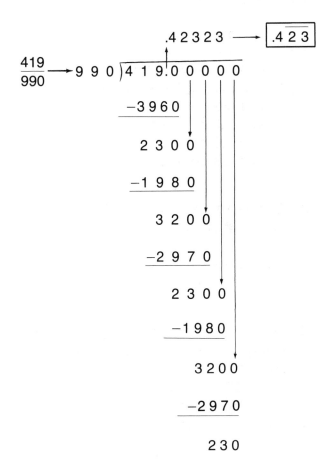

Lesson: The fraction a/b will repeat after at most b divisions since there can be at most b remainders, namely, 0, 1, 2, 3, . . ., $b - 1$.

Drill and Practice:

Set 1

Convert to repeating decimals.

1. $\dfrac{35}{99}$ 2. $\dfrac{125}{999}$ 3. $\dfrac{47}{66}$ 4. $\dfrac{3}{7}$

- *STOP.*
- Check your answers on page 345.
- Correct the problems you missed.
- Go on to Set 2.

Set 2

Convert to repeating decimals.

1. $\dfrac{25}{99}$ 2. $\dfrac{5}{11}$ 3. $\dfrac{50}{111}$ 4. $\dfrac{2}{3}$

- *STOP.*
- Check your answers on page 345.
- Correct the problems you missed.
- Go on to Set 3 or 4.

Set 3

Convert to repeating decimals.

1. $\dfrac{3}{8}$ 2. $\dfrac{1}{11}$ 3. $\dfrac{1}{2}$ 4. $\dfrac{2}{9}$

- *STOP.*
- Check your answers on page 345.
- Correct the problems you missed.
- Go on to Set 4.

Set 4

1. Why the emphasis on converting fractions to repeating decimals?

- *STOP*
- Check your answers on page 346.
- Correct the problems you missed.
- Shade box 13 opposite "working with decimals" on page xix.
- If this was the last subskill you had to work on in this section, take the test on page 244.
- If you have other subskills to work on in this section, go on to the next one.

SUBSKILL 14: Converting Repeating Decimals to Fractions

Problem: Convert $.4\overline{25} = .4252525 \ldots$ to a fraction.

Solution: Make four equations.

- Make first equation by letting N equal decimal.

- Make second equation by multiplying both sides of first equation by power of ten to where decimal point goes just *up* to repeating part.

- Make third equation by multiplying both sides of first equation by power of ten to where decimal point goes just *past* repeating part.

- Make fourth equation by subtracting both sides of second equation from both sides of third equation.

- Divide both sides of fourth equation by coefficient of N.

- Simplify.

First equation:
$$N = .4\overline{25}$$

Second equation:
$$10N = 4.\overline{25}$$

Third equation:
$$1000N = 425.\overline{25}$$

Fourth equation:
$$1000N = 425.\overline{25}$$

$$\begin{aligned} 1000N &= 425.\overline{25} \\ -10N &= -4.\overline{25} \\ \hline 990N &= 421 \end{aligned} \quad \rightarrow \quad \boxed{N = \frac{421}{990}}$$

Lesson: The objective is to do away with the infinite part of the repeating decimal.

Drill and Practice:

Set 1

Convert to fractions.

1. $.\overline{704}$ 2. $.\overline{19}$ 3. $.0\overline{24}$ 4. $.3\overline{6}$

- *STOP.*
- Check your answers on page 346.
- Correct the problems you missed.
- Go on to Set 2.

Set 2

Convert to fractions.

1. $.1\overline{23}$ 2. $.\overline{3}$ 3. $.\overline{9}$ 4. $.\overline{142857}$

- *STOP.*
- Check your answers on page 346.
- Correct the problems you missed.
- Go on to Set 3 or 4.

Set 3

Convert to fractions.

1. $.34\overline{10}$ 2. $.4\overline{9}$ 3. $.5\overline{0}$ 4. $.\overline{63}$

- *STOP.*
- Check your answers on page 346.
- Correct the problems you missed.
- Go on to Set 4.

Set 4

1. Why the emphasis on converting repeating
   decimals to fractions?

- *STOP*

- Check your answers on page 346.

- Correct the problems you missed.

- Shade box 14 opposite "working with decimals" on page xix.

- Take the test on page 244.

Inventory Post Test for
Working with Decimals

1. Write the decimal.

2. Write the verbal equivalent of 3055.025.

3. Which exhibit unnecessary zeros?

    a. .400   b. .040   c. .004   d. 400   e. 40.0   f. 4.00

4. Which indicates the preciseness of the measurement of the distance from *A* to *B*?

    a. .400   b. .40   c. .4   d. 4

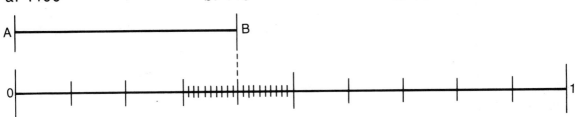

5. Convert 15.18 to a mixed number.

6. Round 9.184 to the nearest hundredth.

7. Convert $9\frac{5}{11}$ to a decimal to the nearest thousandth.

8. 503.109 + 18.03 + 213 + 5.8 = ?

9. 3159.3 − 406.502 = ?

10. 31.62 × .012 = ?

11. Determine 30.2 ÷ .03 to the nearest tenth.

12. 20.125 × 1000000 = ?

13. Convert $\frac{58}{111}$ to a repeating decimal.

14. Convert $\overline{.431}$ = .431431431 . . . to a fraction.

- *STOP*

- Check your answers with the instructor.

- As before, work through the subskills in this section which correspond to the problems you missed, except work the *even* drill-and-practice problems.

- Take the test on page 247.

SECTION 15

SKILL
Working with Percents

Inventory Pretest for
Working with Percents

1. What percent is shaded?

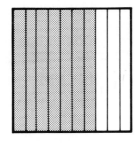

2. Convert 2.015 to a percent.

3. Convert $\frac{3}{7}$ to a percent.

4. Convert 250.5% to a decimal.

5. Convert 12.5% to a fraction.

6. Forty-five percent of 20 is what number?

7. What percent of 250 is 60?

8. Ninety-eight percent of what number is 500?

- *STOP*

- Check your answers on page 346.

- Shade the boxes opposite "working with percents" on page xix which correspond to the problems you got right.

- If you got all of them right, take the test on page 265.

- If you missed some of them, start working on the subskills in this section which correspond to the ones you missed.

- For each subskill, look at the example, study the solution, think about the lesson, and work the *odd* drill-and-practice problems.

SUBSKILL 1: Meaning of Percent

Problem: What percent is shaded?

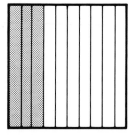

Solution: • Regard as hundredths.

  • Write *numerator.*

  • Attach percent sign.

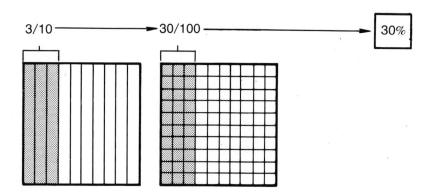

Lesson: Percent means "per 100" like "per the number of *cents* in a dollar." It is denoted %, a sort of scrambled 100.

Drill and Practice:

Set 1

1. What percent is shaded?

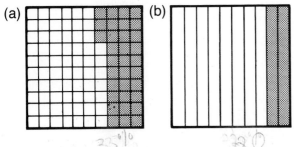

(a) (b)

2. What percent is indicated?

(a)

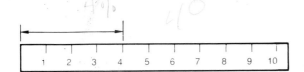

(b)

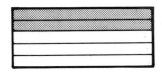

3. What percent is shaded?

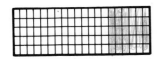

4. Shade 60%.

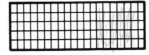

- *STOP.*
- Check your answers on page 346.
- Correct the problems you missed.
- Go on to Set 2.

Set 2

1. What percent is shaded?

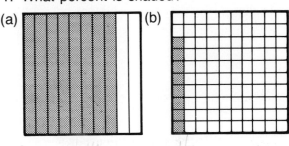

(a) (b)

2. What percent is indicated?

(a)

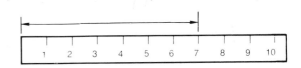

(b)

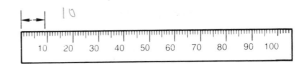

3. What percent is shaded?

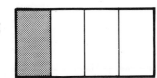

4. Shade 75%.

- *STOP.*
- Check your answers on page 346.
- Correct the problems you missed.
- Go on to Set 3 or 4.

Set 3

1. What percent is shaded?

(a) 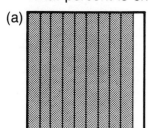 (b)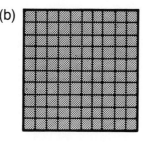

2. What percent is indicated?

(a)

(b)

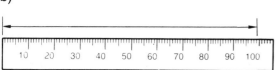

3. What percent is shaded?

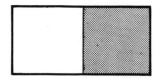

4. Shade 100%.

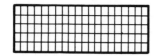

- *STOP.*
- Check your answers on page 346.
- Correct the problems you missed.
- Go on to Set 4.

Set 4

1. What percent of a dollar are
   (a) two dimes?

   (b) 37 cents?

2. What percent of a meter are
   (a) seven decimeters? (ten decimeters = one meter)

   (b) 41 centimeters? (100 centimeters = one meter)

3. Of 100 students, 53 are girls. What percent are girls?

4. Of 100 radish seeds, 93 sprouted. What percent sprouted?

5. Of 50 diesel trucks, 45 honked. What percent honked?

- *STOP*
- Check your answers on page 346.
- Correct the problems you missed.
- Shade box 1 opposite "working with percents" on page xix.
- If this was the only subskill you had to work on in this section, take the test on page 263.
- If you have other subskills to work on in this section, go on to the next one.

SUBSKILL 2: Converting Decimals
to Percents

Problem: Convert 1.305 to a percent.

Solution: • Move decimal point to the *right*
two places.

  $1 . 3 0 5 = \boxed{1\,3\,0\,5\ \%}$

  • Attach percent sign.

Lesson: The decimal point was moved two places to the right to turn the decimal into hundredths.

$$1.305 = 1.305 \times 1 = \frac{1.305}{1} \times \boxed{\frac{100}{100}} = \frac{1.305 \times 100}{1 \times 100} = \frac{130.5}{100} = 130.5\%$$

Drill and Practice:

Set 1

Convert to percents.

1. 2.102 2. .45 3. .8 4. .1005 5. 1.6666

- *STOP.*
- Check your answers on page 346.
- Correct the problems you missed.
- Go on to Set 2.

Set 2

Convert to percents.

1. 3.6   2. .75 3. .5 4. .025 5. 1.2

- *STOP.*
- Check your answers on page 346.
- Correct the problems you missed.
- Go on to Set 3 or 4.

Set 3

Convert to percents.

1. 4.5 2. .25 3. .9 4. .09 5. 1.252525

- *STOP.*
- Check your answers on page 346.
- Correct the problems you missed.
- Go on to Set 4.

Set 4

1. .075 of your salary is withheld for retirement. What percent of your salary is that?

2. .18 of your salary is withheld for federal income tax. What percent of your salary is that?

3. You budget .3 of your salary for food. What percent of your salary is that?

4. You lose .1 of your weight. What percent of your weight is that?

5. You bat .250. What percent of the time do you get a hit?

- *STOP*

- Check your answers on page 346.

- Correct the problems you missed.

- Shade box 2 opposite "working with percents" on page xix.

- If this was the last subskill you had to work on in this section, take the test on page 263.

- If you have other subskills to work on in this section, go on to the next one.

SUBSKILL 3: Converting Fractions and Mixed Numbers to Percents

Problem: Convert $\frac{5}{6}$ to a percent.

Solution:
- Convert to decimal to nearest hundredth.

- Move decimal point to the *right* two places.

- Attach percent sign.

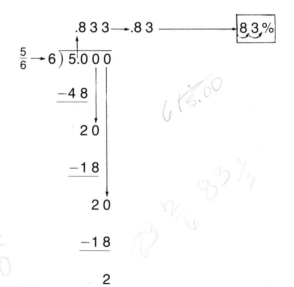

Lesson: To be more precise, $\frac{5}{6} = 83\frac{1}{3}\%$. To illustrate:

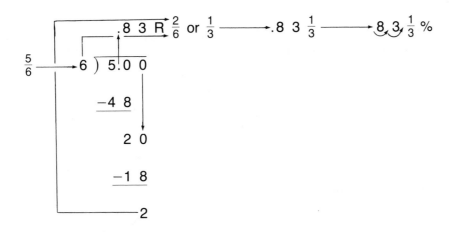

Drill and Practice:

Set 1

Convert to percents.

1. $\frac{4}{25}$ 2. $1\frac{17}{50}$ 3. $\frac{3}{8}$ 4. $1\frac{1}{3}$

- *STOP.*
- Check your answers on page 346.
- Correct the problems you missed.
- Go on to Set 2.

Set 2

Convert to percents.

1. $\frac{3}{5}$ 2. $2\frac{3}{10}$ 3. $\frac{5}{11}$ 4. $2\frac{5}{12}$

- *STOP.*
- Check your answers on page 346.
- Correct the problems you missed.
- Go on to Set 3 or 4.

Set 3

Convert to percents.

1. $\frac{1}{2}$ 2. $3\frac{1}{4}$ 3. $\frac{4}{9}$ 4. $3\frac{2}{3}$

- *STOP.*
- Check your answers on page 346.
- Correct the problems you missed.
- Go on to Set 4.

Set 4

1. Fuel combustion is responsible for 21/100 of the air pollution in the United States. Express this statistic as a percent.

2. Industry is responsible for 3/5 of the water pollution in the United States. Express this statistic as a percent.

3. Forty-three out of 57 people responded a certain way to an item on a questionnaire. What percent of the people responded that way?

4. One hundred twelve out of 132 sweet peas germinated. What percent of the sweet peas germinated?

- *STOP*

- Check your answers on page 346.

- Correct the problems you missed.

- Shade box 3 opposite "working with percents" on page xix.

- If this was the last subskill you had to work on in this section, take the test on page 263.

- If you have other subskills to work on in this section, go on to the next one.

SUBSKILL 4: Converting Percents to Decimals

Problem: Convert 130.5% to a decimal.

Solution:
- Pinpoint decimal point.

- Move decimal point to the *left* two places.

$$130.5\% = \boxed{1\underset{\curvearrowleft}{.305}}$$

- Discard percent sign.

Lesson: Percent means "per 100" like "per the number of *cents* in a dollar." Knowing this,

$$130.5\% = \frac{130.5}{100} = 1.305.$$

Drill and Practice:

Set 1
Convert to decimals.

1. 210.25%   2. 50%   3. $1\frac{1}{2}$%

4. 7.05%   5. 200%   6. $\frac{4}{5}$ %

- *STOP.*
- Check your answers on page 346.
- Correct the problems you missed.
- Go on to Set 2.

Set 2
Convert to decimals.

1. 360.95%   2. 75%   3. $4\frac{1}{4}$%

4. 5.5%   5. 300%   6. $\frac{1}{2}$%

- *STOP.*
- Check your answers on page 346.
- Correct the problems you missed.
- Go on to Set 3 or 4.

Set 3
Convert to decimals.

1. 450%   2. 35%   3. $7\frac{3}{4}$%

4. 1%   5. 100%   6. $\frac{2}{3}$%

- *STOP.*
- Check your answers on page 346.
- Correct the problems you missed.
- Go on to Set 4.

Set 4
1. Why the emphasis on converting percents to decimals?

- *STOP*
- Check your answers on page 346.
- Correct the problems you missed.
- Shade box 4 opposite "working with percents" on page xix.
- If this was the last subskill you had to work on in this section, take the test on page 263.
- If you have other subskills to work on in this section, go on to the next one.

SUBSKILL 5: Converting Percents to Fractions and Mixed Numbers

Problem: Convert $1\frac{2}{3}\%$ to a fraction.

Solution: • Convert to decimal.

$$1\frac{2}{3}\% \longrightarrow 1.67\% = .0167 = \boxed{\frac{167}{10000}}$$

• Convert to fraction or mixed number.

• Simplify.

Lesson: To be more precise, $1\frac{2}{3}\% = \frac{1}{60}$. To illustrate:

$$1\frac{2}{3}\% = \frac{5}{3}\% = \frac{5}{3} \div 100 = \frac{5}{3} \div \frac{100}{1} = \frac{5}{3} \times \frac{1}{100} = \frac{5 \times 1}{3 \times 100} = \frac{5}{300} = \frac{1}{60}$$

Drill and Practice:

Set 1

Convert to fractions or mixed numbers.

1. $2\frac{1}{2}\%$ 2. 45%   3. 150.5%

4.   12.5%   5.   5%

- *STOP.*
- Check your answers on page 346.
- Correct the problems you missed.
- Go on to Set 2.

Set 2

Convert to fractions or mixed numbers.

1. $4\frac{3}{4}\%$ 2. 50%   3. 100.25%

4.   99.9%   5.   10%

- *STOP.*
- Check your answers on page 346.
- Correct the problems you missed.
- Go on to Set 3 or 4.

Set 3

Convert to fractions or mixed numbers.

1. $5\frac{1}{3}\%$ 2. 325% 3. 201.75%

4. .1%   5. 1%

- *STOP.*
- Check your answers on page 346.
- Correct the problems you missed.
- Go on to Set 4.

Set 4

1. Why the emphasis on converting percents to fractions and
   mixed numbers?

- *STOP*

- Check your answers on page 346.

- Correct the problems you missed.

- Shade box 5 opposite "working with percents" on page xix.

- If this was the last subskill you had to work on in this section, take the test on page 263.

- If you have other subskills to work on in this section, go on to the next one.

SUBSKILL 6: Finding a Percent of a Number

Problem: Thirty-five percent of 15 is what number?

Solution: • Convert percent to decimal.

         • Multiply.

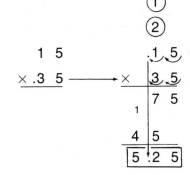

Lesson: The word *of* means multiply as in "half of ten is five."

$$\text{(Half of ten} \longrightarrow \frac{1}{2} \times 10 = \frac{1}{2} \times \frac{10}{1} = \frac{1 \times 10}{2 \times 1} = \frac{10}{2} = 5.)$$

Drill and Practice:

Set 1

1. 20% of 30 = ?   2. 50% of 18 = ?
3. 5% of 10 = ?   4. 75% of 50 = ?

- *STOP.*
- Check your answers on page 346.
- Correct the problems you missed.
- Go on to Set 2.

Set 2

1. 1% of 150 = ?   2. 99% of 150 = ?
3. 7.5% of 12,500 = ?   4. .01% of 30,000 = ?

- *STOP.*
- Check your answers on page 346.
- Correct the problems you missed.
- Go on to Set 3 or 4.

Set 3

1. 25% of 80 = ?   2. 60% of 300 = ?
3. 10% of 45 = ?   4. 8% of 1000 = ?

- *STOP.*
- Check your answers on page 346.
- Correct the problems you missed.
- Go on to Set 4.

Set 4

1. How much would a salesperson earn if he or she were to sell a $37,500 house for an 8% commission?

2. How much would a buyer save by buying a $12,000 piece of property with cash if the property were to be discounted 15%?

3. Given a 6% state sales tax, how much tax would a person pay if he or she were to purchase an automobile for $6995?

4. If a new automobile depreciates 37.5% of its value the first year, how much will a new automobile costing $4990 depreciate the first year?

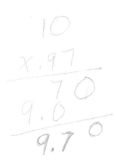

5. Ninety-seven percent of the weight of a watermelon is water. How much of a ten-pound watermelon is water?

6. Pick a number. Multiply by five. Add ten. Find 60%. Divide by three. Subtract the number you picked. Your answer is two. Surprised?

7. Would you actually save 40% on the pocket calculator?

• *STOP*

• Check your answers on page 346.

• Correct the problems you missed.

• Shade box 6 opposite "working with percents" on page xix.

• If this was the last subskill you had to work on in this section, take the test on page 263.

• If you have other subskills to work on in this section, go on to the next one.

SUBSKILL 7: Finding the Percent One Number Is of Another

Problem: What percent of 300 is 75?

Solution: • Divide first number into second number to nearest hundredth.

• Convert to percent.

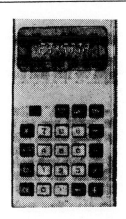

Lesson: Knowing that the word *of* means multiply, the question "What percent of 300 is 75?" can be answered by *dividing* 300 into 75 just as the question "What times four is 12?" could be answered by dividing four into 12.

Drill and Practice:

Set 1

1. ?% of 80 = 40
2. ?% of 75 = 25
3. ?% of 60 = 72
4. ?% of 20 = 21

- *STOP.*
- Check your answers on page 347.
- Correct the problems you missed.
- Go on to Set 2.

Set 2

1. ?% of 50 = 30
2. ?% of 16 = 2
3. ?% of 6000 = 4800
4. ?% of 1800 = 1000

- *STOP.*
- Check your answers on page 347.
- Correct the problems you missed.
- Go on to Set 3 or 4.

Set 3

1. ?% of 75 = 115
2. ?% of 18 = 6
3. ?% of 80 = 100
4. ?% of 150 = 75

- *STOP.*
- Check your answers on page 347.
- Correct the problems you missed.
- Go on to Set 4.

Set 4

1. If a football team won ten games out of 12 for a season, what percent of its games did it win?

2. If a man spent $7500 of a $9000 inheritance, what percent of the inheritance did he spend?

3. If the rent for a $220-a-month apartment was increased by $25, what percent was the rent increased?

4. If you traveled 425 miles of a 600-mile trip, what percent of the trip did you travel?

- *STOP*

- Check your answers on page 347.

- Correct the problems you missed.

- Shade box 7 opposite "working with percents" on page xix.

- If this was the last subskill you had to work on in this section, take the test on page 263.

- If you have other subskills to work on in this section, go on to the next one.

SUBSKILL 8: Finding a Number Given a Percent of the Number

Problem: Twelve percent of what number is six?

$$\begin{array}{r} 5\ 0 \\ .12\overline{)6} \rightarrow 12\overline{)6\ 00} \\ -6\ 0 \\ \hline 0 \\ -0 \\ \hline \end{array}$$

Solution:
- Convert percent to decimal.

- Divide decimal into number.

Lesson: Knowing that the word *of* means multiply, the question "Twelve percent of what number is six?" can be answered by *dividing* the decimal equivalent of 12% into six just as the question "Three times what number is 12?" could be answered by dividing three into 12.

Drill and Practice:

Set 1

1. 15% of ? = 30

2. 3% of ? = 45

3. 75% of ? = 18

4. 105% of ? = 6

- *STOP.*
- Check your answers on page 347.
- Correct the problems you missed.
- Go on to Set 2.

Set 2

1. 18% of ? = 50   2. 1% of ? = 72
3. 50% of ? = 20   4. 200% of ? = 8

- *STOP.*
- Check your answers on page 347.
- Correct the problems you missed.
- Go on to Set 3 or 4.

Set 3

1. 25% of ? = 15   2. 7% of ? = 21
3. 80% of ? = 100   4. 250% of = 15

- *STOP.*
- Check your answers on page 347.
- Correct the problems you missed.
- Go on to Set 4.

Set 4

1. A real-estate agent sold a house for a 5% commission and received $1787.50 for the sale. How much did the agent sell the house for?

2. A car salesman earned $214.30 or 68.5% of his income for the week on one sale. What was his income for the week?

3. A shirt sold retail for $12.50. If this was 160% of the cost of the shirt to the merchant, how much did the merchant pay for the shirt?

4. If you paid $3000 or 28% of your income for the year in rent, what was your income for the year?

5. What was the original price on the towels?

> **Save 20% on our color-coordinated bath towels. Now just $3.19**

- *STOP*

- Check your answers on page 347.

- Correct the problems you missed.

- Shade box 8 opposite "working with percents" on page xix.

- Take the test on page 263.

Inventory Post Test for
Working with Percents

1. What percent is shaded?

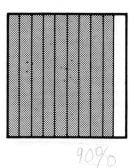

90%

2. Convert 1.105 to a percent.

3. Convert $\frac{5}{8}$ to a percent.

4. Convert 7.5% to a decimal.

5. Convert 37.5% to a fraction.

6. Fifteen percent of 40 is what number?

7. What percent of 120 is 25?

8. Four percent of what number is three?

- *STOP*

- Check your answers with the instructor.

- As before, work through the subskills in this section which correspond to the problems you missed, except work the *even* drill-and-practice problems.

- Take the test on page 265.

General Survey Tests for Decimals, Percents, Estimation, Integers, Less Than, Greater Than, Exponents, and Roots

General Survey Post Test for Decimals and Percents

1. Convert 17.505 to a mixed number.

2. Convert $6\frac{5}{8}$ to a decimal to the nearest tenth.

3. 12.096 + 83.7 + 21 + 16.59 = ?

4. 412.3 × 6.19 = ?

5. Determine 3.74 ÷ .024 to the nearest hundredth.

6. Convert $\frac{11}{12}$ to a percent.

7. Convert 312.08% to a decimal.

8. Seven and one-half percent of 210 is what number?

9. What percent of 420 is 75?

10. Seventeen percent of what number is 30?

- *STOP*

- Check your answers with the instructor.

- Enter the number correct and today's date in the spaces provided on page XX.

- Figure your growth and take pleasure in it.

- If you got nine or more right, take the test on page 266.

- If you got less than nine right, take the inventory pretests for decimals and percents again beginning with the one on page 205.

- As before, work through the subskills which correspond to the problems you miss.

General Survey Pretest for Estimation, Integers, Less Than, Greater Than, Exponents, and Roots

1. Estimate $\frac{9}{17} \times 438$. Do *not* compute.

2. $^+3 - {}^-5 = ?$

3. $^-8 \times {}^+6 = ?$

4. $2 + 3 \times 5 = ?$

5. True or false, $8 < 10$?

6. Which is greater, $\frac{9}{19}$ or $\frac{14}{29}$?

7. $3^3 = ?$

8. Add or subtract exponents: $10^3 \times 10^4$

9. Express in scientific notation: 4070.3855

10. $\sqrt{36}$ = ?

- *STOP*
- Check your answers on page 347.
- Enter the number correct and today's date in the spaces provided on page XX.
- If you got nine or more right, you are a master of basic mathematics, and you can give this book to someone else!
- If you got less than nine right, take the test on page 269.

SKILL
Estimation

Inventory Pretest for Estimation

1. Estimate $25.89 + $3.15 + $12.75. Do *not* compute.

2. Estimate 449107 ÷ 14. Do *not* compute.

3. Estimate 27% of 48. Do *not* compute.

4. Estimate the length of segment *AB* to the nearest centimeter. Do *not* measure.

AB

- *STOP*
- Check your answers on page 347.
- Shade the boxes opposite "estimation" on page xix which correspond to the problems you got right.
- If you got all of them right, take the test on page 281.
- If you missed some of them, start working on the subskills in this section which correspond to the ones you missed.
- For each subskill, look at the example, study the solution, think about the lesson, and work the *odd* drill-and-practice problems.

SUBSKILL 1: Estimating Sums and Differences

Problem: Estimate.

(a) $4.57 + $5.29 +$6.73

(b) 27861 − 8203

Solution: • Disregard relatively small numbers.

• Round remaining numbers to numbers you can work with in head.

• Add or subtract.

(a) $4.57 + $5.29 + $6.73
      ↓   ↓   ↓
      $5   + $5   + $7   = $17

(b)   27861 − 8203
         ↘   ↘
      30000 − 8000 = 22000

Lesson: Estimation is an art. Sometimes you hit. Sometimes you miss. The objective is to stay within reason, that is, within 10% of the answer. To improve your estimation of *sums*, round half the numbers up, half the numbers down. To improve your estimation of *differences*, round both numbers either up or down.

(a) $4.57 + $5.29 + $6.73 = $16.59 (Seventeen dollars was a hit.)

(b) 27861 − 8203 = 19658 (Twenty-two thousand was a miss.)

Drill and Practice:

Set 1

1. Select the bigger number.
   (a) 4 + 19 + 1 or 22 + 9

   (b) 82 − 3 or 101 − 45

2. Estimate.
   (a) $3.89 + $11.15 + $7.62

   (b) 36401 − 6195

   (c) 959 + 327 + 314 + 187

   (d) $17.89 − $11.58

(e)   3462
       598
        34
     +2201

(f) 2930
    − 457

(g) 245.62
      38.5
    +498.03

(h) 39.4578
    − 8.0032

• *STOP.*
• Check your answers on page 347.
• Correct the problems you missed.
• Go on to Set 2.

Set 2

1. Select the bigger number.
   (a) 83 + 95 or 141 + 57 + 3

   (b) 456 − 219 or 307 − 21

2. Estimate.

   (a) $4.07 + $9.98 + $405.50

   (b) 98021 − 40703

   (c) 4076 + 119 + 3721 + 695

   (d) $283.95 − $15.73

   (e)   36925   (f) 385   (g) 3879.99   (h) 1.885
          4001   − 29   402.387   − .92
           289   6598.387
            15   + 294.102
        +59920

- *STOP.*
- Check your answers on page 347.
- Correct the problems you missed.
- Go on to Set 3 or 4.

Set 3

1. Select the bigger number.

   (a) 208 + 319 + 508 or 1083 + 394

   (b) 8043 − 219 or 10520 − 3316

2. Estimate.

   (a) $52.95 + $17.98 + $34.55

   (b) 9021 − 895

   (c) 79854 + 3826 + 2003 + 42305

   (d) $9.25 − $4.95

   (e)   382599   (f) 56   (g) 38.4056   (h) 307.9
          42006   − 8   17.0095   − 25.2
           3025   6.2817
          99999   + 1.95
        +287158

- *STOP.*
- Check your answers on page 347.
- Correct the problems you missed.
- Go on to Set 4.

Set 4

1. You are standing in line at a fish and chips place and are about to order. You have $10. Quickly, can you order two No. 1's, two No. 2's, and one No. 5?

$\mathfrak{Special\ Seafoods}$	
NO. 1 2 Fish & Chips	**1.69**
NO. 2 2 Fish, Chips & Slaw	**1.99**
NO. 3 1 Fish & Chips	**1.07**
NO. 4 3 Fish & Chips	**2.31**
NO. 5 1 Fish & 3 Shrimp	**1.94**
NO. 6 3 Shrimp, 1 Fish & Chips	**2.39**
NO. 7 2 Chick & Chips	**1.89**
NO. 8 1 Chick & Chips	**1.17**
NO. 9 3 Chick & Chips	**2.61**
NO. 10 5 Shrimp & Chips	**2.65**
FISH FILET (ea)	**.62**
CHICKEN FILET (ea.)	**.72**

2. You are taking orders for some friends. They give you $9.35. Quickly, did they give you enough for five large hamburgers, three large fries, two small fries, one chocolate shake, one vanilla shake, two large colas, and one medium root beer?

3. You are standing in line and are about to order dinner. You have $2.08 in loose change. Quickly, what might you order?

CHARLIE'S FRIED CHICKEN MENU

No. 1 Regular	.84	No. 4 Large	1.26
2 Large Pieces		3 Large Pieces	
No. 2 Regular	.94	No. 5 Large	1.41
2 Large Pieces—Dark		3 Large Pieces—Dark	
No. 3 Regular	.99	No. 6 Large	1.48
2 Large Pieces—White		3 Large Pieces—White	

Family Size	4.14	Super Family Size	6.19
10 Large Pieces		15 Large Pieces	
With French Fries for 3	4.96	With French Fries for 5	7.49

Dinner Pack	1.39	Hot Fruit Pie	.29
2 Large Pieces, French Fries, Jalapeño Pepper and Cole Slaw		Pecan Pie	.35
		Jalapeño Pepper	.08
Chicken Snack	.51	Cole Slaw	
1 Large Piece with Roll		3 oz.	.29
With French Fries	.75	12 oz.	.79
French Fries	.29	Drinks .17—.27—.37	

4. You are fooling around with a pocket calculator. You add 42.983, 382.07, and 19.207. You get 738.951. Quickly, did you push the right buttons?

5. You give a clerk a $20-bill for an item costing $12.65. The clerk gives you $8.35 in change. Quickly, what do you do?

#	ITEMS	1	2	3	4	5	$	C
	H' BURGERS	.35	.70	1.05	1.40	1.75		
	C' BURGERS	.40	.80	1.20	1.60	2.00		
	DBL. HAM	.65	1.30	1.95	2.60	3.25		
	DBL. CHEESE	.75	1.50	2.25	3.00	3.75		
	Q H' BG	.75	1.50	2.25	3.00	3.75		
	Q C' BG	.85	1.70	2.55	3.40	4.25		
	FILET	.60	1.20	1.80	2.40	3.00		
	BIG BURGERS	.85	1.70	2.55	3.40	4.25		
	FRIES L.	.45	.90	1.35	1.80	2.25		
	FRIES S.	.30	.60	.90	1.20	1.50		
	APPLE/CHERRY PIE	.30	.60	.90	1.20	1.50		
	COOKIES	.20	.40	.60	.80	1.00		
	C - SHAKES	.45	.90	1.35	1.80	2.25		
	S - SHAKES	.45	.90	1.35	1.80	2.25		
	V - SHAKES	.45	.90	1.35	1.80	2.25		
COLA	COLA SM.	.25	.50	.75	1.00	1.25		
	COLA M.	.30	.60	.90	1.20	1.50		
	COLA L.	.40	.80	1.20	1.60	2.00		
ORANGE	ORANGE SM.	.25	.50	.75	1.00	1.25		
	ORANGE M.	.30	.60	.90	1.20	1.50		
	ORANGE L.	.40	.80	1.20	1.60	2.00		
R' BEER	R' BEER SM.	.25	.50	.75	1.00	1.25		
	R' BEER M.	.30	.60	.90	1.20	1.50		
	R'BEER L.	.40	.80	1.20	1.60	2.00		
	MILK	.25	.50	.75	1.00	1.25		
	O.J./HOT CHOC.	.25	.50	.75	1.00	1.25		
	COFFEE SM C/S	.25	.50	.75	1.00	1.25		
	SC. EGGS W/MUFFIN	.49	.98	1.47	1.96	2.45		
	EGG & MUFFIN	.85	1.70	2.55	3.40	4.25		
	SAUSAGE & EGGS	.99	1.98	2.97	3.96	4.95		
	MUFFINS	.25	.50	.75	1.00	1.25		
	H' CAKES & SAUS.	.90	1.80	2.70	3.60	4.50		
	HOT CAKES	.39	.78	1.17	1.56	1.95		
	DONUTS	.20	.40	.60	.80	1.00		
	BROWNIES	.35	.70	1.05	1.40	1.75		

☐ Qtr Dbl K M Pi O Ch Pl SUB

☐ Qtr Dbl K M Pi O Ch Pl TAX

☐ M S L Pi O Ch Pl TOTAL

☐ Filet Ts Ch K M Pl

NAME _____

- *STOP*
- Check your answers on page 347.
- Correct the problems you missed.
- Shade box 1 opposite "estimation" on page xix.
- If this was the only subskill you had to work on in this section, take the test on page 280.
- If you have other subskills to work on in this section, go on to the next one.

SUBSKILL 2: Estimating Products and Quotients

Problem: Estimate.

  (a) 768 × 32   (b) 438064 ÷ 44

Solution: ● Round numbers to numbers you can work with in your head.

  ● If product, multiply non-zero part of numbers and attach zeros of numbers to product.

  ● If quotient, divide non-zero part of numbers and attach zeros of dividend minus zeros of divisor to quotient.

(a) 768 × 32

  800 × 30 = 2 4 0 0 0

(b) 438064 ÷ 44

  440000 ÷ 40 = 1 1 0 0 0 0

Lesson: *Estimation* is an art. Sometimes you hit. Sometimes you miss. The objective is to stay within reason, that is, within 10% of the answer. To improve your estimation of products, round one number up, one number down. To improve your estimation of quotients, round both numbers either up or down.

  (a) 768 × 32 = 24576 (Twenty-four thousand was a hit.)

  (b) 438064 ÷ 44 = 9956 (Eleven thousand was a miss.)

Drill and Practice:

Set 1

1. Select the biggest number.

  (a) 39 × 41, 52 × 28, or 19 × 98

  (b) 385 ÷ 35, 281 ÷ 13, or 97 ÷ 5

2. Estimate.

  (a)   25 × 403   (d)   89 ÷ 17

  (b)   380
        × 19   (e)   203)‾1‾4‾9‾5‾

  (c)   2.905
        × 1.83   (f)   8)‾1‾1‾5‾.‾0‾3‾8‾

  ● *STOP.*
  ● Check your answers on page 347.
  ● Correct the problems you missed.
  ● Go on to Set 2.

Set 2

1. Select the biggest number.

  (a) 98 × 14, 121 × 7, or 65 × 30

  (b) 218 ÷ 48, 86 ÷ 13, or 461 ÷ 58

2. Estimate.

  (a)   305 × 6   (d)   819 ÷ 4

(b)   39
      ×15

(e) 98)7532

(c)   92.04
      ×11.05

(f) 23)48.02

- *STOP.*
- Check your answers on page 347.
- Correct the problems you missed.
- Go on to Set 3 or 4.

Set 3

1. Select the biggest number.

   (a) 12 × 8 × 5, 500, or 9 × 3 × 6 × 4

   (b) 16 ÷ 7, 1.9, or 48 ÷ 25

2. Estimate.

   (a) 8 × 31

   (d) 807 ÷ 421

   (b)   81
        × 9

   (e) 3)1825

   (c)   407.5
        × 5.16

   (f) 409)15321.06

- *STOP.*
- Check your answers on page 347.
- Correct the problems you missed.
- Go on to Set 4.

Set 4

1. Which is best, an estimate or an exact count for

   (a) the number of trees in a five-acre apple orchard?

   (b) the number of apples in an apple orchard?

   (c) the number of apples in a bag at the grocery store?

   (d) the number of apples in a lunch box?

(e) the number of apples it takes to make one gallon of apple cider?

2. Twenty-four packages of hamburgers—48 hamburgers in each package: About how many hamburgers?

3. Nineteen pounds of cheese slices—18 slices in each pound: About how many slices?

4. Six hundred and seventy-eight acres— about 200 trees per acre: How many trees?

5. One million human hairs—about 120,000 hairs per human: How many humans?

6. Quickly, how many ten-foot 2×6's for a $20-bill?

- *STOP*
- Check your answers on page 347.
- Correct the problems you missed.
- Shade box 2 opposite "estimation" on page xix.
- If this was the last subskill you had to work on in this section, take the test on page 280.
- If you have other subskills to work on in this section, go on to the next one.

SUBSKILL 3: Estimating with Fractions, Decimals, and Percents

Problem: Estimate.

(a) $\frac{5}{19} \times 217$

(b) $8907 \div .475$

(c) 35% of 28

Solution: • Round fraction, decimal, or percent to a fraction like 1/2, 1/3, or 1/4 that you can work with in your head.

• Round remaining number to a number you can work in your head.

• If multiplying, think *piece of number* same as *piece of pie.*

• If dividing, think *number into pieces* same as *pie into pieces.*

(a) $\frac{5}{19} \times 217$ ⟶ one-fourth of 200

or $\boxed{50}$

(b) $8907 \div .475$ ⟶ nine thousand into halves

or $\boxed{18000}$

(c) 35% of 28 ⟶ one-third of 30

or $\boxed{10}$

Lesson: Estimation is an art. Sometimes you hit. Sometimes you miss. The objective is to stay within reason, that is, within 10% of the answer.

(a) $\frac{5}{19} \times 217 = 57.11$ to nearest hundredth (Fifty was a miss.)

(b) $8907 \div .475 = 18751.58$ to nearest hundredth (Eighteen thousand was a hit.)

(c) 35% of 28 = 9.8 (Ten was a hit.)

Drill and Practice:

Set 1

1. Select the biggest number.

$\frac{4}{9} \times 635$, $50 \div .19$, or 25% of 789

2. Estimate.

(a) $\frac{7}{13} \times 498$ (d) $15 \div \frac{6}{19}$

(b) $2057 \div .249$ (e) $1189 \times .675$

(c)   78% of 12   (f)   53% of 385

- *STOP.*
- Check your answers on page 347.
- Correct the problems you missed.
- Go on to Set 2.

Set 2

1. Select the biggest number.

$47 \div \frac{9}{17}$, $1834 \times .09$, or 32% of 345

2. Estimate.

(a) $74 \div \frac{3}{11}$ (d) $\frac{2}{7} \times 139$

(b) $118 \times .2041$ (e) $357 \div .491$

(c)   48% of 316   (f)   8% of $1200

- *STOP.*
- Check your answers on page 347.
- Correct the problems you missed.
- Go on to Set 3 or 4.

Set 3

1. Select the biggest number.

$\frac{3}{29} \times 1107$, $42 \div .35$, or 89% of 112

2. Estimate.

(a) $\frac{11}{15} \times 598$ (d) $146 \div \frac{3}{11}$

(b) $38 \div .0831$ (e) 39×1.24

(c) $7\frac{1}{2}\% \times \$240$ (f) $8\frac{3}{4}\% \times \$5895.50$

- *STOP.*
- Check your answers on page 347.
- Correct the problems you missed.
- Go on to Set 4.

Set 4

1. Which is true?

   a. The smaller the divisor, the bigger the quotient.

   b. The smaller the multiplier, the bigger the product.

2. Quickly, which is longer, 5/16 of 13 feet or 5/8 of eight feet?

3. Quickly, which is more, 21% of $516 or 47% of $283?

4. You have been given $10 to buy six dozen donuts for a party. You enter a donut shop and see a sign stating that donuts are $1.93 per dozen with a 20% discount on orders of five dozen or more. Quickly, what do you do?

- *STOP*
- Check your answers on page 347.
- Correct the problems you missed.
- Shade box 3 opposite "estimation" on page xix.
- If this was the last subskill you had to work on in this section, take the test on page 280.
- If you have other subskills to work on in this section go on to the next one.

SUBSKILL 4: Estimating Lengths

Problem: Estimate the length of segment *AB*

(a) to the nearest half-inch

(b) to the nearest centimeter

A ———————————————————————————— B

Solution: • Use a part of your body as an estimation guide.

(a) Complete Table 17.1 using the inch rule in Figure 17.1. Then use a part of your body as an estimation guide and estimate the length of segment *AB* to the nearest inch. A good estimate would be seven inches.

Table 17.1 Length of Parts of Body to Nearest Inch

Part of body	Length to nearest inch
	one inch
	two inches
	six inches
	one foot (12 inches)

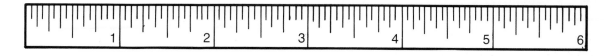

Figure 17.1

(b) Complete Table 17.2 using the centimeter rule in Figure 17.2. Then use a part of your body as an estimation guide and estimate the length of segment *AB* to the nearest centimeter. A good estimate would be 18 centimeters.

Table 17.2 Length of Parts of Body to Nearest Centimeter

Part of body	Length to nearest centimeter
	one centimeter
	two centimeters
	one decimeter (ten centimeters)
	one meter (100 centimeters)

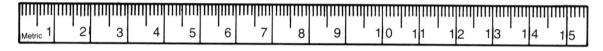

Figure 17.2

Lesson: Every measurement is an estimation. Some are just better than others.

Drill and Practice:

Set 1

1. Select the longer line.

> ——————— l ——————— <

← ———————— m ———————— →

2. Estimate the lengths to the nearest half-inch.

(a) ├————————————┤

(b) ├—————————————————┤

3. Estimate the lengths to the nearest centimeter.

(a) ├——————┤

(b) ├————————————————┤

- *STOP.*
- Check your answers on page 347.
- Correct the problems you missed.
- Go on to Set 2.

Set 2

1. Select the longer line.

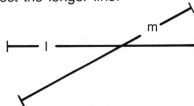

2. Estimate the lengths to the nearest half-inch.

   (a) ├────────────┤

   (b) ├────────────────────────────┤

3. Estimate the lengths to the nearest centimeter.

   (a) ├──────────────┤

   (b) ├────────────────────┤

- *STOP.*
- Check your answers on page 348.
- Correct the problems you missed.
- Go on to Set 3 or 4.

Set 3

1. Select the longer line.

2. Estimate the lengths to the nearest half-inch.

   (a) ├──────────────┤

   (b) ├────────────────────────┤

3. Estimate the lengths to the nearest centimeter.

   (a) ├──────────────────┤

   (b) ├────────────────────────┤

- *STOP.*
- Check your answers on page 348.
- Correct the problems you missed.
- Go on to Set 4.

Set 4

1. Estimate the length of the following to the nearest half-inch or foot.
   - (a) new pencil
   - (b) meter stick

2. Estimate the length of the following to the nearest centimeter or meter.
   - (a) dollar bill
   - (b) Volkswagen

3. Using the dimensions of a brick as an estimation guide, estimate the height of a brick building.

4. Using the dimensions of a paving stone as an estimation guide, estimate the distance between two buildings.

- *STOP*

- Check your answers on page 348.

- Correct the problems you missed.

- Shade box 4 opposite "estimation" on page xix.

- Take the test on page 280.

Inventory Post Test for Estimation

1. Estimate $117.10 + $82.95 + $9.95. Do *not* compute.

2. Estimate 583079 ÷ 19. Do *not* compute.

3. Estimate 48% of 38. Do *not* compute.

4. Estimate the length of segment *AB* to the nearest centimeter. Do *not* measure.

   A ├───┤B

- *STOP*

- Check your answers with the instructor.

- As before, work through the subskills in this section which correspond to the problems you missed, except work the *even* drill-and-practice problems.

- Take the test on page 281.

SKILL
Integers

SUBSKILL 1:

Problem: Whic

(a)

Solu

Inventory Pretest for Integ

1. Which letter corresponds to -5? D

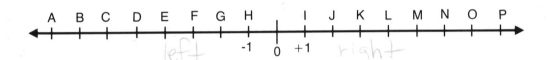

```
    A   B   C   D   E   F   G   H       I   J   K   L   M   N   O   P
  ◄─┼───┼───┼───┼───┼───┼───┼───┼───┼───┼───┼───┼───┼───┼───┼───┼──►
                              left      -1  0  +1   right
```

2. $^+9 - {}^-4 = ?$ $+13$

3. $\left| {}^+6 + {}^-2 \right| = ?$

4. $^+20 \div {}^-4 = ?$ -5

5. $6 + 2 \times 3 - 4 \div 2 = ?$

6. $\left\{ \left[(4 + 2) \times 5 + 2 \right] \div 8 - 3 \right\} \times 15 = ?$ 15

   6×5 $\frac{4}{8\sqrt{32}}$ -3 $1 \times 15 = 1$

- *STOP*
- Check your answers on page 348.
- Shade the boxes opposite "integers" on page xix which correspond to the problems you got right.
- If you got all of them right, take the test on page 297.
- If you missed some of them, start working on the subskills in this section which correspond to the ones you missed.
- For each subskill, look at the example, study the solution, think about the lesson, and work the *odd* drill-and-practice problems.

Meaning of Integers

h letter corresponds to

+3? (b) ⁻1? (c) ⁻7? (d) 6?

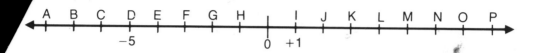

A B C D E F G H I J K L M N O P

−5   0 +1

ion: • K, H, B, and N, respectively.
Positive numbers lie to the right
of zero on the number line,
negative numbers to the left. A
number without a positive or
negative sign in front of it is
understood to be a positive
number.

Lesson: A *raised* plus sign in the context of a number line means *to the right of zero.* It does *not*
mean *add.* Similarly, a *raised* minus sign in the context of a number line means *to the*
left of zero. It does *not* mean *subtract.* To illustrate,

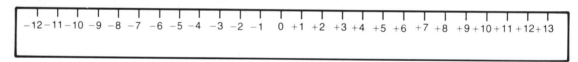

−12 −11 −10 −9 −8 −7 −6 −5 −4 −3 −2 −1 0 +1 +2 +3 +4 +5 +6 +7 +8 +9 +10 +11 +12 +13

Drill and Practice:

Set 1

1. Which letter corresponds to
   (a) ⁺5?   (b) ⁻3?   (c) ⁻6?   (d) 4?

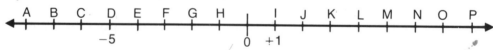

A B C D E F G H I J K L M N O P

−5   0 +1

2. What number corresponds to
   (a) *A?*   (b) *J?*   (c) *D?*   (d) *M?*

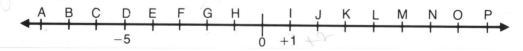

A B C D E F G H I J K L M N O P

−5   0 +1

• *STOP.*
• Check your answers on page 348.
• Correct the problems you missed.
• Go on to Set 2.

Set 2

1. Which letter corresponds to

   (a) ⁻8?   (b) ⁺2?   (c) ⁻2?   (d) 8?

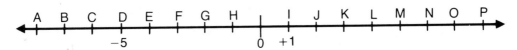

2. What number corresponds to

   (a) *B*?   (b) *N*?   (c) *G*?   (d) *P*?

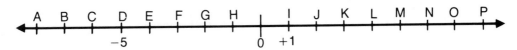

- *STOP.*
- Check your answers on page 348.
- Correct the problems you missed.
- Go on to Set 3 or 4.

Set 3

1. Which letter corresponds to

   (a) ⁺1?   (b) ⁻5?   (c) 7?   (d) ⁻4?

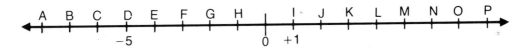

2. What number corresponds to

   (a) *L*?   (b) *E*?   (c) *N*?   (d) *C*?

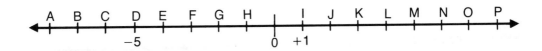

- *STOP.*
- Check your answers on page 348.
- Correct the problems you missed.
- Go on to Set 4.

Set 4

1. What temperature centigrade is shown on the thermometer?

2. Shade each thermometer to show the given temperature.

(a) 40°C   (b) 84°C   (c) 0°C   (d) ⁻6°C

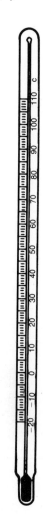

3. If finding $8 is denoted ⁺8, how would losing $3 be denoted?

4. If two meters north is denoted ⁻2, how would seven meters south be denoted?

- *STOP*

- Check your answers on page 348.

- Correct the problems you missed.

- Shade box 1 opposite "integers" on page xix.

- If this was the only subskill you had to work on in this section, take the test on page 296.

- If you have other subskills to work on in this section, go on to the next one.

SUBSKILL 2: Addition and Subtraction of Integers

Problem: Add or subtract.

(a) $^-3 + {}^-5$ *−8*

(b) $^-4 + {}^+9$ *+5*

(c) $^+6 - {}^-7$ *−1*

(d) $^+2 - {}^+8$ *+10*

(e) $^-1 + {}^-6 - {}^+4$

−11

(a) $^-3 + {}^-5 =$ *−8* $\boxed{^-8}$

(b) $^-4 + {}^+9 =$ *+5* $\boxed{^+5}$

(c) $^+6 - {}^-7 -1$ $^+6 + {}^+7 = +13$

$\boxed{^+13}$

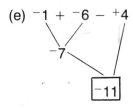

(d) $^+2 - {}^+8 +10$ $^+2 + {}^-8 = -6$

$\boxed{^-6}$

(e) $^-1 + {}^-6 - {}^+4$

$^-7$

$\boxed{^-11}$

Solution: • Never subtract. Always add *opposite.*

• If like signs, add numbers and attach sign to sum.

• If unlike signs, subtract smaller number from larger number and attach sign of larger number to difference.

Lesson: Addition and subtraction of *whole numbers* has to do with *quantities,* the effects of combining and separating them, respectively. In contrast, addition and subtraction of *integers* has to do with *numbers on a number line,* the effects of "following by" and "following by the *opposite* of," respectively.

(a) $^-3 + {}^-5$ or three to the left followed by five to the left

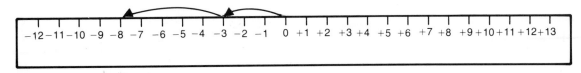

(b) $^-4 + {}^+9$ or four to the left followed by nine to the right

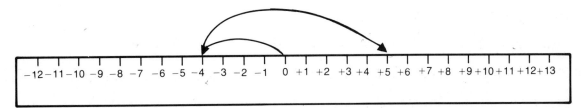

(c) $^+6 - {}^-7$ or six to the right followed by the opposite of seven to the left

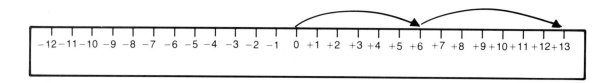

(d) $^+2 - {}^+8$ or two to the right followed by the opposite of eight to the right

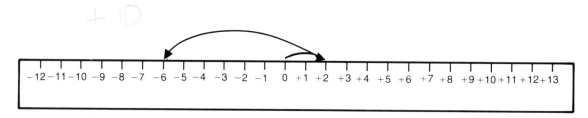

(e) $^-1 + {}^-6 - {}^+4$ or one to the left followed by six to the left followed by the opposite of four to the right

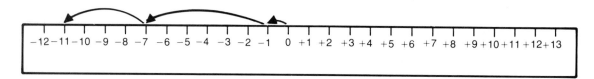

Drill and Practice:

Set 1

1. Add or subtract.
   (a) $^-5 + {}^-2$
   (b) $3 - 7$
   (c) $^-6 + {}^+11$
   (d) $^-10 + {}^+6 - {}^-12$
   (e) $8 - {}^-4$

2. Illustrate $^-9 + {}^-2$.

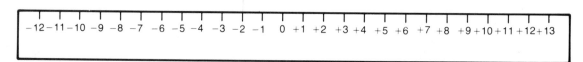

3. Write $^+7 - {}^-3$ as an addition problem.

- *STOP.*
- Check your answers on page 348.
- Correct the problems you missed.
- Go on to Set 2.

Set 2

1. Add or subtract.

   (a) $^-8 + {}^-1$

   (b) $7 - 23$

   (c) $^-12 + {}^+3$

   (d) $53 - 144 + 17 - 5 + 10$

   (e) $9 - {}^-5$

2. Illustrate $^-9 + {}^+20$.

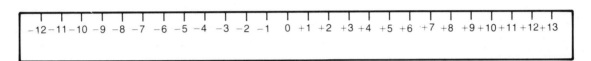

3. Write $^+1 - {}^+10$ as an addition problem

- *STOP.*
- Check your answers on page 348.
- Correct the problems you missed.
- Go on to Set 3 or 4.

Set 3

1. Add or subtract.

   (a) $^+7 - {}^+15$

   (b) $79 - 516$

   (c) $^-11 + {}^+3$

   (d) $53 - 144 + 17 - 5 + 10$

   (e) $102 - {}^-58$

2. Illustrate $^-10 - {}^-21$.

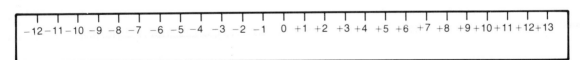

3. Write $^-13 - {}^-25$ as an addition problem.

- *STOP.*
- Check your answers on page 348.
- Correct the problems you missed.
- Go on to Set 4.

Set 4

1. The Jets lost six yards on a first down, gained two yards on a second down. How well did they do?

2. You are dieting. You lose four pounds one week, gain five pounds the next week. How well are you doing?

3. You are playing cards. You lose four cents, win seven cents, win 11 cents, lose 18 cents, lose 12 cents, win six cents, win 13 cents, and lose one cent. How well are you doing?

4. A number is divisible by 11 if the sum of its digits with alternate signs is $^-11$, zero, or $^+11$. To illustrate, 83,479 is divisible by 11 because $^+8 + {}^-3 + {}^+4 + {}^-7 + {}^+9 = {}^+11$.

   Which are divisible by 11?
   a. 75262   b. 187   c. 308
   d. 3948   e. 103818

5. Simplify the following treasure map.

   Start at the cork tree and go 18 meters east, 32 meters south, 15 meters west, 45 meters north, 17 meters west, six meters south, 11 meters east, 13 meters north, and nine meters west. Voila!

6. You are bear hunting. You leave camp and walk south five miles, east five miles, and north five miles, and you come across a bear raiding your camp. What color is the bear?

- *STOP*
- Check your answers on page **348**.
- Correct the problems you missed.
- Shade box 2 opposite "integers" on page **xix**.
- If this was the last subskill you had to work on in this section, take the test on page **296**.
- If you have other subskills to work on in this section, go on to the next one.

SUBSKILL 3: Absolute Value

Problem: Find the absolute values.

   (a) $\left| {}^-7 \right|$

   (b) $\left| {}^+13 \right|$

   (c) $\left| {}^+12 + {}^-8 \right|$

   (d) $\left| 8 - 13 \right|$

Solution:
- The absolute value of a number is just the number.

   (a) $\left| {}^-7 \right| = \boxed{7}$

   (b) $\left| {}^+13 \right| = \boxed{13}$

   (c) $\left| {}^+12 + {}^-8 \right| = \left| {}^+4 \right| = \boxed{4}$

   (d) $\left| 8 - 13 \right| = \left| {}^-5 \right| = \boxed{5}$

Lesson: Absolute value is a *distance* concept. The absolute value of a number is the distance of the number from zero on the number line. The absolute value of the *difference* of numbers is the distance *between* the numbers on the number line.

(a) $\mid {}^-7 \mid$ or the distance from zero to $^-7$

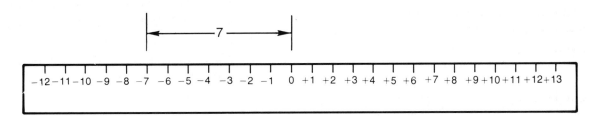

(b) $\mid {}^+13 \mid$ or the distance from zero to $^+13$

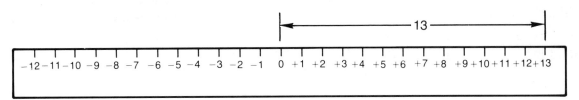

(c) $\mid {}^+12 + {}^-8 \mid$ or the distance between $^+12$ and $^+8$ because $^+12 + {}^-8 =$ $^+12 - {}^+8$

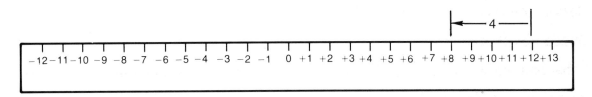

(d) $\mid 8 - 13 \mid$ or the distance between $^+8$ and $^+13$

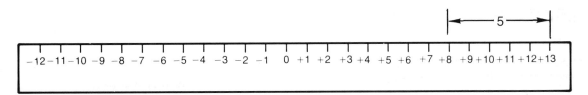

Drill and Practice:

Set 1

1. Find the absolute values.

(a) $\mid {}^-5 \mid$ (c) $\mid {}^+6 + {}^-3 \mid$

(b) $\mid {}^+21 \mid$ (d) $\mid 5 - {}^-4 \mid$

2. Illustrate $\mid {}^-10 \mid$.

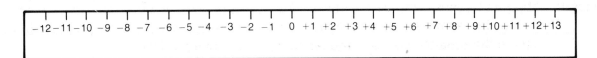

3. Illustrate $\left| {}^{+}8 - {}^{-}3 \right|$.

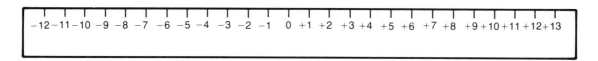

- *STOP.*
- Check your answers on page 348.
- Correct the problems you missed.
- Go on to Set 2.

Set 2

1. Find the absolute values.

   (a) $\left| {}^{+}9 \right|$ (c) $\left| {}^{-}15 - {}^{-}20 \right|$

   (b) $\left| {}^{-}12 \right|$ (d) $\left| 12 - 35 \right|$

2. Illustrate $\left| {}^{+}6 \right|$.

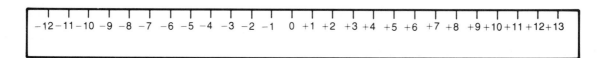

3. Illustrate $\left| {}^{-}9 - {}^{-}4 \right|$.

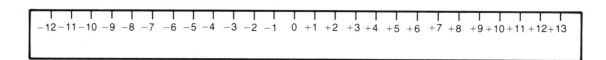

- *STOP.*
- Check your answers on page 348.
- Correct the problems you missed.
- Go on to Set 3 or 4.

Set 3

1. Find the absolute values.

   (a) $\left| {}^{-}25 \right|$ (c) $\left| {}^{-}18 + {}^{+}5 \right|$

   (b) $\left| {}^{+}105 \right|$ (d) $\left| 75 - 225 \right|$

2. Illustrate $\left| {}^{-}5 \right|$.

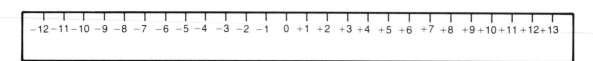

3. Illustrate $|\,^-6 + \,^-7\,|$.

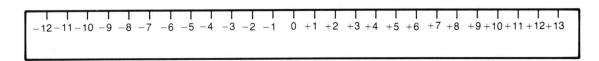

- *STOP.*
- Check your answers on page 348.
- Correct the problems you missed.
- Go on to Set 4.

Set 4

1. Why the emphasis on absolute value?

- *STOP*
- Check your answers on page 348.
- Correct the problems you missed.
- Shade box 3 opposite "integers" on page xix.
- If this was the last subskill you had to work on in this section, take the test on page 296.
- If you have other subskills to work on in this section, go on to the next one.

SUBSKILL 4: Multiplication and Division of Integers

Problem: Multiply or divide.

(a) $^+5 \times \,^-7$ ⌐0

(b) $^-8 \times \,^-9$ $+^-$

(c) $^-16 \div \,^+2$ 8

(d) $^+25 \div \,^+5$ $+$ 5

Solution:
- Disregard signs.
- Multiply or divide.

- If like signs, make answer positive.
- If unlike signs, make answer negative.

(a) $^+5 \times \,^-7 = \boxed{^-35}$

(b) $^-8 \times \,^-9 = \boxed{^+72}$

(c) $^-16 \div \,^+2 = \boxed{^-8}$

(d) $^+25 \div \,^+5 = \boxed{^+5}$

Lesson: The rules for multiplying integers arise naturally from the following number pattern beginning with $^+3 \times {}^+3 = {}^+9$. The rules for dividing integers arise similarly.

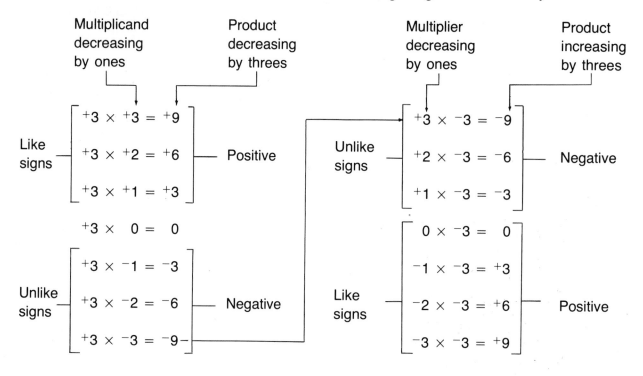

Drill and Practice:

Set 1

1. $^+4 \times {}^-6 = ?$ — 24

2. $^-12 \times {}^-3 = ?$ $+36$

3. $^-24 \div 8 = ?$ — 3

- *STOP.*
- Check your answers on page 348.
- Correct the problems you missed.
- Go on to Set 2.

Set 2

1. $^-8 \times {}^+32 = ?$

2. $^+15 \times {}^+6 = ?$

3. $72 \div {}^-6 = ?$

4. $14 \div 2 = ?$ $+7$

5. $^-51 \times 8 = ?$ —

4. $^-121 \div {}^-11 = ?$

5. $^-75 \times 40 = ?$

- *STOP.*
- Check your answers on page 348.
- Correct the problems you missed.
- Go on to Set 3 or 4.

Set 3

1. $^+7 \times {}^+9 = ?$

2. $^-5 \times {}^+13 = ?$

3. $^+39 \div {}^-13 = ?$

4. $81 \div {}^-3 = ?$

5. $12 \times {}^-8 = ?$

- *STOP.*
- Check your answers on page 348.
- Correct the problems you missed.
- Go on to Set 4.

Set 4

1. You walk three blocks east five times. Describe your walk as simply as possible.

2. You are playing cards. You play six times and win seven cents each time. How well are you doing?

3. You are dieting. You lose two pounds a week for six weeks. How well are you doing?

4. A frog is at the bottom of a ten-foot well. It jumps six feet and slides back four. The frog will need how many jumps to get out of the well?

5. If you film the water draining from a bathtub and project the film backwards, what will you see?

- *STOP*
- Check your answers on page 348.
- Correct the problems you missed.
- Shade box 4 opposite "integers" on page xix.
- If this was the last subskill you had to work on in this section. take the test on page 296.
- If you have other subskills to work on in this section, go on to the next one.

SUBSKILL 5: Order of Operations

Problem: $5 + 3 \times 6 - 4 \div 2 = ?$

Solution:
- Work from left to right.
- Multiply or divide.
- Add or subtract.

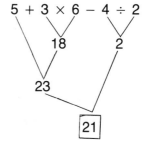

Lesson: If you do not do *exactly* as stated, you will typically get a different answer. To illustrate, if you just work from left to right on the above, you will get 22.

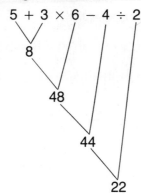

Drill and Practice:

Set 1

1. $6 + 2 \times 5 - 14 \div 7 = ?$

2. $2 \times 8 + 1 - 6 \div 3 = ?$

3. $8 \div 4 \div 2 = ?$

4. $^{+}5 - {}^{+}3 \times {}^{-}2 \div {}^{+}6 + {}^{+}1 = ?$

- *STOP.*
- Check your answers on page 349.
- Correct the problems you missed.
- Go on to Set 2.

Set 2

1. $8 - 30 \div 10 + 5 \times 6 = ?$

2. $12 \div 3 - 8 + 2 \times 5 = ?$

3. $2 \times 3 \times 4 = ?$

4. $^{+}1 + {}^{-}1 \times {}^{-}1 \times {}^{-}1 = ?$

- *STOP.*
- Check your answers on page 349.
- Correct the problems you missed.
- Go on to Set 3 or 4.

Set 3

1. $2 + 3 - 4 \times 5 \div 2 \times 3 = ?$

2. $36 \div 12 \times 3 - 5 + 1 - 8 \times 5 = ?$

3. $2 \times 6 \div 4 \div 3 = ?$

4. $^{-}8 \div {}^{+}4 \times {}^{-}5 + {}^{-}7 - {}^{-}2 = ?$

- *STOP.*
- Check your answers on page 349.
- Correct the problems you missed.
- Go on to Set 4.

Set 4

1. Why the emphasis on order of operations?

- *STOP*
- Check your answers on page 349.
- Correct the problems you missed.
- Shade box 5 opposite "integers" on page xix.
- If this was the last subskill you had to work on in this section, take the test on page 296.
- If you have other subskills to work on in this section, go on to the next one.

SUBSKILL 6: Parentheses, Brackets, and Braces

Problem: $\{[(6 + 4) \div 2 + 7] \div 3 - 2\}$
$\times 5 = ?$

$\{[(6 + 4) \div 2 + 7] \div 3 - 2\} \times 5 =$

$\{[10 \div 2 + 7] \div 3 - 2\} \times 5 =$

$\{12 \div 3 - 2\} \times 5 = 2 \times 5 = \boxed{10}$

Solution:
- Work from inside out, doing what is grouped *first.*

- Discard grouping symbols.

Lesson: Grouping symbols are to mathematics what periods, commas, and question marks are to English. They *punctuate.* They indicate what is to be done *first.* The convention is to group first with parentheses ( ), second with brackets [ ], and third with braces { }.

Drill and Practice:

Set 1

1. $(6 + 2) \times 5 - 14 \div 7 = ?$

2. $2 \times (8 + 1 - 6) \div 3 = ?$

3. $8 \div (4 \div 2) = ?$

4. Insert parentheses to get eight:
   $3 + 5 \times 4 - 3$

- *STOP.*
- Check your answers on page 349.
- Correct the problems you missed.
- Go on to Set 2.

Set 2

1. $[8 - 30 \div (10 + 5)] \times 6 = ?$

2. $[6 \times (2 + 3) - 5] \div 5 = ?$

3. $5 \times [1 + 8 \div (2 - 4)] = ?$

4. Insert parentheses and brackets to get three:
   $4 + 8 \times 1 - 6 \div 2$

- *STOP.*
- Check your answers on page 349.
- Correct the problems you missed.
- Go on to Set 3 or 4.

Set 3

1. $\{[3 + (4 - 3) \times 5] \div 4 + 3\} \div 5 = ?$

2. $\{[(1 + 2) \times 3 + 4] \times 5 - 65\} \times 1 = ?$

3. $5 \div \{5 \times [2 \times (5 - 3) - 3] - 10\} = ?$

4. Insert parentheses, brackets, and braces to get ten:
   $1 + 2 \times 3 + 6 \div 5 + 2 \times 2$

- *STOP.*
- Check your answers on page 349.
- Correct the problems you missed.
- Go on to Set 4.

Set 4

1. Why the emphasis on parentheses, brackets, and braces?

- *STOP*

- Check your answers on page 349.

- Correct the problems you missed.

- Shade box 6 opposite "integers" on page xix.

- Take the test on page 296.

Inventory Post Test for Integers

1. Which letter corresponds to $^-6$?

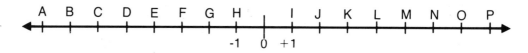

2. $^+11 - {}^-5 = ?$

3. $\left| {}^-2 + {}^+10 \right| = ?$

4. $^-18 \div {}^+6 = ?$

5. $1 + 5 \times 3 - 8 \div 4 = ?$

6. $\{2 + [(1 + 2) \times 3 - 5] \times 2\} \div 5 = ?$

- *STOP*

- Check your answers with the instructor.

- As before, work through the subskills in this section which correspond to the problems
- you missed, except work the *even* drill-and-practice problems.

- Take the test on page 297.

SKILL
Less Than and Greater Than

Inventory Pretest for
Less Than and Greater Than

1. Which are true?

             a. $7 < 9$ b. $30 > 24$ c. $103 > 130$

2. Which is greater, $\dfrac{4}{7}$ or $\dfrac{6}{11}$?

3. Which is greater, 1.051 or 1.501?

4. Which is greater, 5% or 50%?

5. Which are true?

             a. $^-3 > {}^-1$ b. $^+2 > {}^-5$ c. $^-7 < {}^+4$

- *STOP*

- Check your answers on page **349**.

- Shade the boxes opposite "less than and greater than" on page xix which correspond to the problems you got right.

- If you got all of them right, take the test on page **308**.

- If you missed some of them, start working on the subskills in this section which correspond to the ones you missed.

- For each subskill, look at the example, study the solution, think about the lesson, and work the *odd* drill-and-practice problems.

SUBSKILL 1: Meaning of Less Than and Greater Than

Problem: Which are true?

a. 5 < 7 b. 20 > 11 c. 19 > 91

Solution: a and b Just think of < and > as *greedy* mouths that always eat the *bigger* number.

Lesson: The symbols < and > are read *less than* and *greater than,* respectively. They are used to compare unequal numbers.

Drill and Practice:

Set 1

1. Which are true?
   a. 7 < 9   b. 35 > 19   c. 23 > 32

2. Write a *less than* sentence for the centimeter cubes.

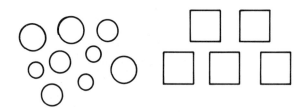

3. Write a *greater than* sentence for the circles and squares.

- *STOP.*
- Check your answers on page 349.
- Correct the problems you missed.
- Go on to Set 2.

Set 2

1. Which is true?
   a. 5 < 1   b. 20 > 30   c. 11 < 111

2. Write a *greater than* sentence for the centimeter cubes.

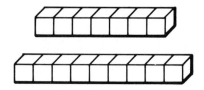

3. Write a *less than* sentence for the triangles and trapezoids.

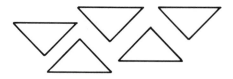

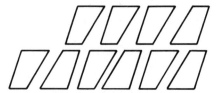

- *STOP.*
- Check your answers on page 349.
- Correct the problems you missed.
- Go on to Set 3 or 4.

Set 3

1. Which are true?

 a. 6 > 8   b. 21 > 12   c. 0 < 15

2. Write a *less than* sentence for the centimeter cubes.

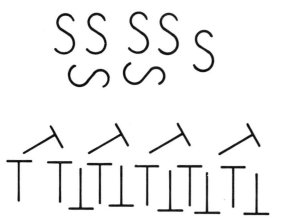

3. Write a *greater than* sentence for the S's and T's.

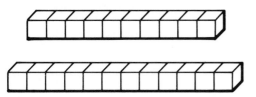

- *STOP.*
- Check your answers on page 349.
- Correct the problems you missed.
- Go on to Set 4.

Set 4

1. Which is more?

a.   b.

2. Which is shorter?

a.   b.

3. Which is longer?

a.

b.

4. Which is better?

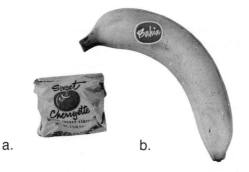

a.   b.

5. Which is more, three pennies and two nickels or one quarter?

- *STOP*
- Check your answers on page 349.
- Correct the problems you missed.
- Shade box 1 opposite "less than and greater than" on page xix.
- If this was the only subskill you had to work on in this section, take the test on page 306.
- If you have other subskills to work on in this section, go on to the next one.

SUBSKILL 2: Comparing Fractions

Problem: Which is greater, $\dfrac{3}{5}$ or $\dfrac{7}{12}$?

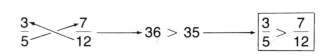

Solution:
- Cross multiply.

- Greater fraction corresponds to greater whole number.

Lesson: The greater the fraction, the greater the numerator *with respect to* the denominator.

$$\frac{3}{5} = \frac{3}{5} \times 1 = \frac{3}{5} \times \frac{12}{12} = \frac{3 \times 12}{5 \times 12} = \frac{36}{60}$$

$$\frac{7}{12} = \frac{7}{12} \times 1 = \frac{7}{12} \times \frac{5}{5} = \frac{7 \times 5}{12 \times 5} = \frac{35}{60}$$

Drill and Practice:

Set 1

Which is greater?

1. $\dfrac{1}{2}$ or $\dfrac{2}{3}$?

2. $\dfrac{1}{3}$ or $\dfrac{3}{4}$?

3. $\dfrac{5}{6}$ or $\dfrac{2}{3}$?

4. $\dfrac{1}{4}$ or $\dfrac{1}{5}$?

Set 2

Which is less?

1. $\dfrac{3}{4}$ or $\dfrac{4}{5}$?

2. $\dfrac{5}{6}$ or $\dfrac{6}{7}$?

3. $\dfrac{8}{9}$ or $\dfrac{14}{25}$?

4. $\dfrac{9}{10}$ or $\dfrac{99}{100}$?

- *STOP.*
- Check your answers on page 349.
- Correct the problems you missed.
- Go on to Set 2.

- *STOP.*
- Check your answers on page 349.
- Correct the problems you missed.
- Go on to Set 3 or 4.

Set 3

Which is greater?

1. $\dfrac{3}{8}$ or $\dfrac{4}{15}$?   2. $\dfrac{7}{16}$ or $\dfrac{1}{2}$?

3. $\dfrac{9}{20}$ or $\dfrac{13}{25}$?   4. $\dfrac{4}{17}$ or $\dfrac{5}{21}$?

- *STOP.*
- Check your answers on page 349.
- Correct the problems you missed.
- Go on to Set 4.

Set 4

1. Which is longer, 7/8 of an inch or 15/16 of an inch?

2. Which is less, 1/2 a pound of ground round or 3/4 of a pound of ground round?

3. Which is more, 1/4 finished or 1/3 finished?

4. Which is the better buy,

   (a) six 12-ounce bottles of cola for 78 cents or eight 12-ounce bottles of cola for 98 cents?

   (b) one six-ounce can of tuna for 54 cents or one nine-ounce can of tuna for 80 cents?

   (c) three oranges for 22 cents or four apples for 25 cents?

   (d) 100 pages of typing paper for 39 cents or 250 pages of typing paper for 99 cents?

- *STOP*

- Check your answers on page 349.

- Correct the problems you missed.

- Shade box 2 opposite "less than and greater than" on page xix.

- If this was the last subskill you had to work on in this section, take the test on page 306.

- If you have other subskills to work on in this section, go on to the next one.

SUBSKILL 3: Comparing Decimals

Problem: Which is greater, 2.17 or 2.036?

Solution: • Compare whole number parts.

   • Greater decimal corresponds to greater whole number part.

   • Compare fraction parts.

   • Greater decimal corresponds to greater fraction part.

$$\dfrac{17}{100} \diagdown \dfrac{36}{1000} \longrightarrow 17000 > 3600$$

$$\dfrac{17}{100} > \dfrac{36}{1000} \longrightarrow .17 > .036$$

$$\boxed{2.17 > 2.036}$$

Lesson: The greater the decimal, the greater the corresponding improper fraction.

$$2.17 = 2\frac{17}{100} = \frac{217}{100} = \frac{217}{100} \times 1 = \frac{217}{100} \times \boxed{\frac{10}{10}} = \frac{217 \times 10}{100 \times 10} = \frac{2170}{1000}$$

$$2.036 = 2\frac{36}{1000} = \frac{2036}{1000}$$

Drill and Practice:

Set 1

Which is greater?

1. 3.58 or 3.071? 2. 1.95 or 1.99?

3. .0123 or .1023? 4. 4.09 or 3.95?

- *STOP.*
- Check your answers on page 349.
- Correct the problems you missed.
- Go on to Set 2.

Set 2

Which is less?

1. 17.0021 or 17.0201? 2. 5.89 or 5.98?

3. .1253 or .1242? 4. 1.25 or .908?

- *STOP.*
- Check your answers on page 349.
- Correct the problems you missed.
- Go on to Set 3 or 4.

Set 3

Which is greater?

1. 250.45 or 250.46? 2. 9.023 or 9.203?

3. .0005 or .5005? 4. 5.1 or 4.99999?

- *STOP.*
- Check your answers on page 349.
- Correct the problems you missed.
- Go on to Set 4.

Set 4

1. Which is less, $5.08 or $5.80?

2. Which is longer, 12.305 meters or 12.350 meters?

3. Which is the greater tolerance, .001 of an inch or .0001 of an inch?

4. Which weighs more, 1.125 kilograms or 1.150 kilograms?

- *STOP*
- Check your answers on page 349.
- Correct the problems you missed.
- Shade box 3 opposite "less than and greater than" on page xix.
- If this was the last subskill you had to work on in this section, take the test on page 306.
- If you have other subskills to work on in this section, go on to the next one.

SUBSKILL 4: Comparing Percents

Problem: Which is greater, 10% or 20%?

Solution: • Compare numeric parts.

  • Greater percent corresponds to greater numeric part.

$$10 < 20 \longrightarrow \boxed{10\% < 20\%}$$

Lesson: The greater the percent, the greater the numerator of the hundredths the percent represents.

$$10\% = \frac{10}{100}$$

$$20\% = \frac{20}{100}$$

Drill and Practice:

Set 1

Which is greater?

1. 5% or 15% ?   2. 7% or 70% ?

3. 25% or 50% ?   4. 75% or 125% ?

• *STOP.*
• Check your answers on page 349.
• Correct the problems you missed.
• Go on to Set 2.

Set 2

Which is less?

1. 8% or 10% ?   2. 15% or 20% ?

3. 1.5% or 1% ?   4. $7\frac{1}{2}$% or 5% ?

• *STOP.*
• Check your answers on page 349.
• Correct the problems you missed.
• Go on to Set 3 or 4.

Set 3

Which is greater?

1. 2% or 20% ?   2. 33% or 34% ?

3. 7.5% or 7.75% ?   4. $5\frac{3}{4}$% or $6\frac{1}{2}$%?

• *STOP.*
• Check your answers on page 349.
• Correct the problems you missed.
• Go on to Set 4.

Set 4

1. Which is the better discount, 10% or 15%?

2. Which is the better interest rate for buying a house, 6¾% or 7½%?

3. Which is the better interest rate for a savings account, 4½% or 5¼%?

4. Which is more, 30% of a lot or 50% of a little?

- *STOP*

- Check your answers on page 349.

- Correct the problems you missed.

- Shade box 4 opposite "less than and greater than" on page xix.

- If this was the last subskill you had to work on in this section, take the test on page 306.

- If you have other subskills to work on in this section, go on to the next one.

SUBSKILL 5: Comparing Integers

Problem: Which are true?

    a. $^-7 < {}^-5$ b. $^+1 > {}^-3$ c. $^-5 > {}^+2$

Solution: a and b An integer is less than another integer if it would lie to the other's *left* on a number line. Correspondingly, an integer is greater than another integer if it would lie to the other's *right* on a number line.

Lesson:

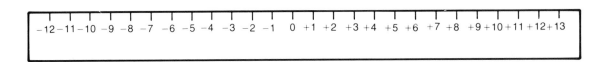

Drill and Practice:

Set 1

1. Which are true?

    a. $^-5 < {}^-1$ b. $^+2 > {}^-6$ c. $^-6 > {}^+4$

2. Which is less, *A* or *B*?

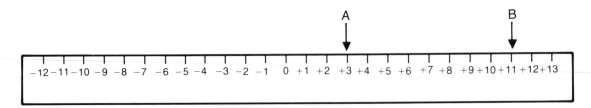

- *STOP.*
- Check your answers on page 349.
- Correct the problems you missed.
- Go on to Set 2.

Set 2

1. Which are true?

   a. $^+8 > ^+10$ b. $^-12 < ^-9$ c. $0 < ^+5$

2. Which is more, *A* or *B*?

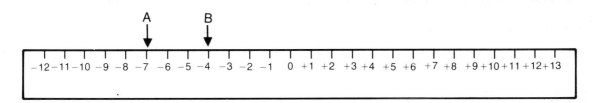

- *STOP.*
- Check your answers on page 349.
- Correct the problems you missed.
- Go on to Set 3 or 4.

Set 3

1. Which are true?

   a. $^-3 < 2$ b. $0 > ^-2$ c. $^-10 > ^+10$

2. Which is less, *A* or *B*?

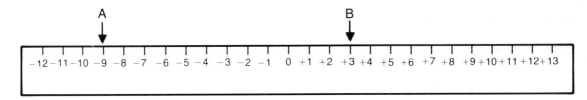

- *STOP.*
- Check your answers on page 349.
- Correct the problems you missed.
- Go on to Set 4.

Set 4

1. Which is colder, $^-6°C$ or $^-10°C$?   2. Which is hotter, 72°F or 102°F?

3. Which checkbook is more in the "red," the one with a balance of $^-$$18 or the one with a balance of $^-$$102?

4. Which business is more in the "black," the one with a balance of $4023 or the one with a balance of $13,500?

- *STOP*

- Check your answers on page 349.

- Correct the problems you missed.

- Shade box 5 opposite "less than and greater than" on page xix.

- Take the test on page 306.

Inventory Post Test for
Less Than and Greater Than

1. Which are true?

    a. $4 < 8$ b. $40 > 21$ c. $218 > 412$

2. Which is greater, $\dfrac{3}{10}$ or $\dfrac{6}{15}$?

3. Which is greater, 7.302 or 7.032?

4. Which is greater, $\dfrac{1}{2}\%$ or 50%?

5. Which are true?

    a. $^-6 > ^-2$ b. $^+8 > ^-12$ c. $^-9 < ^+1$

- *STOP*

- Check your answers with the instructor.

- As before, work through the subskills in this section which correspond to the problems you missed, except work the *even* drill-and-practice problems.

- Take the test on page 307.

SKILL

Exponents and Roots

Inventory Pretest for Exponents and Roots

1. $4^2 = ?$

2. Add or subtract exponents: $6^2 \times 6^3$

3. Multiply exponents: $(3^2 5^4)^7$

4. $2^{-2} = ?$

5. Express in scientific notation: 20503.751

6. $\sqrt{121} = ?$

7. Simplify: $\sqrt{18}$

8. $\sqrt[3]{343} = ?$

9. $216^{\frac{2}{3}} = ?$

- *STOP*

- Check your answers on page 350.

- Shade the boxes opposite "exponents and roots" on page xix which correspond to the problems you got right.

- If you got all of them right, take the test on page 329.

- If you missed some of them, start working on the subskills in this section which correspond to the ones you missed.

- For each subskill, look at the example, study the solution, think about the lesson, and work the *odd* drill-and-practice problems.

SUBSKILL 1: Meaning of Exponents

Problem: $3^4 = ?$

Solution: • 3^4 is shorthand for three times *itself* four times.

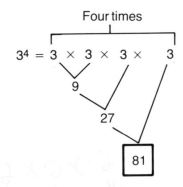

Lesson: M^N is called a *power of M* and is read "*M* to the *N*th power" or simply "*M* to the *N*th." It stands for *M* times itself *N* times. (*M* is called a *base* and *N* an *exponent*. Also, $M^1 = M$ and $M^0 = 1$ for all *M* except zero. $0°$ is undefined.)

Drill and Practice:

Set 1

1. Which equals 3^2?

    a. 3×3 b. 2×3

    c. 3×2 d. $2 \times 2 \times 2$

2. Evaluate.

    (a) 2^2 (b) 2^3 (c) 4^4 (d) 5^2 (e) 7^1 (f) 8^0

3. Express with exponents.

    (a) $2 \times 2 \times 2 \times 2$ (c) 8

    (b) $5 \times 5 \times 5 \times 5 \times 5 \times 5$ (d) 27

• *STOP.*
• Check your answers on page 350.
• Correct the problems you missed.
• Go on to Set 2.

Set 2

1. Which equals 4^3?

    a. 3×4 b. 4×3

    c. $3 \times 3 \times 3 \times 3$ d. $4 \times 4 \times 4$

2. Evaluate.

    (a) 3^4 (c) 5^3 (e) 10^5

    (b) 1^2 (d) 15^0 (f) 25^1

3. Express with exponents.

    (a) $10 \times 10 \times 10$ (c) 16

    (b) $6 \times 6 \times 6$ (d) 625

• *STOP.*
• Check your answers on page 350.
• Correct the problems you missed.
• Go on to Set 3 or 4.

Set 3

1. Which equals 2^4?

    a. $2 \times 2 \times 2 \times 2$ b. 4×2

    c. 2×4 d. 4×4

2. Evaluate.

    (a) 2^5 (c) 10^{12} (e) 1^6

    $2 \times 2 \times$

    (b) 3^5 (d) 79^1 (f) 0^0

3. Express with exponents.

    (a) $8 \times 8 \times 8 \times 8$ (c) 64

    8^4

    (b) $15 \times 15 \times 15$ (d) 10000

    15^3

- *STOP.*
- Check your answers on page 350.
- Correct the problems you missed.
- Go on to Set 4.

Set 4

1. Find the area of the square using $A = s^2$ for the area A of a square of side s.

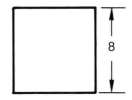

2. Find the volume of the cube using $V = s^3$ for the volume V of a cube of side s.

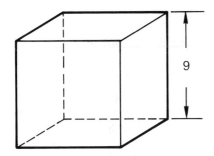

3. Find the area of the circle using $\pi = 3.14$ and $A = \pi r^2$ for the area A of a circle of radius r.

10

4. Find the surface area of the can of tomato sauce using $\pi = 3.14$ and $S = 2\pi r^2 + 2\pi rh$ for the surface area S of a cylinder of radius r and height h.

7 cm

5. Find the volume of the can of tomato sauce using $\pi = 3\frac{1}{7}$ and $V = \pi r^2 h$ for the volume V of a cylinder of radius r and height h.

6. A piece of paper one mile long, one mile wide and 1/1000 of an inch thick is cut in half to form two halves. The halves are then stacked one on top of another and cut in half to form four fourths. The fourths are then stacked one on top of another and cut in half to form eight eighths, and so on, with the pieces of paper doubling in number and halving in area after each cutting.

    (a) How many pieces of paper would there be after 100 cuttings?

    (b) Calculate the height in miles of a stack of this many papers.

- *STOP*

- Check your answers on page 350.

- Correct the problems you missed.

- Shade box 1 opposite "exponents and roots" on page xix.

- If this was the only subskill you had to work on in this section, take the test on page 326.

- If you have other subskills to work on in this section, go on to the next one.

SUBSKILL 2: Adding and Subtracting Exponents

Problem: Add or subtract exponents if possible.

(a) $5^3 + 5^4$ (e) $8^3 - 7^2$

(b) $2^3 \times 2^4$ (f) $3^8 \div 3^5$

(c) $4^2 \times 5^2$ (g) $6^4 \div 2^2$

(d) $10^2 \times 10^3$ (h) $\dfrac{3^5}{5^3}$

Solution:
- Add exponents if *multiplying* like bases.

- Subtract exponents if *dividing* like.

(a) Cannot add or subtract exponents. Not multiplying or dividing.

(b) $2^3 \times 2^4 = 2^{3+4} = \boxed{2^7}$

(c) Cannot add or subtract exponents. Not like bases.

(d) $10^2 \times 10^3 = 10^{2+3} = \boxed{10^5}$

(e) Cannot add or subtract exponents. Not multiplying or dividing.

(f) $3^8 \div 3^5 = 3^{8-5} = \boxed{3^3}$

(g) Cannot add or subtract exponents. Not like bases.

(h) Cannot add or subtract exponents. Not like bases.

Lesson:

$$\text{(b)} \quad 2^3 \times 2^4 = \underbrace{\overbrace{2 \times 2 \times 2}^{\text{Three times}} \times \overbrace{2 \times 2 \times 2 \times 2}^{\text{Four times}}}_{\text{Seven times}} = 2^7$$

Two times   Three times

(d) $10^2 \times 10^3 = \overbrace{10 \times 10}^{\text{Two times}} \times \overbrace{10 \times 10 \times 10}^{\text{Three times}} = 10^5$

Five times

Eight times

(f) $3^8 \div 3^5 = \dfrac{3^8}{3^5} = \dfrac{\overbrace{3 \times 3 \times 3 \times 3 \times 3 \times 3 \times 3 \times 3}^{\text{Eight times}}}{\underbrace{3 \times 3 \times 3 \times 3 \times 3}_{\text{Five times}}} = 3^3$

Five times   Three times

Drill and Practice:

Set 1

Add or subtract exponents if possible.

1. $5^2 + 5^6$ 2. $6^5 - 6^3$ 3. $3^4 \times 3^7$

4. $4^9 \div 4^2$ 5. $2^3 \times 3^2$ 6. $4^{10} \div 2^5$

7. $5^2 \times 5^3$ 8. $\dfrac{2^7}{2^4}$

- *STOP.*
- Check your answers on page 350.
- Correct the problems you missed.
- Go on to Set 2.

Set 2

Add or subtract exponents if possible.

1. $2^6 \times 2^7$ 2. $7^5 \div 7^3$ 3. $4^1 + 6^2$

4. $4^3 - 3^2$ 5. $10^6 \div 10^6$ 6. $3^2 \times 4^2$

7. $6^9 \times 6^3$ 8. $\dfrac{10^6}{10^2}$

- *STOP.*
- Check your answers on page 350.
- Correct the problems you missed.
- Go on to Set 3 or 4.

Set 3

Add or subtract exponents if possible.

1. $8^3 - 8^2$ 2. $10^3 + 10^4$ 3. $1^2 \times 3^4$

4. $13^5 \times 13^8$ 5. $29^{11} \div 29^{10}$ 6. $8^5 \div 7^5$

7. $4^2 \times 4$ 8. $\dfrac{5^3}{5}$

- *STOP.*
- Check your answers on page 350.
- Correct the problems you missed.
- Go on to Set 4.

Set 4

1. Find 2^{100} on a pocket calculator without using the x^n button.

2. Why the emphasis on adding and subtracting exponents?

- *STOP*
- Check your answers on page 350.
- Correct the problems you missed.
- Shade box 2 opposite "exponents and roots" on page xix.
- If this was the last subskill you had to work on in this section, take the test on page 326.
- If you have other subskills to work on in this section, go on to the next one.

SUBSKILL 3: Multiplying Exponents

Problem: Multiply exponents if possible.

    (a) $(2^3)^4$ (e) $(3^2)^5$

    (b) $(6^2 4^5)^3$ (f) $\left(\dfrac{7}{9^3}\right)^2$

    (c) $(2^3 + 2^4)^5$ (g) $(3^2 - 4^3)^2$

    (d) $(10^4)^2$ (h) $(5^2)^3$

Solution: • Multiply exponents by exponent outside parentheses if no addition or subtraction.

(a) $(2^3)^4 = 2^{3 \times 4} = \boxed{2^{12}}$

(b) $(6^2 4^5)^3 = 6^{2 \times 3} 4^{5 \times 3} = \boxed{6^6 4^{15}}$

(c) Cannot multiply exponents. Addition present.

(d) $(10^4)^2 = 10^{4 \times 2} = \boxed{10^8}$

(e) $(3^2)^5 = 3^{2 \times 5} = \boxed{3^{10}}$

(f) $\left(\dfrac{7}{9^3}\right)^2 = \dfrac{7^{1 \times 2}}{9^{3 \times 2}} = \boxed{\dfrac{7^2}{9^6}}$

(g) Cannot multiply exponents. Subtraction present.

(h) $(5^2)^3 = 5^{2 \times 3} = \boxed{5^6}$

Lesson:

                  Four times

(a) $(2^3)^4 = \overbrace{2^3 \times 2^3 \times 2^3 = 2^3} = 2^{3 + 3 + 3 + 3} = 2^{12}$

                  Three times

(b) $(6^2 4^5)^3 = \overbrace{6^2 4^5 \times 6^2 4^5 \times 6^2 4^5} = 6^2 \times 6^2 \times 6^2 \times 4^5 \times 4^5 \times 4^5 =$

    $6^{2 + 2 + 2} \times 4^{5 + 5 + 5} = 6^6 4^{15}$

Two times

(d)　$(10^4)^2 = \overbrace{10^4 \times 10^4}^{} = 10^{4 + 4} = 10^8$

Five times

(e)　$(3^2)^5 = \overbrace{3^2 \times 3^2 \times 3^2 \times 3^2 \times 3^2}^{} = 3^{2 + 2 + 2 + 2 + 2} = 3^{10}$

Two times

(f)　$\left(\dfrac{7}{9^3}\right)^2 = \overbrace{\dfrac{7}{9^3} \times \dfrac{7}{9^3}}^{} = \dfrac{7 \times 7}{9^3 \times 9^3} = \dfrac{7^2}{9^{3 + 3}} = \dfrac{7^2}{9^6}$

Three times

(h)　$(5^2)^3 = \overbrace{5^2 \times 5^2 \times 5^2}^{} = 5^{2 + 2 + 2} = 5^6$

Drill and Practice:

Set 1
Multiply exponents if possible.

1. $(4^3)^2$　　2. $(5^4)^6$　　　　3. $(3^5 4^2)^5$

4. $\left(\dfrac{6}{7^4}\right)^4$　　5. $(10^4 + 10^5)^2$　　6. $(3^8 - 8^5)^7$

7. $(12^5)^6$　　　　8. $(2^2)^2$

- *STOP.*
- Check your answers on page 350.
- Correct the problems you missed.
- Go on to Set 2.

Set 2
Multiply exponents if possible.

1. $(10^3)^8$　　　　2. $(6^5)^4$　　　3. $\left(\dfrac{5^3}{2^5}\right)^3$

4. $(8^3 15^7)^4$　　　5. $(4^8 - 4^2)^5$

6. $(5^{10} + 10^{15})^{20}$　　7. $(10^0)^{25}$　　8. $(5^1)^5$

- *STOP.*
- Check your answers on page 350.
- Correct the problems you missed.
- Go on to Set 3 or 4.

Set 3
Multiply exponents if possible.

1. $(7^4)^5$　　2. $(10^8)^9$　　　　3. $(2^7 5^{11})^8$

4. $\left(\dfrac{1}{2^4}\right)^3$　　5. $(3^2 + 3)^{10}$　　6. $(6^3 - 6^2)^2$

7. $(15^{20})^6$　　　　8. $(100^{35})^5$

- *STOP.*
- Check your answers on page 350.
- Correct the problems you missed.
- Go on to Set 4.

Set 4
1. Why the emphasis on multiplying exponents?

- *STOP*
- Check your answers on page 350.
- Correct the problems you missed.
- Shade box 3 opposite "exponents and roots" on page xix.
- If this was the last subskill you had to work on in this section, take the test on page 326.
- If you have other subskills to work on in this section, go on to the next one.

SUBSKILL 4: Negative Exponents

Problem: $3^{-2} = ?$

Solution: To work with a negative exponent, *change to a positive exponent* by

- Putting base with exponent in denominator if in numerator, in numerator if in denominator.

- Changing sign of exponent.

$$3^{-2} = \frac{3^{-2}}{1} = \boxed{\frac{1}{3^2}}$$

Lesson: A term with a negative exponent is the *reciprocal* of the term with a positive exponent. To illustrate,

$$3^{-2} = 3^{0-2} = 3^0 \div 3^2 = \frac{3^0}{3^2} = \frac{1}{3^2}$$

Drill and Practice:

Set 1

1. Evaluate.
   (a) 2^{-3} (b) 4^{-3} (c) 5^{-2} (d) 10^{-4}
2. Evaluate $4^2 \div 4^5$.
3. Write with positive exponents.
   (a) 5^{-9} (b) 8^{-3} (c) $\frac{1}{6^{-5}}$ (d) $\frac{10^{-3}}{9^{-5}}$

- *STOP.*
- Check your answers on page 350.
- Correct the problems you missed.
- Go on to Set 2.

Set 2

1. Evaluate.

   (a) 8^{-2} (b) 2^{-5} (c) 25^{-1} (d) 1^{-8}

2. Evaluate $10^3 \div 10^6$.

3. Write with positive exponents.

   (a) 15^{-3} (b) 9^{-5} (c) $\dfrac{2}{5^{-3}}$ (d) $\dfrac{3^{-2}}{4^{-4}}$

- *STOP.*
- Check your answers on page 350.
- Correct the problems you missed.
- Go on to Set 3 or 4.

Set 3

1. Evaluate.

   (a) 5^{-3} (b) 10^{-2} (c) 4^{-1} (d) 6^{-3}

2. Evaluate $2^{15} \div 2^{19}$.

3. Write with positive exponents.

   (a) 10^{-5} (b) 5^{-10} (c) $\dfrac{6^{-2}}{3}$ (d) $\dfrac{10^{-3}}{10^{-5}}$

- *STOP.*
- Check your answers on page 350.
- Correct the problems you missed.
- Go on to Set 4.

Set 4

1. Why the emphasis on negative exponents?

- *STOP*
- Check your answers on page 350.
- Correct the problems you missed.
- Shade box 4 opposite "exponents and roots" on page xix.
- If this was the last subskill you had to work on in this section, take the test on page 326.
- If you have other subskills to work on in this section, go on to the next one.

SUBSKILL 5: Scientific Notation

Problem: Express in scientific notation.

(a) 34765.829

(b) .00004957

Solution: ● Move decimal point to immediate right of first non-zero digit.

(a) $34765.829 \longrightarrow 3.4\,7\,6\,5\,8\,2\,9$

$$\boxed{3.4765829 \times 10^4}$$

● Multiply by ten to number of places moved if moved to *left*.

(b) $.00004957 \longrightarrow 0\,0\,0\,0\,4.9\,5\,7$

$$\boxed{4.957 \times 10^{-5}}$$

● Multiply by ten to *negative* of number of places moved if moved to *right*.

Lesson: Scientific notation is used with pocket calculators. A readout like "2.3570081 4" would mean 2.3570081×10^4 or 23570.081. A readout like "1.3099102 −3" would mean 1.3099102×10^{-3} or .0013099102.

Drill and Practice:

Set 1

1. Express in scientific notation.
   (a) 50016.525   (c) 3805

   (b) .00003861   (d) .0595

2. Write as decimals.
   (a) 2.9800121×10^2 (c) 5.301×10^3

   (b) 1.48×10^{-5} (d) 4.76×10^{-4}

● *STOP.*
● Check your answers on page 350.
● Correct the problems you missed.
● Go on to Set 2.

Set 2

1. Express in scientific notation.
   (a) 4001.59   (c) 125056

   (b) .001275   (d) .000007

2. Write as decimals.
   (a) 3.45801×10^4 (c) 5.15×10^3

   (b) 2.00576×10^{-3} (d) 6.01×10^{-2}

● *STOP.*
● Check your answers on page 351.
● Correct the problems you missed.
● Go on to Set 3 or 4.

Set 3

1. Express in scientific notation.

   (a) 15051000000   (c) 250

   (b) .00000000121   (d) .5

2. Write as decimals.

   (a) 9.0012×10^6 (c) 1.59×10^2

   (b) 2.156×10^{-1} (d) 3.487×10^{-5}

- *STOP.*
- Check your answers on page 351.
- Correct the problems you missed.
- Go on to Set 4.

Set 4

1. A fast-food chain has sold more than 20 billion hamburgers. Express this number in scientific notation.

2. The star *Epsilon Eridani* is .000025 times as bright as the sun. Express this number in scientific notation.

3. The U.S. Bureau of Mines reports that from 1967 to 1970, inclusive, 2,259,682,000 tons of coal were produced in this country. Express this number in scientific notation.

4. The average wavelength of infrared light is .000001407 meters. Express this number in scientific notation.

- *STOP*

- Check your answers on page 351.

- Correct the problems you missed.

- Shade box 5 opposite "exponents and roots" on page xix.

- If this was the last subskill you had to work on in this section, take the test on page 326.

- If you have other subskills to work on in this section, go on to the next one.

SUBSKILL 6 Meaning of Square Roots

Problem: $\sqrt{64}$ = ?

Solution: $\sqrt{64}$ is shorthand for the number that times itself is 64.

$\sqrt{64}$ = $\boxed{8}$ because $8 \times 8 = 64$

Lesson: $\sqrt{N}$ is called a *square root* and is read "the square root of N." It stands for the number that times itself is N. As such, it stands for the *length of an edge of a square of area N.* To find a square root, use a table like Table 20.1 or a pocket calculator. To find one otherwise is too tedious and time consuming.

Table 20.1 Squares of one to 100 and Square Roots of one to 1000

n	n^2	$\sqrt{n}$	$\sqrt{10n}$	n	n^2	$\sqrt{n}$	$\sqrt{10n}$
1	1	1.000	3.162	51	2601	7.141	22.583
2	4	1.414	4.472	52	2704	7.211	22.804
3	9	1.732	5.477	53	2809	7.280	23.022
4	16	2.000	6.325	54	2916	7.348	23.238
5	25	2.236	7.071	55	3025	7.416	23.452
6	36	2.449	7.746	56	3136	7.483	23.664
7	49	2.646	8.367	57	3249	7.550	23.875
8	64	2.828	8.944	58	3364	7.616	24.083
9	81	3.000	9.487	59	3481	7.681	24.290
10	100	3.162	10.000	60	3600	7.746	24.495
11	121	3.317	10.488	61	3721	7.810	24.698
12	144	3.464	10.954	62	3844	7.874	24.900
13	169	3.606	11.402	63	3969	7.937	25.100
14	196	3.742	11.832	64	4096	8.000	25.298
15	225	3.873	12.247	65	4225	8.062	25.495
16	256	4.000	12.649	66	4356	8.124	25.690
17	289	4.123	13.038	67	4489	8.185	25.884
18	324	4.243	13.416	68	4624	8.246	26.077
19	361	4.359	13.784	69	4761	8.307	26.268
20	400	4.472	14.142	70	4900	8.367	26.458
21	441	4.583	14.491	71	5041	8.426	26.646
22	484	4.690	14.832	72	5184	8.485	26.833
23	529	4.796	15.166	73	5329	8.544	27.019
24	576	4.899	15.492	74	5476	8.602	27.203
25	625	5.000	15.811	75	5625	8.660	27.386
26	676	5.099	16.125	76	5776	8.718	27.568
27	729	5.196	16.432	77	5929	8.775	27.749
28	784	5.292	16.733	78	6084	8.832	27.928
29	841	5.385	17.029	79	6241	8.888	28.107
30	900	5.477	17.321	80	6400	8.944	28.284
31	961	5.568	17.607	81	6561	9.000	28.460
32	1024	5.657	17.889	82	6724	9.055	28.636
33	1089	5.745	18.166	83	6889	9.110	28.810
34	1156	5.831	18.439	84	7056	9.165	28.983
35	1225	5.916	18.708	85	7225	9.220	29.155
36	1296	6.000	18.974	86	7396	9.274	29.326
37	1369	6.083	19.235	87	7569	9.327	29.496
38	1444	6.164	19.494	88	7744	9.381	29.665
39	1521	6.245	19.748	89	7921	9.434	29.833
40	1600	6.325	20.000	90	8100	9.487	30.000
41	1681	6.403	20.248	91	8281	9.539	30.166
42	1764	6.481	20.494	92	8464	9.592	30.332
43	1849	6.557	20.736	93	8649	9.644	30.496
44	1936	6.633	20.976	94	8836	9.695	30.659
45	2025	6.708	21.213	95	9025	9.747	30.822
46	2116	6.782	21.448	96	9216	9.798	30.984
47	2209	6.856	21.679	97	9409	9.849	31.145
48	2304	6.928	21.909	98	9604	9.899	31.305
49	2401	7.000	22.136	99	9801	9.950	31.464
50	2500	7.071	22.361	100	10000	10.000	31.623

Drill and Practice:

Set 1

1. Find the square roots.

   (a) $\sqrt{9}$ (b) $\sqrt{81}$ (c) $\sqrt{45}$ (d) $\sqrt{950}$

2. Multiply 4.472 by itself to see how good an approximation of $\sqrt{20}$ it is.

3. Without using Table 20.1 or a pocket calculator, determine the first digit of $\sqrt{50}$.

   • *STOP.*
   • Check your answers on page 351.
   • Correct the problems you missed.
   • Go on to Set 2.

Set 2

1. Find the square roots.

   (a) $\sqrt{4}$ (b) $\sqrt{100}$ (c) $\sqrt{32}$ (d) $\sqrt{830}$

2. Multiply 5.916 by itself to see how good an approximation of $\sqrt{35}$ it is.

3. Without using Table 20.1 or a pocket calculator, determine the first digit of $\sqrt{75}$.

   • *STOP.*
   • Check your answers on page 351.
   • Correct the problems you missed.
   • Go on to Set 3 or 4.

Set 3

1. Find the square roots.

   (a) $\sqrt{16}$ (b) $\sqrt{25}$ (c) $\sqrt{17}$ (d) $\sqrt{26}$

2. Multiply 21.679 by itself to see how good an approximation of $\sqrt{470}$ it is.

3. Without using Table 20.1 or a pocket calculator, determine the first digit of $\sqrt{110}$.

   • *STOP.*
   • Check your answers on page 351.
   • Correct the problems you missed.
   • Go on to Set 4.

Set 4

1. Find the length of an edge of the square.

   $$A = 25$$

2. What is the length of an edge of a square of area 350?

3. Find the length of the hypotenuse of the right triangle using $a^2 + b^2 = c^2$ for the legs a and b and hypotenuse c of a right triangle.

   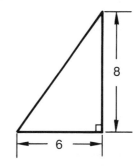

4. How long should the rafters for the roof be?

   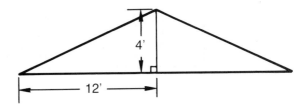

- *STOP*

- Check your answers on page 351.

- Correct the problems you missed.

- Shade box 6 opposite "exponents and roots" on page xix.

- If this was the last subskill you had to work on in this section, take the test on page 326.

- If you have other subskills to work on in this section, go on to the next one.

SUBSKILL 7: Simplifying Square Roots

Problem: Simplify if possible.

     (a) $\sqrt{32}$ (c) $\sqrt{21}$

     (b) $\sqrt{45}$ (d) $\sqrt{40}$

Solution:
- Factor in terms of $\sqrt{4}$, $\sqrt{9}$, $\sqrt{16}$, $\sqrt{25}$, $\sqrt{36}$, $\sqrt{49}$, $\sqrt{64}$, $\sqrt{81}$, or $\sqrt{100}$.

- Substitute two for $\sqrt{4}$, three for $\sqrt{9}$, four for $\sqrt{16}$, five for $\sqrt{25}$, six for $\sqrt{36}$, seven for $\sqrt{49}$, eight for $\sqrt{64}$, nine for $\sqrt{81}$, and ten for $\sqrt{100}$.

(a) $\sqrt{32} = \sqrt{16}\sqrt{2} = 4\sqrt{2}$

(b) $\sqrt{45} = \sqrt{9}\sqrt{5} = 3\sqrt{5}$

(c) Cannot simplify. Factors in terms of $\sqrt{3}$ and $\sqrt{7}$.

(d) $\sqrt{40} = \sqrt{4}\sqrt{10} = 2\sqrt{10}$

Lesson: $\sqrt{N}$ stands for the number that times itself is *N.* As such, it stands for the *length of an edge of a square of area N.*

(a) One large square with an area of 32 and edges of length $\sqrt{32}$, or four small squares each with an area of two and edges of length $\sqrt{2}$.

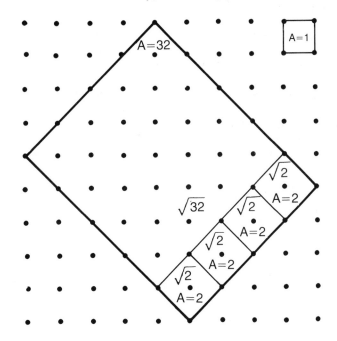

(b) One large square with an area of 45 and edges of length $\sqrt{45}$, or three small squares each with an area of five and edges of length $\sqrt{5}$

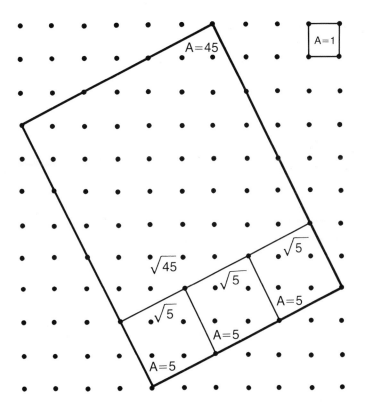

(d) One large square with an area of 40 and edges of length $\sqrt{40}$, or two small squares each with an area of ten and edges of length $\sqrt{10}$.

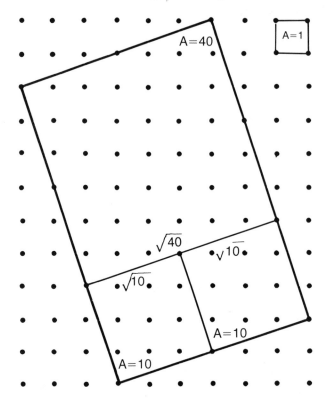

Drill and Practice:

Set 1

1. Simplify if possible.

   (a) $\sqrt{50}$ (b) $\sqrt{30}$ (c) $\sqrt{48}$ (d) $\sqrt{20}$

2. Simplify and combine like terms

   (a) $\sqrt{20} + \sqrt{45}$ (b) $\sqrt{48} - \sqrt{27}$

- *STOP.*
- Check your answers on page 351.
- Correct the problems you missed.
- Go on to Set 2.

Set 2

1. Simplify if possible.

   (a) $\sqrt{8}$ (b) $\sqrt{12}$ (c) $\sqrt{35}$ (d) $\sqrt{98}$

2. Simplify and combine like terms.

   (a) $\sqrt{72} - \sqrt{8}$ (b) $\sqrt{242} + \sqrt{200}$

- *STOP.*
- Check your answers on page 351.
- Correct the problems you missed.
- Go on to Set 3 or 4.

Set 3
1. Simplify if possible.
   (a) $\sqrt{24}$ (b) $\sqrt{80}$ (c) $\sqrt{108}$ (d) $\sqrt{70}$
2. Simplify and combine like terms.
   (a) $\sqrt{128} + \sqrt{162}$ (b) $\sqrt{300} - \sqrt{147}$

- *STOP.*
- Check your answers on page 351.
- Correct the problems you missed.
- Go on to Set 4.

Set 4

1. Why the emphasis on simplifying square roots?

- *STOP*

- Check your answers on page 351.

- Correct the problems you missed.

- Shade box 7 opposite "exponents and roots" on page xix.

- If this was the last subskill you had to work on in this section, take the test on page 326.

- If you have other subskills to work on in this section, go on to the next one.

SUBSKILL 8: Meaning of Mth Roots

Problem: $\sqrt[3]{8} = ?$

Solution: $\sqrt[3]{8}$ is shorthand for the number that times itself three times is eight.

$\sqrt[3]{8} = \boxed{2}$ because $\overbrace{2 \times 2 \times 2}^{\text{Three times}} = 8$

Lesson: $\sqrt[M]{N}$ is called a *radical* and is read "the *M*th root of *N*." It stands for the number that times itself *M* times is *N*. If *M* is omitted, it stands for the square root of *N*. ($\sqrt{}$ is called a *radical sign, M* an *index,* and *N* a *radicand.*)

Drill and Practice:

Set 1

Find the roots.

1. $\sqrt[3]{27}$ 2. $\sqrt[3]{125}$ 3. $\sqrt[3]{216}$

4. $\sqrt{36}$ 5. $\sqrt[3]{1000}$ 6. $\sqrt[6]{1}$

- *STOP.*
- Check your answers on page 351.
- Correct the problems you missed.
- Go on to Set 2.

Set 2

Find the roots.

1. $\sqrt[3]{64}$ 2. $\sqrt[7]{128}$ 3. $\sqrt[4]{81}$

4. $\sqrt{49}$ 5. $\sqrt[4]{10000}$ 6. $\sqrt[10]{0}$

- *STOP.*
- Check your answers on page 351.
- Correct the problems you missed.
- Go on to Set 3 or 4.

Set 3

Find the roots.

1. $\sqrt[4]{16}$ 2. $\sqrt[5]{243}$ 3. $\sqrt[8]{256}$

4. $\sqrt{64}$ 5. $\sqrt[5]{100000}$ 6. $\sqrt[12]{1}$

- *STOP.*
- Check your answers on page 351.
- Correct the problems you missed.
- Go on to Set 4.

Set 4

1. Why the emphasis on roots?

- *STOP*
- Check your answers on page 351.
- Correct the problems you missed.
- Shade box 8 opposite "exponents and roots" on page xix.
- If this was the last subskill you had to work on in this section, take the test on page 326.
- If you have other subskills to work on in this section, go on to the next one.

SUBSKILL 9: Fractional Exponents

Problem: $8^{\frac{2}{3}} = ?$

$$8^{\frac{2}{3}} = \sqrt[3]{8^2} = \sqrt[3]{64} = \boxed{4}$$

because $\overbrace{4 \times 4 \times 4}^{\text{Three times}} = 64$

Solution: $8^{\frac{2}{3}}$ is another way of writing $\sqrt[3]{8^2}$.

Lesson: $8^{\frac{2}{3}} = \sqrt[3]{8^2}$ because $8^{\frac{2}{3}} \times 8^{\frac{2}{3}} \times 8^{\frac{2}{3}} = 8^{\frac{2}{3}+\frac{2}{3}+\frac{2}{3}} = 8^{\frac{6}{3}} = 8^2$.

Drill and Practice:

Set 1

1. Which equals $16^{\frac{3}{4}}$?

    a. $16 \times \frac{3}{4}$ b. $\frac{3}{4} \times 16$ c. $\sqrt[4]{16^3}$ d. $\sqrt[3]{16^4}$

    e. $16^{\frac{3}{4}} \times 16^{\frac{3}{4}} \times 16^{\frac{3}{4}} \times 16^{\frac{3}{4}}$

2. Evaluate.

    (a) $27^{\frac{2}{3}}$ (b) $81^{\frac{3}{4}}$ (c) $9^{\frac{1}{2}}$ (d) $1000^{\frac{2}{3}}$

- *STOP.*
- Check your answers on page 351.
- Correct the problems you missed.
- Go on to Set 2.

Set 2

1. Which equals $32^{\frac{2}{5}}$?

    a. $\frac{2}{5} \times 32$ b. $32 \times \frac{2}{5}$ c. $\sqrt[2]{32^5}$ d. $\sqrt[5]{32^2}$

    e. $32^{\frac{2}{5}} \times 32^{\frac{2}{5}} \times 32^{\frac{2}{5}} \times 32^{\frac{2}{5}} \times 32^{\frac{2}{5}}$

2. Evaluate.

    (a) $64^{\frac{2}{3}}$ (b) $32^{\frac{3}{5}}$ (c) $125^{\frac{1}{3}}$ (d) $10000^{\frac{3}{4}}$

- *STOP.*
- Check your answers on page 351.
- Correct the problems you missed.
- Go on to Set 3 or 4.

Set 3

1. Which equals $27^{\frac{2}{3}}$?

   a. $27 \times \frac{2}{3}$ b. $\frac{2}{3} \times 27$ c. $\sqrt[3]{27^2}$ d. $\sqrt[2]{27^3}$

   e. $27^{\frac{2}{3}} \times 27^{\frac{2}{3}} \times 27^{\frac{2}{3}}$

2. Evaluate.

   (a) $125^{\frac{2}{3}}$ (b) $64^{\frac{5}{6}}$ (c) $16^{\frac{1}{4}}$ (d) $100000^{\frac{4}{5}}$

- *STOP.*
- Check your answers on page 351.
- Correct the problems you missed.
- Go on to Set 4.

Set 4

1. Why the emphasis on fractional exponents?

- *STOP*

- Check your answers on page 351.

- Correct the problems you missed.

- Shade box 9 opposite "exponents and roots" on page xix.

- Take the test on page 326.

Inventory Post Test for Exponents and Roots

1. $2^6 = ?$

2. Add or subtract exponents: $2^8 \div 2^4$

3. Multiply exponents: $(8^4 10^5)^6$

4. $2^{-4} = ?$

5. Express in scientific notation: .00008395

6. $\sqrt{144} = ?$

7. Simplify: $\sqrt{192}$

8. $\sqrt[4]{256} = ?$

9. $625^{\frac{3}{4}} = ?$

- *STOP*

- Check your answers with the instructor.

- As before, work through the subskills in this section which correspond to the problems you missed, except work the *even* drill-and-practice problems.

- Take the test on page 329.

General Survey Post Test for Estimation, Integers, Less Than, Greater Than, Exponents, and Roots

1. Estimate 316 ÷ .1903. Do *not* compute.

2. $^+4 - {}^-2 = ?$ 3. $^-7 \times {}^+3 = ?$ 4. $6 - 4 \div 2 = ?$

5. True or false, $15 > 20$?

6. Which is greater, $\dfrac{7}{15}$ or $\dfrac{12}{25}$?

7. $5^4 = ?$

8. Add or subtract exponents: $6^{15} \div 6^3$

9. Express in scientific notation: .00295036

10. $\sqrt{49} = ?$

- *STOP*

- Check your answers with the instructor.

- Enter the number correct and today's date in the space provided on page XX.

- Figure your growth and take pleasure in it.

- If you got nine or more right, you are a master of basic mathematics, and you can give this book to someone else!

- If you got less than nine right, take the inventory pretests for estimation, integers, less than, greater than, exponents, and roots again beginning with the one on page 269.

- As before, work through the subskills which correspond to the problems you miss.

ANSWERS

General Survey Pretest for Whole Numbers:

1. 15   *2.* 68   *3.* 95   *4.* 522   *5.* 68,629
6. 7   *7.* 24   *8.* 45   *9.* 383   *10.* 14,179
11. 54   *12.* 81   *13.* 236   *14.* 116,928
15. 12,815,400   *16.* 5R2   *17.* 12R2

18. 90R2   *19.* 203R17   *20.* $15\frac{8}{36}$ or $15\frac{2}{9}$

SKILL
Addition of Whole Numbers

Inventory Pretest:

1. 13   *2.* 14   *3.* 49   *4.* 83   *5.* 628
6. 762   *7.* 831   *8.* 70,430

Drill and Practice Sets by Subskill:

SUBSKILL 1:

Set 1
1. 11   *3.* 12   *5.* 16   *7.* 8   *9.* 9
Set 2
1. 18   *3.* 10   *5.* 15   *7.* 9   *9.* 14
Set 3
1. 17   *3.* 15   *5.* 10   *7.* 2   *9.* 8
Set 4
1. 8   *3.* (a) 13   (b) 14   *5.* $3

SUBSKILL 2:

Set 1
1. 16   *3.* 12   *5.* 15
Set 2
1. 14   *3.* 9   *5.* 14
Set 3
1. 24   *3.* 27   *5.* 20
Set 4
1. 14   *3.* Every sum is 15.   *5.* 22 cents

SUBSKILL 3:

Set 1
1. 597   *3.* 75   *5.* 4599

Set 2
1. 879   *3.* 99   *5.* 93,399
Set 3
1. 638   *3.* 77   *5.* 455,308
Set 4
1. 58 cents   *3.* Eight miles per hour
5. 12 feet, seven inches

SUBSKILL 4:

Set 1
1. 61   *3.* 67   *5.* 391
Set 2
1. 50   *3.* 80   *5.* 8671
Set 3
1. 40   *3.* 92   *5.* 66,962
Set 4
1. 40 cents   *3.* Twenty-fifth floor   *5.* 552

SUBSKILL 5:

Set 1
1. 744   *3.* 659   *5.* 2847
Set 2
1. 618   *3.* 702   *5.* 46,379
Set 3
1. 638   *3.* 506   *5.* 308,918
Set 4
1. 659   *3.* $228   *5.* 618

SUBSKILL 6:

Set 1
1. 834   *3.* 610   *5.* 1830
Set 2
1. 410   *3.* 902   *5.* 15,898
Set 3
1. 900   *3.* 443   *5.* 574,921
Set 4
1. $1   *3.* 211 pounds   *5.* 918

SUBSKILL 7:

Set 1
1. 762   3. 761   5. 3935

Set 2
1. 675   3. 630   5. 13,729

Set 3
1. 910   3. 789   5. 130,864

Set 4
1. $241   3. $111   5. 743

SUBSKILL 8:

Set 1
1. 68,352   3. 70,700

Set 2
1. 85,285   3. 55,115

Set 3
1. 70,032   3. 47,018

Set 4
1. $10,201   3. $1302   5. 1980

SKILL
Subtraction of Whole Numbers

Inventory Pretest:

1. 4   2. 6   3. 321   4. 45   5. 383
6. 366   7. 37,575   8. 37,546

Drill and Practice Sets by Subskill:

SUBSKILL 1:

Set 1
1. 3   3. 3   5. 8

Set 2
1. 7   3. 1   5. 4

Set 3
1. 6   3. 9   5. 0

Set 4
1. $7 - 2 = 5,\ 7 - 5 = 2$
3. 4   5. 3

SUBSKILL 2:

Set 1
1. 9   3. 7   5. 8

Set 2
1. 4   3. 1   5. 5

Set 3
1. 7   3. 3   5. 6

Set 4
1. (a) $14 - 5 = 9,\ \ 14 - 9 = 5$
   (b) $13 - 6 = 7,\ \ 13 - 7 = 6$
3. 5   5. 3

SUBSKILL 3:

Set 1
1. 353   3. 62   5. 2201

Set 2
1. 124   3. 45   5. 411,253

Set 3
1. 404   3. 11   5. 83,132,001

Set 4
1. 12 cents   3. Three inches
5. Six minutes, 12 seconds

SUBSKILL 4:

Set 1
1. 29   3. 29   5. 126

Set 2
1. 19   3. 27   5. 3714

Set 3
1. 27   3. 23   5. 547

Set 4
1. 39 cents   3. 27 miles per hour   5. 48

SUBSKILL 5:

Set 1
1. 173   3. 283   5. 4341

Set 2
1. 291   3. 673   5. 46,182

Set 3
1. 281   3. 26   5. 4284

Set 4
1. $190   3. 32

SUBSKILL 6:

Set 1
1. 247   3. 189   5. 2089

Set 2
1. 179   3. 689   5. 23,049

Set 3
1. 289   3. 187   5. 2088

Set 4

1. $1369   *3.* 457   *5.* 67

7. See answers for Set 1.

SUBSKILL 7:

Set 1

1. 28,647   *3.* 48,773

Set 2

1. 38,888   *3.* 18,586

Set 3

1. 18,278   *3.* 48,845

Set 4

1. $877   *3.* 754 pages   *5.* 978 feet

SUBSKILL 8:

Set 1

1. 36,859   *3.* 266

Set 2

1. 27,662   *3.* 481

Set 3

1. 18,835   *3.* 127

Set 4

1. 207   *3.* 999,000   *5.* 1105 miles

SKILL
Multiplication of Whole Numbers

Inventory Pretest:

1. 56   *2.* 68   *3.* 84   *4.* 608   *5.* 741

6. 66,240   *7.* 86,760   *8.* 1,664,505

9. 1,500,065,000   *10.* 15,674,884

Drill and Practice Sets by Subskill:

SUBSKILL 1:

Set 1

1. 56   *3.* 63   *5.* 24   *7.* 49   *9.* 48

Set 2

1. 0   *3.* 8   *5.* 27   *7.* 16   *9.* 81

Set 3

1. 10   *3.* 21   *5.* 48   *7.* 56   *9.* 18

Set 4

1. 12   *3.* 12   *5.* 35   *7.* 24

9. (a) 4   *(b)* 16   *11.* 48

13. 32

SUBSKILL 2:

Set 1

1. 64   *3.* 60   *5.* 42,686

Set 2

1. 84   *3.* 80   *5.* 936,906

Set 3

1. 23   *3.* 0   *5.* 8,888,888

Set 4

1. 80   *3.* 996 meters.

5. (a) *266* (b) *399*

SUBSKILL 3:

Set 1

1. 70   *3.* 84   *5.* 3672

Set 2

1. 78   *3.* 95   *5.* 90,375

Set 3

1. 98   *3.* 96   *5.* 802,654

Set 4

1. 75   *3.* $3.25   *5.* 78   *7.* 80 cubic decimeters.

SUBSKILL 4:

Set 1

1. 459   *3.* 900   *5.* 3426

Set 2

1. 788   *3.* 960   *5.* 84,288

Set 3

1. 847   *3.* 960   *5.* 206,528

Set 4

1. 250   *3.* 126   *5.* 128

SUBSKILL 5:

Set 1

1. 777   *3.* 972   *5.* 6876

Set 2

1. 896   *3.* 810   *5.* 36,132

Set 3

1. 804   *3.* 712   *5.* 426,734

Set 4

1. $6.02   *3.* $13.87   *5.* 120 square meters

SUBSKILL 6:

Set 1

1. 93,824   *3.* 48,759

Set 2

1. 111,846   *3.* 193,936

Set 3

1. 215,685   3. 50,924

Set 4

1. (a) 21 times   (b) 90 times   (c) 1095 times
3. 2600
5. (a) 35 cents   (b) $1.50   (c) $18.25

SUBSKILL 7:

Set 1

1. 121,662   3. 37,352   5. 3,809,512

Set 2

1. 146,250   3. 24,912   5. 3,488,289

Set 3

1. 381,292   3. 43,956   5. 502,458

Set 4

1. 938

3. (a) 91 pounds   (b) 390 pounds
   (c) 4745 pounds
5. $1800
7. See answers for Set 1

SUBSKILL 8:

Set 1

1. 678,326   3. 168,015   5. 354,865,344

Set 2

1. 2,356,144   3. 189,805   5. 3,110,856,140

Set 3

1. 1,089,418   3. 405,594
5. 5,443,942,863,462

Set 4

1. (a) 4320 times   (b) 103,680 times
   (c) 3,110,400 times   (d) 37,843,200 times
3. 5,349,360
5. See answers for Set 1.

SUBSKILL 9:

Set 1

1. 2,176,050,000   3. 217,808,500

Set 2

1. 1,664,020,000   3. 147,271,500

Set 3

1. 4,860,180,000   3. 33,333,000

Set 4

1. 5000   3. (a) 350   (b) 1500   (c) 18,250
5. (a) 3500 pounds   (b) 15,000 pounds
   (c) 182,500 pounds

7. (a) 120,000,000   (b) 7,200,000,000
   (c) 172,800,000,000
   (d) 63,072,000,000,000

SUBSKILL 10:

Set 1

1. 6,249,585   3. 858,893

Set 2

1. 29,243,309   3. 2,403,800

Set 3

1. 41,134,969   3. 2,794,500

Set 4

1. 32,235   3. $847,350

SKILL
Division of Whole Numbers

Inventory Pretest:

1. 2R4   2. 12R2   3. 75R2   4. 1281R2
5. 5061R3   6. 21R27   7. 202R27
8. 82R220   9. $21\frac{6}{24}$ or $21\frac{1}{4}$ 10. 45.285

Drill and Practice Sets by Subskill:

SUBSKILL 1:

Set 1

1. 3   3. 2   5. 1R7

Set 2

1. 7   3. 2R1   5. 17

Set 3

1. 5   3. Undefined   5. 6

Set 4

1. 2R9   3. (a) 4   (b) 2   5. 0, 1, 2, 3, 4, 5, 6

SUBSKILL 2:

Set 1

1. 25R1   3. 13   5. 7R7

Set 2

1. 12R1   3. 13R2   5. 2R3

Set 3

1. 16R2   3. 11R2   5. 7R2

Set 4

1. 26   3. 14   5. 16

SUBSKILL 3:

Set 1

1. 245   3. 122   5. 86R3

Set 2

1. 276R1   3. 111   5. 91R1

Set 3

1. 112   3. 77   5. 24R6

Set 4

1. 416   3. 262

SUBSKILL 4:

Set 1

1. 14R3   3. 1115

Set 2

1. 22R1   3. 1213

Set 3

1. 11R4   3. 1561

Set 4

1. 16 cents   3. $2982

SUBSKILL 5:

Set 1

1. 306R1   3. 1504R6

Set 2

1. 307R1   3. 6504R4

Set 3

1. 20R3   3. 2208R2

Set 4

1. 106   3. 603

SUBSKILL 6:

Set 1

1. 21R6   3. 11R18

Set 2

1. 25   3. 8R28

Set 3

1. 42R9   3. 9R76

Set 4

1. 3   3. 9   5. 26

7. See answers for Set 1.

SUBSKILL 7:

Set 1

1. 209R9   3. 20,803

Set 2

1. 108R15   3. 200,565R8

Set 3

1. 307R14   3. 204,005R4

Set 4

1. 105   3. 1

SUBSKILL 8:

Set 1

1. 20R23   3. 4573R951

Set 2

1. 20R75   3. 568R4241

Set 3

1. 20   3. 20R206,902

Set 4

1. 4   3. 601,093

SUBSKILL 9:

Set 1

1. $4\frac{2}{4}$ or $4\frac{1}{2}$ 3. $22\frac{1}{37}$

Set 2

1. $6\frac{2}{8}$ or $6\frac{1}{4}$ 3. $10\frac{33}{48}$ or $10\frac{11}{16}$

Set 3

1. $8\frac{8}{9}$ 3. $20\frac{20}{23}$

Set 4

1. $8\frac{1}{3}$ 3. $9\frac{1}{2}$ 5. $6\frac{1}{2}$

SUBSKILL 10:

Set 1

1. 91.714   3. 339.640

Set 2

1. 65.87   3. 163.17

Set 3

1. 91.7   3. 172.3

Set 4

1. 5.35

3. (a) 16.6   (b) 6.94   (c) 144.675

General Survey Pretest for Fractions:

1. a   2. b   3. $\frac{2}{3}$ or 2:3

4. $\frac{2}{3} = \frac{4}{6} = \frac{10}{15}$, $\frac{8}{18} = \frac{4}{9}$, $\frac{1}{2} = \frac{8}{16}$

5. $4\frac{1}{9} = \frac{37}{9}$, $\frac{11}{5} = 2\frac{1}{5}$, $\frac{7}{5} = 1\frac{2}{5}$, $1\frac{4}{9} = \frac{13}{9}$

6. a, d

7. The LCD is 60 and

$$\frac{2}{3} = \frac{40}{60}, \quad \frac{1}{5} = \frac{12}{60}, \quad \text{and} \quad \frac{5}{12} = \frac{25}{60}.$$

8. The GCF is four. *9.* $\frac{3}{4}$ *10.* $1\frac{1}{12}$ *11.* $8\frac{1}{10}$

12. $\frac{1}{2}$ *13.* $\frac{5}{24}$ *14.* $2\frac{7}{12}$ *15.* $\frac{3}{8}$ *16.* 4

17. 15   *18.* $1\frac{1}{3}$ *19.* $\frac{3}{4}$ *20.* $\frac{3}{4}$

SKILL
Fractions: Basic Concepts

Inventory Pretest:

1. c   *2.* b

3. $A = \frac{7}{8}$, $B = \frac{12}{8} = \frac{6}{4} = \frac{3}{2} = 1\frac{4}{8} = 1\frac{2}{4} = 1\frac{1}{2}$,

and $C = \frac{17}{8} = 2\frac{1}{8}$

4. $\frac{4}{9}$ or 4:9   *5.* $\frac{3}{4}$ or 3:4   *6.* $N = 24$

7. $\frac{1}{3} = \frac{6}{18}$, $\frac{6}{15} = \frac{2}{5} = \frac{12}{30}$, $\frac{5}{6} = \frac{10}{12}$

8. $\frac{11}{8} = 1\frac{3}{8}$, $3\frac{1}{5} = \frac{16}{5}$, $\frac{25}{8} = 3\frac{1}{8}$, $1\frac{3}{5} = \frac{8}{5}$

9. a, c, e   *10.* $\frac{5}{6}$

11. $\frac{18}{24}$ *12.* c, d, f, g

13. The GCF is six. *14.* $2\frac{1}{5}$

15. a, b, d   *16.* $2 \times 2 \times 2 \times 3$

17. The LCM is 30.

18. The LCD is 30 and $\frac{1}{3} = \frac{10}{30}$, $\frac{3}{5} = \frac{18}{30}$,

and $\frac{5}{6} = \frac{25}{30}$.

19. $\frac{4}{3}$

Drill and Practice Sets by Subskill:

SUBSKILL 1:

Set 1

1. c

3. or or

Set 2

1. a

3.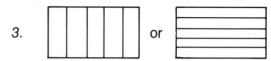

Set 3

1. a *3.*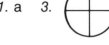

Set 4

1. a, e

3. *(a)* 1/100   *(b)* 1/1000   *(c)* 1/1000
   (d) 1/1000

5. One milliliter.

SUBSKILL 2:

Set 1

1. c   *3.*

Set 2

1. a

3. or or

Set 3

1. c   *3.*

Set 4

1. a

3. *(a)* 3/16   *(b)* 11/16   *(c)* 7/16   *(d)* 15/16

5. *(a)* 23/100   *(b)* 957/1000   *(c)* 9/1000
   (d) 483/1000

7. Riddle: What has five eyes and rests on a
         water bed?
   Answer: The Mississippi river.

SUBSKILL 3:

Set 1

1. $A = \frac{1}{4}$, $B = \frac{3}{4}$, $C = \frac{4}{4} = 1$,

   $D = \frac{8}{4} = \frac{4}{2} = \frac{2}{1} = 2$, $E = \frac{14}{4} = \frac{7}{2} = 3\frac{1}{2}$

Set 2

1. $A = \frac{1}{16}$, $B = \frac{8}{16} = \frac{4}{8} = \frac{2}{4} = \frac{1}{2}$,

$C = \frac{18}{16} = \frac{9}{8} = 1\frac{2}{16} = 1\frac{1}{8}$, $D = \frac{25}{16} = 1\frac{9}{16}$,

$E = \frac{36}{16} = \frac{18}{8} = \frac{9}{4} = 2\frac{4}{16} = 2\frac{2}{8} = 2\frac{1}{4}$

Set 3

1. $A = \frac{1}{10}$, $B = \frac{6}{10} = \frac{3}{5}$, $C = \frac{10}{10} = \frac{5}{5} = 1$,

$D = \frac{24}{10} = \frac{12}{5} = 2\frac{4}{10} = 2\frac{2}{5}$, $E = \frac{39}{10} = 3\frac{9}{10}$

Set 4

1. (a) $\frac{13}{16}$ (b) $3\frac{11}{16}$ or $3\frac{3}{4}$

3. (a) 10 (b) 100 (c) 1000

SUBSKILL 4:

Set 1

1. $\frac{4}{7}$ or 4:7   3. $\frac{4}{8}$, $\frac{1}{2}$, or 1:2

Set 2

1. $\frac{1}{6}$ or 1:6   3. $\frac{4}{11}$ or 4:11

Set 3

1. $\frac{5}{9}$ or 5:9   3. $\frac{3}{9}$, $\frac{1}{3}$, or 1:3

Set 4

1. $\frac{4}{5}$ or 4:5   3. $\frac{24}{25}$ or 24:25

5. $\frac{3}{7}$ or 3:7

SUBSKILL 5:

Set 1

1. $\frac{2}{3}$ or 2:3   3. $\frac{42}{18}$, $\frac{7}{3}$, or 7:3

Set 2

1. $\frac{7}{3}$ or 7:3   3. $\frac{20}{20}$, $\frac{1}{1}$, or 1:1

Set 3

1. $\frac{4}{7}$ or 4:7   3. $\frac{25}{25}$, $\frac{1}{1}$, or 1:1

Set 4

1. $\frac{40}{1}$ or 40:1   3. $\frac{2}{1}$ or 2:1

5. $\frac{1\frac{1}{2}}{1} = \frac{3}{2}$ or 3:2

SUBSKILL 6:

Set 1

1. $N = 21$ 3. $N = 1$

Set 2

1. $N = 15$ 3. $N = 2\frac{2}{3}$

Set 3

1. $N = 12$ 3. $N = 1\frac{1}{3}$

Set 4

1. 80   3. 240   5. 480 miles   7. 25
9. 240 pounds   11. $25
13. $4.95

SUBSKILL 7:

Set 1

1. $\frac{1}{2} = \frac{4}{8} = \frac{3}{6} = \frac{5}{10}$, $\frac{2}{3} = \frac{10}{15} = \frac{16}{24}$, $\frac{9}{12} = \frac{3}{4}$,

$\frac{4}{5} = \frac{8}{10}$

3. $\frac{4}{12} = \frac{1}{3}$

Set 2

1. $\frac{1}{2} = \frac{8}{16} = \frac{2}{4}$, $\frac{2}{6} = \frac{5}{15} = \frac{1}{3}$, $\frac{3}{4} = \frac{6}{8}$,

$\frac{1}{5} = \frac{3}{15} = \frac{2}{10}$

3. $\frac{6}{24} = \frac{1}{4}$

Set 3

1. $\frac{1}{2} = \frac{12}{24}$, $\frac{1}{4} = \frac{2}{8} = \frac{3}{12}$, $\frac{10}{25} = \frac{4}{10} = \frac{2}{5}$,

$\frac{5}{6} = \frac{15}{18} = \frac{10}{12}$

3. $\frac{24}{40} = \frac{3}{5}$

Set 4

1. (a) 2   (b) 1/2
3. (a) 6   (b) 3/4
5. (a) 15   (b) 3/20

SUBSKILL 8:

Set 1

1. $1\frac{1}{8} = \frac{9}{8}$, $\frac{39}{16} = 2\frac{7}{16}$, $2\frac{1}{4} = \frac{9}{4}$, $\frac{3}{2} = 1\frac{1}{2}$,

$$3\frac{3}{10} = \frac{33}{10}$$

3. (a) $\frac{9}{2}$　(b) $\frac{11}{4}$　(c) $\frac{25}{8}$

Set 2

1. $1\frac{5}{8} = \frac{13}{8}, \frac{13}{4} = 3\frac{1}{4}, 2\frac{5}{8} = \frac{21}{8}, \frac{11}{4} = 2\frac{3}{4},$

   $2\frac{3}{5} = \frac{13}{5}$

3. (a) $\frac{21}{4}$　(b) $\frac{19}{8}$　(c) $\frac{51}{16}$

Set 3

1. $2\frac{1}{16} = \frac{33}{16}, \frac{9}{5} = 1\frac{4}{5}, 2\frac{3}{16} = \frac{35}{16}, \frac{11}{5} = 2\frac{1}{5},$

   $2\frac{5}{16} = \frac{37}{16}$

3. (a) $\frac{27}{8}$　(b) $\frac{69}{16}$　(c) $\frac{93}{10}$

Set 4

1. (a) 11　(b) $2\frac{3}{4}$　3. (a) 8　(b) $2\frac{2}{3}$

5. (a) 11　(b) $1\frac{5}{6}$

SUBSKILL 9:

Set 1

1. a, b, d, e

Set 2

1. b, c, e, f

Set 3

1. a, b, d, e

Set 4

1. (a) 2　(b) 1　3. (a) 6　(b) 1

5. (a) 12/12　(b) 3/3　(c) 16/16　(d) 2/2
   (e) 2/2　(f) 4/4

7. The whole thing　　　9. $99\frac{99}{99}$

SUBSKILL 10:

Set 1

1. $\frac{1}{2}$　3. $\frac{5}{6}$

Set 2

1. $\frac{1}{3}$　3. $\frac{7}{10}$

Set 3

1. $\frac{2}{5}$　3. $\frac{7}{12}$

Set 4

1. The fraction

3. You always get the number you started with.

SUBSKILL 11:

Set 1

1. $\frac{8}{12}$　3. $\frac{15}{36}$

Set 2

1. $\frac{6}{12}$　3. $\frac{8}{10}$

Set 3

1. $\frac{55}{60}$　3. $\frac{20}{36}$

Set 4

1. Infinitely many

3. They amount to doing the same thing.

SUBSKILL 12:

Set 1

1. c, d, e, f, g, h　3. a, d

5. (a) 1, 2, 7, 14
   (b) 1, 2, 3, 5, 6, 10, 15, 30
   (c) 1, 3, 5, 15
   (d) 1, 2, 3, 6, 9, 17, 18, 34, 51, 102, 153, 306

Set 2

1. c, d, e, f, g, h　3. a, c

5. (a) 1, 2, 4, 5, 10, 20
   (b) 1, 2, 4, 5, 8, 10, 20, 40
   (c) 1, 3, 17, 51
   (d) 1, 5, 7, 23, 35, 115, 161, 805

Set 3

1. c, f, h　3. a, b, d

5. (a) 1, 3, 13, 39
   (b) 1, 2, 4, 5, 8, 10, 16, 20, 40, 80
   (c) 1, 47
   (d) 1, 7, 11, 13, 77, 91, 143, 1001

Set 4

1. Being able to determine factors is prerequisite to being able to simplify fractions.

SUBSKILL 13:

Set 1

1. 2　3. 6

1. 9   *3.* 15

Set 3

1. 2   *3.* 13

Set 4

1. It is the best number with which to simplify fractions.

SUBSKILL 14:

Set 1

1. $1\frac{1}{2}$ *3.* $2\frac{4}{5}$ *5.* $1\frac{1}{3}$

Set 2

1. $1\frac{1}{2}$ *3.* $1\frac{1}{3}$ *5.* $2\frac{2}{3}$

Set 3

1. $1\frac{1}{3}$ *3.* 3   *5.* $2\frac{1}{2}$

Set 4

1. (a) 1/6   (b) 1/3   (c) 2/3   (d) 5/6
(e) 1/4   (f) 1/2   (g) 3/4

3. (a) One centimeter
(b) 1/4 of a meter
(c) 1/2 of a meter
(d) 4/5 of a meter

5. (a) 1/4 of a kilogram
(b) 1/20 of a kilogram
(c) 3/4 of a kilogram
(d) 4/5 of a kilogram

SUBSKILL 15:

Set 1

1. c, f, h

Set 2

1. b, f, h

Set 3

1. c, f, g, i

Set 4

1. They are the essence of whole numbers. Every whole number is either prime or can be written as a product of primes.

SUBSKILL 16:

Set 1

1. 2 × 3 × 3   *3.* 2 × 2 × 3 × 3
5. 2 × 2 × 2 × 2 × 3 × 3 × 3 × 3 × 5

Set 2

1. 2 × 2 × 5   *3.* 2 × 5 × 5
5. 2 × 2 × 2 × 2 × 3 × 3 × 3 × 3 × 3 × 5 × 5

Set 3

1. 3 × 13   *3.* 2 × 2 × 3 × 3 × 3
5. 2 × 2 × 2 × 3 × 3 × 3 × 5

Set 4

1. First, whereas a whole number might have many factorizations, it has just one prime factorization. Second, the prime factorization of a whole number tells you what it is divisible by.

SUBSKILL 17:

Set 1

1. 12   *3.* 60

Set 2

1. 24   *3.* 12

Set 3

1. 6   *3.* 12

Set 4

1. Being able to find LCM's is prerequisite to being able to find LCD'S.

SUBSKILL 18:

Set 1

1. The LCD is 12 and $\frac{2}{3} = \frac{8}{12}$ and $\frac{3}{4} = \frac{9}{12}$.

3. The LCD is 30 and $\frac{1}{2} = \frac{15}{30}$, $\frac{2}{3} = \frac{20}{30}$, and $\frac{2}{5} = \frac{12}{30}$.

Set 2

1. The LCD is 20 and $\frac{1}{4} = \frac{5}{20}$ and $\frac{3}{5} = \frac{12}{20}$.

3. The LCD is 30 and $\frac{1}{6} = \frac{5}{30}$, $\frac{3}{10} = \frac{9}{30}$, and $\frac{4}{15} = \frac{8}{30}$.

Set 3

1. The LCD is six and $\frac{1}{2} = \frac{3}{6}$ and $\frac{1}{3} = \frac{2}{6}$.

3. The LCD is 72 and $\frac{1}{2} = \frac{36}{72}$, $\frac{3}{8} = \frac{27}{72}$, and $\frac{4}{9} = \frac{32}{72}$.

Set 4

1. No. Any CD or common denominator will do.

SUBSKILL 19:

Set 1

1. $\dfrac{5}{4}$ 3. $\dfrac{1}{8}$ 5. $\dfrac{7}{30}$

Set 2

1. $\dfrac{4}{3}$ 3. $\dfrac{1}{10}$ 5. $\dfrac{3}{20}$

Set 3

1. $\dfrac{3}{2}$ 3. $\dfrac{1}{12}$ 5. $\dfrac{6}{35}$

Set 4

1. You have to know how to invert to divide fractions.

SKILL
Addition of Fractions

Inventory Pretest

1. $\dfrac{2}{3}$ 2. $1\dfrac{7}{15}$ 3. $7\dfrac{11}{12}$ 4. $6\dfrac{3}{10}$

Drill and Practice Sets by Subskill:

SUBSKILL 1:

Set 1

1. $1\dfrac{1}{2}$ 3. $1\dfrac{1}{3}$

Set 2

1. $1\dfrac{1}{6}$ 3. $1\dfrac{2}{5}$

Set 3

1. $1\dfrac{1}{4}$ 3. $1\dfrac{3}{7}$

Set 4

1. (a) 8   (b) $1\dfrac{1}{3}$

3. $3/4 + 2/4 = 1\dfrac{1}{4}$, $2/4 + 3/4 = 1\dfrac{1}{4}$

SUBSKILL 2:

Set 1

1. $1\dfrac{5}{12}$ 3. $1\dfrac{3}{10}$

Set 2

1. $1\dfrac{1}{8}$ 3. $1\dfrac{1}{12}$

Set 3

1. $1\dfrac{1}{10}$ 3. $1\dfrac{7}{15}$

Set 4

1. (a) $3/8 + 1/4 = 5/8$ (b) $3/8 + 2/8 = 5/8$

3. (a) $3/4 + 7/8 = 1\dfrac{5}{8}$ (b) $6/8 + 7/8 = 1\dfrac{5}{8}$

5. 17/20

SUBSKILL 3:

Set 1

1. $5\dfrac{1}{2}$ 3. $7\dfrac{11}{12}$

Set 2

1. $9\dfrac{8}{9}$ 3. $7\dfrac{7}{8}$

Set 3

1. $7\dfrac{11}{18}$ 3. $3\dfrac{13}{15}$

Set 4

1. (a) $2\dfrac{1}{4} + 1\dfrac{5}{12} = 3\dfrac{2}{3}$ (b) $2\dfrac{3}{12} + 1\dfrac{5}{12} = 3\dfrac{8}{12}$

3. $3\dfrac{7}{8}$

SUBSKILL 4:

Set 1

1. $7\dfrac{7}{12}$ 3. $14\dfrac{1}{6}$

Set 2

1. $10\dfrac{2}{9}$ 3. $18\dfrac{2}{5}$

Set 3

1. $10\dfrac{11}{20}$ 3. $6\dfrac{13}{30}$

Set 4

1. (a) $1\dfrac{3}{4} + 2\dfrac{2}{3} = 4\dfrac{5}{12}$ (b) $1\dfrac{9}{12} + 2\dfrac{8}{12} = 4\dfrac{5}{12}$

3. $4\dfrac{3}{8}$

SKILL
Subtraction of Fractions

Inventory Pretest:

1. $\frac{1}{5}$ *2.* $\frac{7}{40}$ *3.* $2\frac{5}{12}$ *4.* $2\frac{5}{8}$

Drill and Practice Sets by Subskill:

SUBSKILL 1:

Set 1

1. $\frac{1}{4}$ *3.* $\frac{5}{12}$

Set 2

1. $\frac{1}{3}$ *3.* $\frac{2}{5}$

Set 3

1. $\frac{2}{5}$ *3.* $\frac{7}{15}$

Set 4

1. 2/3 − 1/3 = 1/3
3. 3/4 − 1/4 = 2/4, 3/4 − 2/4 = 1/4

SUBSKILL 2:

Set 1

1. $\frac{1}{6}$ *3.* $\frac{3}{10}$

Set 2

1. $\frac{1}{4}$ *3.* $\frac{1}{12}$

Set 3

1. $\frac{3}{10}$ *3.* $\frac{1}{2}$

Set 4

1. (a) 3/4 − 1/8 = 5/8
  (b) 6/8 − 1/8 = 5/8
3. (a) 1/2 − 1/4 = 1/4
  (b) 2/4 − 1/4 = 1/4
5. 7/20

SUBSKILL 3:

Set 1

1. $2\frac{2}{5}$ *3.* $5\frac{2}{3}$

Set 2

1. $2\frac{1}{4}$ *3.* $5\frac{3}{8}$

Set 3

1. $2\frac{1}{6}$ *3.* $3\frac{11}{40}$

Set 4

1. (a) $3\frac{3}{4} - 1\frac{1}{2} = 2\frac{1}{4}$ *(b)* $3\frac{3}{4} - 1\frac{2}{4} = 2\frac{1}{4}$

3. $1\frac{3}{8}$

SUBSKILL 4:

Set 1

1. $1\frac{7}{12}$ *3.* $2\frac{5}{6}$

Set 2

1. $1\frac{9}{10}$ *3.* $6\frac{3}{10}$

Set 3

1. $1\frac{13}{18}$ *3.* $\frac{19}{24}$

Set 4

1. (a) $3\frac{1}{2} - 1\frac{2}{3} = 1\frac{5}{6}$ *(b)* $2\frac{9}{6} - 1\frac{4}{6} = 1\frac{5}{6}$

3. $\frac{7}{8}$

SKILL
Multiplication of Fractions

Inventory Pretest:

1. $\frac{2}{3}$ *2.* $1\frac{1}{3}$ *3.* $2\frac{4}{9}$ *4.* $14\frac{1}{2}$ *5.* $16\frac{37}{72}$

Drill and Practice Sets by Subskill:

SUBSKILL 1:

Set 1

1. $\frac{1}{6}$ *3.* $\frac{1}{4}$

Set 2

1. $\frac{2}{3}$ *3.* 3

Set 3

1. $\frac{5}{27}$ *3.* 6

Set 4

1. 2/3 × 3/4 = 1/2, 3/4 × 2/3 = 1/2
3. 7/16 *5.* 1/6

SUBSKILL 2:

Set 1

1. $\frac{1}{2}$ 3. $1\frac{1}{2}$

Set 2

1. 2   3. $1\frac{2}{3}$

Set 3

1. $2\frac{1}{2}$ 3. 6

Set 4

1. $2\frac{1}{4}$ 3. 20 pounds   5. $31\frac{1}{2}$

7. *(a)* 25 miles   *(b)* 325 miles   *(c)* 75 miles
   (d) 625 miles

9. 50

SUBSKILL 3:

Set 1

1. $\frac{2}{3}$ 3. $\frac{3}{4}$

Set 2

1. $\frac{4}{9}$ 3. $\frac{5}{6}$

Set 3

1. $2\frac{3}{10}$ 3. $2\frac{25}{36}$

Set 4

1. $\frac{2}{3} \times 3\frac{1}{2} = 2\frac{1}{3}$, $3\frac{1}{2} \times \frac{2}{3} = 2\frac{1}{3}$

3. $\frac{5}{8}$ of a cup of soy sauce and

   $1\frac{1}{4}$ teaspoons of ginger

SUBSKILL 4:

Set 1

1. 6   3. $7\frac{1}{4}$

Set 2

1. $3\frac{1}{2}$ 3. 17

Set 3

1. $19\frac{2}{3}$ 3. 57

Set 4

1. $416   3. $4.08   5. 112 years

7. *(a)* 32°F   *(b)* 95°F   *(c)* 68°F
   (d) 212°F

SUBSKILL 5:

Set 1

1. $4\frac{4}{9}$ 3. $10\frac{5}{6}$

Set 2

1. 9   3. $12\frac{1}{4}$

Set 3

1. $27\frac{17}{24}$ 3. $10\frac{1}{3}$

Set 4

1. $2\frac{1}{2} \times 3\frac{1}{3} = 8\frac{1}{3}$, $3\frac{1}{3} \times 2\frac{1}{2} = 8\frac{1}{3}$

3. $6\frac{1}{8}$

SKILL
Division of Fractions

Inventory Pretest:

1. $1\frac{5}{27}$ 2. $\frac{3}{10}$ 3. $5\frac{1}{3}$ 4. $\frac{13}{20}$ 5. $\frac{125}{176}$ 6. $2\frac{1}{3}$

Drill and Practice Sets by Subskill:

SUBSKILL 1:

Set 1

1. 2   3. $1\frac{1}{5}$

Set 2

1. 3   3. $\frac{1}{2}$

Set 3

1. $\frac{5}{7}$ 3. $10\frac{1}{2}$

Set 4

1. $\frac{8}{15}$ 3. $2\frac{2}{5}$

SUBSKILL 2:

Set 1

1. $\frac{2}{5}$ 3. 4

Set 2

1. $\frac{1}{3}$ 3. 2

Set 3

1. $\frac{3}{40}$ 3. $13\frac{1}{3}$

Set 4

1. $3 \div \frac{3}{8} = 8$ 3. 20 times

SUBSKILL 3:

Set 1

1. $3\frac{1}{2}$ 3. 18

Set 2

1. 6   3. 4

Set 3

1. $7\frac{9}{25}$ 3. $3\frac{13}{15}$

Set 4

1. $2\frac{1}{2} \div \frac{5}{8} = 4$ 3. 8

SUBSKILL 4:

Set 1

1. $1\frac{3}{8}$ 3. $1\frac{11}{12}$

Set 2

1. $1\frac{1}{12}$ 3. $\frac{9}{10}$

Set 3

1. $1\frac{15}{32}$ 3. $1\frac{7}{12}$

Set 4

1. $2\frac{1}{2}$ 3. 20

SUBSKILL 5:

Set 1

1. $1\frac{11}{84}$ 3. $\frac{2}{3}$

Set 2

1. $\frac{125}{192}$ 3. $\frac{47}{64}$

Set 3

1. $1\frac{19}{68}$ 3. $3\frac{61}{100}$

Set 4

1. $1\frac{1}{5}$ 3. 173

SUBSKILL 6:

Set 1

1. $\frac{5}{4}$ 3. $\frac{1}{8}$ 5. $\frac{7}{30}$

Set 2

1. $\frac{4}{3}$ 3. $\frac{1}{10}$ 5. $\frac{3}{20}$

Set 3

1. $\frac{3}{2}$ 3. $\frac{1}{12}$ 5. $\frac{6}{35}$

Set 4

1. $\frac{1}{9}$

3. The reciprocal of a number is the same as the multiplicative inverse of the number.

5. Nothing, because you cannot divide by zero.

General Survey Pretest for Decimals and Percents:

1. $12\frac{9}{40}$ 2. 8.6   3. 117.953   4. 1440.087

5. 240.59   6. 64%   7. 4.1605

8. 19.25   9. 28%   10. 178.57

SKILL
Working with Decimals

Inventory Pretest:

1. 1.25

2. Three hundred seventeen and 49 thousandths

3. b, c, d, e   4. c

5. $31\frac{7}{20}$ 6. 7.2   7. 12.429   8. 717.249

9. 3419.118   10. 1435.239   11. 77.13

12. .015025   13. .9$\overline{18}$ 14. $\frac{50}{99}$

Drill and Practice Sets by Subskill:

SUBSKILL 1:

Set 1

1. 2.27

3.

Set 2
1. 12.74

3.

Set 3
1. 101.21

3.

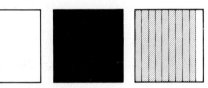

Set 4
1. Four dollars, three dimes, and seven pennies

3. $1.10   *5.* .09   *7.* .139

SUBSKILL 2:
Set 1
1. (a) Seven-tenths
   (b) Eighteen-hundredths
   (c) Eighteen and eight-tenths
   (d) One and 49 hundredths

Set 2
1. (a) Nine-tenths
   (b) Two hundred three thousandths
   (c) Two hundred three and six-tenths
   (d) Three and 456 thousandths

Set 3
1. (a) Thirty-six hundredths
   (b) Four hundred eight thousandths
   (c) One thousand fifty-six and 23 hundredths
   (d) Two hundred ninety and 351 thousandths

Set 4
1. Two hundred three and 45/100 . . .

3. Seven-hundredths

SUBSKILL 3:
Set 1
1. b, c

Set 2
1. b, c, d, f

Set 3
1. b, c, d

Set 4
1. One reason is so you will know how not to use them. Another reason is so you will know when your answer to a problem is the same as an answer book's answer to the problem.

SUBSKILL 4:
Set 1
1. b   *3.* d

Set 2
1. a   *3.* d

Set 3
1. d   *3.* d

Set 4
1. a, b, c   *3.* b

SUBSKILL 5:
Set 1
1. $\frac{3}{5}$ *3.* $42\frac{19}{100}$

Set 2
1. $\frac{1}{2}$ *3.* $51\frac{81}{100}$

Set 3
1. $\frac{3}{10}$ *3.* $62\frac{1}{2}$

Set 4
1. To underscore the equivalence of the two.

SUBSKILL 6:
Set 1
1. (a) 1   *(b)* .9   *(c)* .88

Set 2
1. (a) 4   *(b)* 4.4   *(c)* 4.36

Set 3
1. (a) 0   (b) .2   (c) .18
Set 4
1. $48.94   3. 13,000

SUBSKILL 7:
Set 1
1. .28   3. .571
Set 2
1. .45   3. .27
Set 3
1. .3   3. .6
Set 4
1. One reason is to underscore the equivalence of the two. Another reason is to simplify their addition, subtraction, multiplication, and division on a pocket calculator.

SUBSKILL 8:
Set 1
1. 353.293   3. 4.403   5. 993.2
Set 2
1. 458.219   3. 4.773   5. 633.4
Set 3
1. 31.6068   3. 15.2832   5. 436.5
Set 4
1. $11.99   3. $13.76   5. 9361.23
7. 8.2 centimeters

SUBSKILL 9:
Set 1
1. 4607.141   3. 12.422   5. 21.9128
Set 2
1. 5.9529   3. 116.18   5. 4.8928
Set 3
1. 263.672   3. 20.475   5. 25.9404
Set 4
1. 877.49   3. 189.63
5. 531.037 miles per hour   7. $4.07
9. $20.05

SUBSKILL 10:
Set 1
1. 2367.963   3. .11666

Set 2
1. 24073.28   3. .09338
Set 3
1. 38876.2   3. .39024
Set 4
1. 30   3. 25.12   5. $67.25   7. $7.88

SUBSKILL 11:
Set 1
1. 76.4   3. 15.24
Set 2
1. 321.1   3. 38.3
Set 3
1. 4657.143   3. 436
Set 4
1. 21.4   3. 2.13
5. (a) .18 centimeters   (b) .20 centimeters

SUBSKILL 12:
Set 1
1. .0035   3. .0047   5. 8.95
Set 2
1. 48.3   3. 795   5. 9990
Set 3
1. .00082536   3. .0000000000621   5. .99
Set 4
1. (a) 162.8   (b) 16.28   (c) 1.628
3. (a) 730.4   (b) 73.04   (c) 7.304
5. 2.35   7. .729
9. (a) 1050   (b) 10,500   (c) 105,000
11. (a) 60   (b) 600   (c) 6000
13. (a) .25 centimeters
    (b) 2.5 centimeters
    (c) 25 centimeters

SUBSKILL 13:
Set 1
1. $.3\overline{5}$ 3. $.7\overline{12}$
Set 2
1. $.2\overline{5}$ 3. $.\overline{450}$
Set 3
1. $.375\overline{0}$ 3. $.5\overline{0}$

Set 4

1. One reason is to underscore the equivalence of the two. Another reason is to capture your interest.

SUBSKILL 14:

Set 1

1. $\frac{697}{990}$ *3.* $\frac{8}{333}$

Set 2

1. $\frac{61}{495}$ *3.* 1

Set 3

1. $\frac{844}{2475}$ *3.* $\frac{1}{2}$

Set 4

1. One reason is to underscore the equivalence of the two. Another reason is to capture your interest.

SKILL
Working with Percents

Inventory Pretest:

1. 70% *2.* 201.5% *3.* 43% *4.* 2.505

5. $\frac{1}{8}$ *6.* 9 *7.* 24% *8.* 510.2

Drill and Practice Sets by Subskill:

SUBSKILL 1:

Set 1

1. *(a)* 33% *(b)* 20% *3.* 40%

Set 2

1. *(a)* 80% *(b)* 8% *3.* 25%

Set 3

1. *(a)* 90% *(b)* 100% *3.* 50%

Set 4

1. *(a)* 20% *(b)* 37% *3.* 53% *5.* 90%

SUBSKILL 2:

Set 1

1. 210.2% *3.* 80% *5.* 166.66%

Set 2

1. 360% *3.* 50% *5.* 120%

Set 3

1. 450% *3.* 90% *5.* 125.2525%

Set 4

1. 7.5% *3.* 30% *5.* 25%

SUBSKILL 3:

Set 1

1. 16% *3.* 38%

Set 2

1. 60% *3.* 45%

Set 3

1. 50% *3.* 44%

Set 4

1. 21% *3.* 75%

SUBSKILL 4:

Set 1

1. 2.1025 *3.* .015 *5.* 2

Set 2

1. 3.6095 *3.* .0425 *5.* 3

Set 3

1. 4.5 *3.* .0775 *5.* 1

Set 4

1. The only way you can multiply or divide by a percent is to convert it to a decimal.

SUBSKILL 5:

Set 1

1. $\frac{1}{40}$ *3.* $1\frac{101}{200}$ *5.* $\frac{1}{20}$

Set 2

1. $\frac{19}{400}$ *3.* $1\frac{1}{400}$ *5.* $\frac{1}{10}$

Set 3

1. $\frac{533}{10000}$ or $\frac{4}{75}$ *3.* $2\frac{7}{400}$ or $\frac{4}{75}$ *5.* $\frac{1}{100}$

Set 4

1. To underscore the equivalence of the two.

SUBSKILL 6:

Set 1

1. 6 *3.* .5

Set 2

1. 1.5 *3.* 937.5

Set 3

1. 20 *3.* 4.5

Set 4

1. $3000 *3.* $419.70 *5.* 9.7 pounds

7. Yes

SUBSKILL 7:

Set 1

1. 50%   *3.* 120%

Set 2

1. 60%   *3.* 80%

Set 3

1. 153%   *3.* 125%

Set 4

1. 83%   *3.* 11%

SUBSKILL 8:

Set 1

1. 200   *3.* 24

Set 2

1. 277.78   *3.* 40

Set 3

1. 60   *3.* 125

Set 4

1. $35,750   *3.* $7.81   *5.* $3.99

General Survey Pretest for Estimation, Integers, Less Than, Greater Than, Exponents, and Roots

1. About 225. 231.88 to nearest hundredth.

2. $^+8$ *3.* $^-48$ *4.* 17   *5.* True

6. $\frac{14}{29}$ *7.* 27 *8.* 10^7 *9.* 4.0703855×10^3 *10.* 6

SKILL
Estimation

Inventory Pretest:

1. About $42. $41.79 actual.

2. About 30,000. 32,079.07 to nearest hundredth.

3. About 12. 12.96 actual.

4. About ten centimeters. 9.8 centimeters actual.

Drill and Practice Sets by Subskill:

SUBSKILL 1:

Set 1

1. (a) 22 + 9   *(b)* 82 − 3

Set 2

1. (a) 141 + 57 + 3   *(b)* 307 − 21

Set 3

1. (a) 1083 + 394   *(b)* 8043 − 219

Set 4

1. Yes. $9.30 total plus tax.

3. No. 4 large, french fries, large drink. $1.92 total plus tax. Or no. 5 large, hot fruit pie, medium drink. $1.97 total plus tax. Or the like.

5. Return $1.

SUBSKILL 2:

Set 1

1. (a) 19 × 98   *(b)* 281 ÷ 13

Set 2

1. (a) 65 × 30   *(b)* 461 ÷ 58

Set 3

1. (a) 9 × 3 × 6 × 4   *(b)* 16 ÷ 7

Set 4

1. (a) Exact count

   (b) Estimate

   (c) Estimate

   (d) Exact count

   (e) Estimate

3. About 400. 342 actual.   *5.* 8

SUBSKILL 3:

Set 1

1. $\frac{4}{9} \times 635$

Set 2

1. 1834 × .09

Set 3

1. 42 ÷ .35

Set 4

1. a   *3.* 47% of $283

SUBSKILL 4:

Set 1

1. Optical illusion. Lines the same length.

3. (a) About two centimeters. 2.2 centimeters actual.

   (b) About ten centimeters. 9.8 centimeters actual.

Set 2

1. Optical illusion. Lines the same length.

3. (a) About four centimeters 4.2 centimeters actual.

   (b) About eight centimeters. 7.7 centimeters actual.

Set 3

1. Optical illusion. Lines the same length.

3. (a) About six centimeters. 6.1 centimeters actual.

   (b) About nine centimeters. 9.2 centimeters actual.

Set 4

1. (a) About $7\frac{1}{2}$ inches

   (b) About three feet

3. Answers will vary.

SKILL
Integers

Inventory Pretest:

1. D   2. $^+13$ 3. 4   4. $^-5$ 5. 10   6. 15

Drill and Practice Sets by Subskill:

SUBSKILL 1:

Set 1

1. (a) M   (b) F   (c) C   (d) L

Set 2

1. (a) A   (b) J   (c) G   (d) P

Set 3

1. (a) I   (b) D   (c) O   (d) E

Set 4

1. $+13°C$ 3. -3

SUBSKILL 2:

Set 1

1. (a) $^-7$ (b) $^-4$ (c) $^+5$ (d) $^+8$ (e) $^+12$

3. $^+7 + ^+3$

Set 2

1. (a) $^-9$ (b) $^-16$ (c) $^-9$ (d) $^-15$

(e) $^+14$

3. $^+1 + ^-10$

Set 3

1. (a) $^-8$ (b) $^-437$ (c) $^-8$ (d) $^-69$

(e) $^+160$

3. $^-13 + ^+25$

Set 4

1. Not too good. They lost four yards.

3. Not too bad. You have won two cents.

5. Twelve meters west, 20 meters north

SUBSKILL 3:

Set 1

1. (a) 5   (b) 21   (c) 3   (d) 9

3.

Set 2

1. (a) 9   (b) 12   (c) 5   (d) 23

3.

Set 3

1. (a) 25   (b) 105   (c) 13   (d) 150

3.

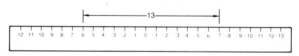

Set 4

1. It has theoretical value. If you ever take calculus, you will need it.

SUBSKILL 4:

Set 1

1. $^-24$ 3. $^-3$ 5. $^-408$

Set 2

1. $^-256$ 3. $^-12$ 5. $^-3000$

Set 3

1. $^+63$ 3. $^-3$ 5. $^-96$

Set 4

1. Fifteen blocks east

3. Pretty good. You have lost 12 pounds.

5. the water filling the bathtub. Thus a negative (draining) and a negative (backwards) is a

positive (filling).

SUBSKILL 5:

Set 1

1. 14 *3.* 1

Set 2

1. 35 *3.* 24

Set 3

1. ⁻25 *3.* 1

Set 4

1. Without some agreement on what to do first, different people would get different answers for the same problems.

SUBSKILL 6:

Set 1

1. 38 *3.* 4

Set 2

1. 36 *3.* ⁻15

Set 3

1. 1 *3.* ⁻1

Set 4

1. Without them, you could not change the order of operations.

SKILL
Less Than and Greater Than

Inventory Pretest:

1. a and b *2.* $\frac{4}{7}$ *3.* 1.501

4. 50% *5.* b and c

Drill and Practice Sets by Subskill:

SUBSKILL 1:

Set 1

1. a and b   *3.* 9 > 5

Set 2

1. c   *3.* 5 < 10

Set 3

1. b and c   *3.* 15 > 7

Set 4

1. b *3.* b

5. Depends. The pennies and nickels are the most coins, but the quarter is the most money.

SUBSKILL 2:

Set 1

1. $\frac{2}{3}$ *3.* $\frac{5}{6}$

Set 2

1. $\frac{3}{4}$ *3.* $\frac{14}{25}$

Set 3

1. $\frac{3}{8}$ *3.* $\frac{13}{25}$

Set 4

1. $\frac{15}{16}$ of an inch

3. $\frac{1}{3}$ finished

SUBSKILL 3:

Set 1

1. 3.58   *3.* .1023

Set 2

1. 17.0021 *3.* .1242

Set 3

1. 250.46   *3.* .5005

Set 4

1. $5.08 *3.* .001 of an inch

SUBSKILL 4:

Set 1

1. 15% *3.* 50%

Set 2

1. 8% *3.* 1%

Set 3

1. 20% *3.* 7.75%

Set 4

1. 15% *3.* $5\frac{1}{4}$%

SUBSKILL 5:

Set 1

1. a and b

Set 2

1. b and c

Set 3

1. a and b

Set 4

1. −10°C

3. The one with a balance of −$102

SKILL
Exponents and Roots

Inventory Pretest:

1. 16   *2.* 6^5 *3.* $3^{14}5^{28}$ *4.* $\frac{1}{4}$

5. 2.0503751×10^4 *6.* 11   *7.* $3\sqrt{2}$ *8.* 7
9. 36

Drill and Practice Sets by Subskill:

SUBSKILL 1:

Set 1

1. a   *3.* (a) 2^4 (b) 5^6 (c) 2^3 (d) 3^3

Set 2

1. d

3. (a) 10^3 (b) 6^3 (c) 4^2 or 2^4 (d) 5^4

Set 3

1. a

3. (a) 8^4 (b) 15^3 (c) 8^2, 4^3, or 2^6
    (d) 100^2 or 10^4

Set 4

1. 64   *3.* 314

5. 225.28 cubic centimeters

SUBSKILL 2:

Set 1

1. Cannot add or subtract exponents. Not multiplying or dividing.

3. 3^{11}

5. Cannot add or subtract exponents. Not like bases.

7. 5^5

Set 2

1. 2^{13}

3. Cannot add or subtract exponents. Not multiplying or dividing.

5. $10^0 = 1$ *7.* 6^{12}

Set 3

1. Cannot add or subtract exponents. Not multiplying or dividing.

3. Cannot add or subtract exponents. Not like bases.

5. 29   *7.* 4^3

Set 4

1. 1.2676504×10^{30}

SUBSKILL 3:

Set 1

1. 4^6 *3.* $3^{25}4^{10}$

5. Cannot multiply exponents. Not multiplying or dividing.

7. 12^{30}

Set 2

1. 10^{24} *3.* $\frac{5^9}{2^{15}}$

5. Cannot multiply exponents. Not multiplying or dividing.

7. $10^0 = 1$ *8.* 5^5

Set 3

1. 7^{20} *3.* $2^{56}5^{88}$

5. Cannot multiply exponents. Not multiplying or dividing.

7. 15^{120}

Set 4

1. You need to know how to multiply exponents in case you ever take algebra.

SUBSKILL 4:

Set 1

1. (a) $\frac{1}{8}$ (b) $\frac{1}{64}$ (c) $\frac{1}{25}$ (d) $\frac{1}{10000}$

3. (a) $\frac{1}{5^9}$ (b) $\frac{1}{8^3}$ (c) 6^5 (d) $\frac{9^5}{10^3}$

Set 2

1. (a) $\frac{1}{64}$ (b) $\frac{1}{32}$ (c) $\frac{1}{25}$ (d) 1

3. (a) $\frac{1}{15^3}$ (b) $\frac{1}{9^5}$ (c) $2(5^3)$ (d) $\frac{4^4}{3^2}$

Set 3

1. (a) $\frac{1}{125}$ (b) $\frac{1}{100}$ (c) $\frac{1}{4}$ (d) $\frac{1}{216}$

3. (a) $\frac{1}{10^5}$ (b) $\frac{1}{5^{10}}$ (c) $\frac{1}{3(6^2)}$ (d) $\frac{10^5}{10^3}$

Set 4

1. You need them for scientific notation.

SUBSKILL 5:

Set 1

1. (a) 5.0016525×10^4 (c) 3.805×10^3

(b) 3.861×10^{-5} *(d)* 5.95×10^{-2}

Set 2

1. (a) 4.00159×10^3 *(c)* 1.25056×10^5

(b) 1.275×10^{-3} *(d)* 7×10^{-6}

Set 3

1. (a) 1.5051×10^{10} *(c)* 2.5×10^2

(b) 1.21×10^{-9} *(d)* 5×10^{-1}

Set 4

1. 2×10^{10} *3.* 2.259682×10^9

SUBSKILL 6:

Set 1

1. (a) 3   *(b)* 9   *(c)* 6.708   *(d)* 30.822   *3.* 7

Set 2

1. (a) 2   *(b)* 10   *(c)* 5.657   *(d)* 28.810

3. 8

Set 3

1. (a) 4   *(b)* 5   *(c)* 4.123   *(d)* 5.099   *3.* 10

Set 4

1. 5   *3.* 10

SUBSKILL 7:

Set 1

1. (a) $5\sqrt{2}$ *(c)* $4\sqrt{3}$ *(d)* $2\sqrt{5}$

Set 2

1. (a) $2\sqrt{2}$ *(b)* $2\sqrt{3}$ *(d)* $7\sqrt{2}$

Set 3

1. (a) $2\sqrt{6}$ *(b)* $4\sqrt{5}$ *(c)* $6\sqrt{3}$

Set 4

1. You need to know how to simplify square roots in case you ever take algebra.

SUBSKILL 8:

Set 1

1. 3   *3.* 6   *5.* 10

Set 2

1. 4   *3.* 3   *5.* 10

Set 3

1. 2   *3.* 2   *5.* 10

Set 4

1. You need to know about roots in case you ever take algebra.

SUBSKILL 9:

Set 1

1. c

Set 2

1. d

Set 3

1. c

Set 4

1. You need to know about fractional exponents in case you ever take algebra.

INDEX